Human Rights in Child Protection

Asgeir Falch-Eriksen
Elisabeth Backe-Hansen
Editors

Human Rights in Child Protection

Implications for Professional Practice and Policy

Editors
Asgeir Falch-Eriksen
Norwegian Social Research
Oslo Metropolitan University
Oslo, Norway

Elisabeth Backe-Hansen
Norwegian Social Research
Oslo Metropolitan University
Oslo, Norway

ISBN 978-3-030-06917-9   ISBN 978-3-319-94800-3 (eBook)
https://doi.org/10.1007/978-3-319-94800-3

© The Editor(s) (if applicable) and The Author(s) 2018 This book is an open access publication.
Softcover re-print of the Hardcover 1st edition 2018
Open Access This book is licensed under the terms of the Creative Commons Attribution 4.0 International License (http://creativecommons.org/licenses/by/4.0/), which permits use, sharing, adaptation, distribution and reproduction in any medium or format, as long as you give appropriate credit to the original author(s) and the source, provide a link to the Creative Commons license and indicate if changes were made.
The images or other third party material in this book are included in the book's Creative Commons license, unless indicated otherwise in a credit line to the material. If material is not included in the book's Creative Commons license and your intended use is not permitted by statutory regulation or exceeds the permitted use, you will need to obtain permission directly from the copyright holder.
The use of general descriptive names, registered names, trademarks, service marks, etc. in this publication does not imply, even in the absence of a specific statement, that such names are exempt from the relevant protective laws and regulations and therefore free for general use.
The publisher, the authors and the editors are safe to assume that the advice and information in this book are believed to be true and accurate at the date of publication. Neither the publisher nor the authors or the editors give a warranty, express or implied, with respect to the material contained herein or for any errors or omissions that may have been made. The publisher remains neutral with regard to jurisdictional claims in published maps and institutional affiliations.

Cover illustration: Matt Caisley via the Noun Project

This Palgrave Macmillan imprint is published by the registered company Springer Nature Switzerland AG
The registered company address is: Gewerbestrasse 11, 6330 Cham, Switzerland

Preface

Next year will mark the thirtieth anniversary of the UN Convention on the Rights of the Child. The convention is a catalogue of rights that, among other things, is meant to safeguard children from maltreatment. Children living in nation-states claiming to abide by the convention should also be able to make a claim based on their right to protection. The child's right to protection, specified in Art. 19 of the convention, is intended to establish child protection services that ensure that children develop and experience their childhoods in safe family environments.

For the anniversary, we seek to move on from discussing the validity and formal content of the convention, and focus on how it can become operative in the field of practice. This book aims at exploring what human rights, and especially the Convention on the Rights of the Child, entail for child protection services, for professional practice and policy.

It has not been an easy book to develop. Theorizing rights-based professional child protection practice is in many ways still in its infancy, as is the development of policy and practice guidelines based on human rights. Thus, writing chapters aiming to do all three has been an interesting challenge to both authors and editors. We hope the results of our efforts will be helpful to child protection workers, and to educators and policymakers who aim to develop rights-based practice in child protection.

We wish to thank the contributors for their efforts and patience during the two to three years it has taken to develop the book. Also, we wish to thank Oslo Metropolitan University for funding open access, and for funding working seminars together with NOVA—Norwegian Social Research.

Oslo, Norway Asgeir Falch-Eriksen
April 2018 Elisabeth Backe-Hansen

Contents

1. Child Protection and Human Rights: A Call for Professional Practice and Policy ... 1
   Asgeir Falch-Eriksen and Elisabeth Backe-Hansen

2. Children's Right to Protection Under the CRC ... 15
   Kirsten Sandberg

3. Rights and Professional Practice: How to Understand Their Interconnection ... 39
   Asgeir Falch-Eriksen

4. The Child's Best Interest Principle across Child Protection Jurisdictions ... 59
   Marit Skivenes and Line Marie Sørsdal

5. Re-designing Organizations to Facilitate Rights-Based Practice in Child Protection ... 89
   Eileen Munro and Andrew Turnell

6 Experts by Experience Infusing Professional Practices in Child Protection 111
Tarja Pösö

7 The Rights of Children Placed in Out-of-Home Care 129
Anne-Dorthe Hestbæk

8 Emergency Placements: Human Rights Limits and Lessons 147
Elisabeth Gording-Stang

9 Rights-Based Practice and Marginalized Children in Child Protection Work 167
Bente Heggem Kojan and Graham Clifford

10 In-home Services: A Rights-Based Professional Practice Meets Children's and Families' Needs 185
Øivin Christiansen and Ragnhild Hollekim

11 Embodied Care Practices and the Realization of the Best Interests of the Child in Residential Institutions for Young Children 209
Cecilie Basberg Neumann

12 Formal and Everyday Participation in Foster Families: A Challenge? 227
Elisabeth Backe-Hansen

13 Conclusion: Towards Rights-Based Child Protection Work 245
Elisabeth Backe-Hansen and Asgeir Falch-Eriksen

Index 255

Notes on Contributors

Editors

Asgeir Falch-Eriksen is a researcher at NOVA/Oslo Metropolitan University. He has a PhD in political science and specializes in political theory, legal philosophy and the sociology of the professions. He has published multiple research reports on Norwegian child protection and further publications on the interconnection between child protection and human rights.

Elisabeth Backe-Hansen is a professor at NOVA/Oslo Metropolitan University. She has published extensively on core aspects of child protection, primarily decision-making, foster/residential care and aftercare. In addition, she has conducted research on children and young people. She has a special interest in ethics in child research and children's participation, with national as well as international publications.

Contributors

Øivin Christiansen is a researcher at the Regional Centre for Child and Youth Mental Health and Child Welfare, University of Bergen. He has substantial experience in research on child protection services in Norway. His main fields of interests are decision-making in child welfare organizations, children receiving preventive services and foster care.

Graham Clifford is Professor Emeritus of Social Work at the Department of Social Work, Norwegian University of Science and Technology. He has extensive research experience within the area of child protection and also other areas of social work.

Elisabeth Gording-Stang is Professor of Law at the Department of Social Services, Oslo Metropolitan University and teaches bachelor students in child protection. Since her PhD dissertation of 2007, on preventive child welfare services from the point of view of the child, she has been publishing extensively on children's rights and more generally on human rights in child protection and related legal arenas. She has also been researching confidentiality issues in interdepartmental collaboration.

Anne-Dorthe Hestbæk has for many years been researching in the field of child abuse and neglect, children with special needs and out-of-home placements in a cross-cultural context at VIVE—The Danish Center for Social Science Research. She was one of the founders of the Danish longitudinal cohort study on children in out-of-home care and still designates children growing up in foster care or residential care as one of her core fields, combined with social work studies.

Ragnhild Hollekim is an associate professor at the Department of Health Promotion and Development at the Faculty of Psychology at the University of Bergen. Her fields of interests are child welfare, children's status and rights, migration, equality and integration.

Bente Heggem Kojan is Associate Professor of Social Work at the Department of Social Work, Norwegian University of Science and Technology. Her particular field of expertise is child protection and inequality.

Eileen Munro is Professor in Social Policy, London School of Economics. Her background in both philosophy and social work has shaped her research interests in reasoning skills in child protection, leading to an interest in how organizational cultures help or hinder good-quality reasoning and practice. Understanding of the complex causal processes in working with families has triggered a critical interest in the philosophy of social science underlying evidence-based policy and practice movements.

Cecilie Basberg Neumann is Professor in Sociology at Oslo Metropolitan University. She is also a Gestalt therapist and is interested in professional social work, gender, class, methodology and social theory. She is the author of Power, ethics and situated research methodology (Palgrave, 2018, together with Iver B. Neumann).

Tarja Pösö is Professor in Social Work at the University of Tampere, Finland. She has studied child protection for many years. Her present research focuses on the notions of 'consent' and 'objection' in child protection decision-making, including risk-intelligent decision-making and how organizations can best support it. She is currently co-editing books about interviewing children (in Finnish) and errors made (in English) in child protection. Her research focus is on child law and children's rights, including the right of the child to be heard, the best interests of the child, child protection and asylum-seeking children.

Kirsten Sandberg is Professor of Law, University of Oslo and a member of the UN Committee on the Rights of the Child 2011–2019, serving as the Committee's chairperson 2013–2015. Her research focus is on child law and children's rights, including the right of the child to be heard, the best interests of the child, child protection and asylum-seeking children. She has lectured on children's rights to lawyers in Harare, Zimbabwe, and to law students in Yunnan, China.

Marit Skivenes is a professor in political science at the Department of Administration and Organization Theory at the University of Bergen, Norway, and the Director of the Centre for Research on Discretion and Paternalism. She has written numerous articles about the role of welfare policies, practices to understand the legitimacy problems modern states face, and child protection systems. She has led a range of international research projects and been awarded several prestigious research grants, including a European Research Council Consolidator Grant in 2016.

Line Marie Sørsdal is a PhD candidate in political science at the Department of Administration and Organization Theory at the University of Bergen, Norway. Her research interests are children's rights, social policy and regulation, and comparative public administration. She is also the research coordinator of an EU H2020 consortium on the digital transformation of the state.

Andrew Turnell is a social worker and a co-creator of the Signs of Safety approach to child protection casework. Andrew acts as a consultant for many international child protection systems focusing on teaching, distilling and describing constructive on-the-ground casework and the organizational practices that support it.

Abbreviations

CASS   The Consolidation Act on Social Services 2017 (Denmark)
CPS/CWS Child Protection Services/Child Welfare Services
CRC   UN Convention on the Rights of the Child
CWA   Child Welfare Act (Finland and Norway)
ECHR   European Convention on Human Rights
GC   General Comment from the UN Committee on the Rights of the Child
TABU   Well-being among children and young people in care (Denmark)

List of Pictures

Picture 5.1	My three houses—photos in a series	96
Picture 5.2	A words and pictures story	103
Picture 5.3	A words and pictures story	103
Picture 5.4	A words and pictures story	104
Picture 5.5	A words and pictures story	105
Picture 5.6	A words and pictures story	106
Picture 5.7	A words and pictures story	106

List of Tables

Table 4.1	Child protection systems, child well-being rank, child rights index	65
Table 4.2	The child protection laws	67
Table 4.3	Codes for identifying themes in the texts	68
Table 4.4	Main findings	70
Table 4.5	Strong discretion and material content	80
Table 4.6	Considerations in legislation that authorizes weak discretion	81
Table 5.1	Signs of safety assessment and planning framework	92
Table 7.1	CRC articles and out-of-home care	133
Table 7.2	Risk indicators in out-of-home care	137
Table 7.3	Satisfaction with life in out-of-home care	140
Table 10.1	Reasons for providing in-home measures	191

1

Child Protection and Human Rights: A Call for Professional Practice and Policy

Asgeir Falch-Eriksen and Elisabeth Backe-Hansen

1 Introduction

Professional practice is a defining trait of modernity, and democratic and constitutional nation-states depend on professional practitioners and their efforts to solve problems and coordinate activity in order to distribute state services as accurately as possible, thus dealing with the particular problem at hand of implementing human rights. Throughout modern history, legislators in different democratic nation-states have developed complex systems of implementation to make sure that public resources are distributed at the street level according to their democratic intent, and in an accurate manner aimed at solving particular problems. In this manner, state services at the street level are provided according to predetermined political and legal distributive standards set by elected officials through regular law-making and constitutional rights norms. Consequently, professional practice is a cen-

---

A. Falch-Eriksen (✉) • E. Backe-Hansen
Norwegian Social Research, Oslo Metropolitan University, Oslo, Norway
e-mail: asgeirer@oslomet.no; ebha@oslomet.no

tral tool in the democratic chain of command in the efforts of legislators to implement democratic policies, and to distribute public goods and burdens. This is also the case with regard to child protection services. Within the system of child protection there are countless practitioners who must abide by the law.

During its nearly thirty years of existence the United Nations Convention on the Rights of the Child (CRC) has become not only an international human rights convention, but also a catalogue of rights that expresses legal norms used by legislators to legitimize systems of child protection. The convention has been embraced across nation-states globally, and by legislators who claim to push for a legal development on a par with the normative *ethos* of the CRC. Hence, by now the CRC is not just a banner, but a toolkit that expresses a normative order, that is, a human rights standard for how to legitimately protect children. Such a standard, which we will return to throughout the book, attempts to capture the underlying normative ethos of human rights and the indivisibility of rights. Incrementally, the CRC has become a point of reference in developing child protection services, as a way to design decision-making procedures, understand what constitutes the child's integrity, and develop professional practice and policy. This potential is what the book sets out to explore.

2 The Aim and Scope of the Book

The main aim of the book is to utilize a human rights standard as a prism, and critically explore what implications human rights have for professional practice and public policy. In this way, the book will explore and utilize a normatively substantial and conceptually rich analytical approach to practices of child protection. Child protection services have deep roots as public services across many modern nation-states (Fox Harding 2014), and they all depend on case workers at street level. Although there are significant variations across nation-states, in recent history most child protection services are bound to argue that they respect, abide by and enforce the CRC. Variations exist as to: what public sector the services belong to; what and how legal rules set the design for child protection services; what interventions are allowed, their frequency, and what measures could be used; how attached services are to education, health- and social services; what type of budgetary priority services are given; and so forth. Rights, on the other hand, are equalizers across nation-states, although they too are open to variation.

This book will transcend nation-bound rhetoric, albeit predominantly referencing nation-based empirical research to anchor discussions in the normative-political development that gradually points in the direction of increasingly implementing the CRC across policy and professional practice. Hence, child protection services are developing towards a widely shared human rights standard across nation-states, which explicitly grant children the right to protection (cf. CRC Art. 19). The CRC constitutes a rights-based normative order that has increasingly infused law-making across the world, and in some nation-states become formal law and even constitutional law.

Through CRC Art. 19.1, every child is provided the right to protection:

> *States Parties shall take all appropriate legislative, administrative, social and educational measures to protect the child from all forms of physical or mental violence, injury or abuse, neglect or negligent treatment, maltreatment or exploitation, including sexual abuse, while in the care of parent(s), legal guardian(s) or any other person who has the care of the child.*

This right can be claimed by any child living within a jurisdiction claiming to abide by the CRC. However, how or whether it will be answered will vary. Although an international human rights standard has gradually become a source for legitimizing the public protection of children, this does not preclude certain strands of politics opposing rights-based protection. Still, rights-based protection has increasingly become a source of reference and a standard to strive for across the globe (Gilbert et al. 2011).

If a child is maltreated, a rights-based public protection of children will enter *in loco parentis*, in the place of the parent, and intervene to sustain the child's personal integrity and aid the child's development. Maltreatment, caused by the violence or neglect of care-givers to the detriment of the child, must lead to interventions proportionally to the needs of the child.

3 'Lady Justice' at Street Level

'Lady Justice' is the personification of rule-of-law and an important symbol as to what merits the legitimate application of legal rules. She holds a sword in one hand and a scale in the other, and she carries a blindfold. Her face shows no significant expression. Rule-of-law is symbolized as blind because every subject under the law is to be treated equally when equal, and unequally when unequal. This is referred to as the formal principle of equality and is best summed up by the catch-phrase 'equality before the law'. The scale symbolizes a transparent process of reasoning, which ensures that each citizen is judged both according to general and known laws *but* also valid laws. Art. 7 of the Universal Declaration of Human Rights stipulates that 'All are equal before the law and are entitled without any discrimination to equal protection of the law.' Art. 7 is traceable to the constitutional traditions of the USA and France, and has its modern roots particularly in John Locke and its classical roots in Aristotle's *Politics* (Aristotle 2014). The CRC has its equivalent in Art. 2—the child's right to not suffer discrimination of any kind.

Justice is not merely a formal precept for equal treatment, but also equal treatment according to legal rules, and therefore the normative and political intent of those rules. Consequently, if rule-of-law is to work, 'Lady Justice's' judgments cannot be in conflict with legal rules, nor with their normative and political intent. If we turn to modern democratic and constitutional nation-states, which all enforce some version of a principle of rule-of-law, 'Lady Justice' must also enforce democratically forged rules. Popular sovereignty thereby becomes embedded into her judgments and judgments become parasitic upon the legitimacy of democracy. In this way, whenever a democratic nation-state passes new rules, she rules accordingly. Finally, 'Lady Justice' carries a sword that symbolizes coercion. The sword is the threat of sanctions whenever there is a breach of the law, and cannot be wielded without the authority of the law.

As already noted, in modern and complex nation-states, enforcement of legal rules often depends on professional practitioners at street level (Lipsky 1980). Legislators do not have the competence, the time or desire to provide the necessary quality of services in every conceivable case that confronts the modern nation-state on which its citizens depends. Legislators thus need to shape decision-making processes, jurisdictions and organizations in such a way that professional practitioners can handle any type of case within their remit. The legislature authorizes professional practitioners at street level through rule-of-law, enabling them to make decisions locally in each case by providing practitioners the mandate to reach decisions. This involves granting practitioners autonomy to reach decisions in specific cases by way of a public mandate. In this manner, we can describe the practitioners as a street-level version of 'Lady Justice'.

4 Child Protection and Discretion

Those who become authorized to work as 'Lady Justice' in child protection are case-workers in child protection services. They are professional practitioners set to become part of the democratic chain of command as implementation agents of politics, and in their capacity as case-workers they enforce the law and become its final arbiters at street level (Molander et al. 2012; Rothstein 1998). When case-workers enforce the law, they have been delegated the authority to exercise *discretion*. This is what Robert Goodin characterizes as the positive aspect of discretion, namely that a case-worker 'can be said to have discretion if and only if he is empowered to pursue some social goal(s) in the context of individual cases in such a way as he judges to be best calculated' (1986). A case-worker who departs from pursuing social goals is on the other hand not enforcing her or his delegated authority in any legitimate manner. In the public sector the social goal is provided as a democratic mandate, especially through legal rules, budgets and administrative directives. This is also where the CRC becomes relevant—namely in that practices that are argued by legislators are supposed to follow the CRC and become mandated through the democratic will to enforce the human rights standard underpinning the CRC, and thus cannot depart from the convention. If practice departs from the human rights standard, it will become challenging to defend a practice as legitimate either according to a principle of democracy or a human rights standard.

A delegation of authority to street level implies that case-workers must reach decisions that are neither in conflict with the law nor in breach of the intention of the law. While the former is a formal and structural restriction where case-workers are obligated to justify decisions, the latter is mainly epistemic and left to the autonomous capabilities of the case-worker. The autonomy of case-workers implies that case-workers must be able to reach decisions and justify them in accordance with a type of knowledge that preserves the intention of the law and the delegated authority (Molander et al. 2012). To this end, Goodin also provides a negative characterization of discretion, encapsulating what can be referred to as epistemic autonomy. Goodin alludes to the fact that discretion does not make sense if it denotes a complete freedom of choice, that is untethered autonomy. Hence, discretionary competence, conveyed by a case-worker, is always in accordance with certain restrictions.

Case-workers in child protection must reach decisions that are in accordance with the restrictions set by the law, and more specifically the CRC. They must practice their autonomy according to not just the letter of the law, but also the normative intent of the law. Goodin refers to this area of autonomy as 'a lacuna in a system of rules'. This aspect of discretion refers to an area 'which is generally governed by rules, but where the dictates of the rules are indeterminate' (Goodin 1986). The authorization of case-workers constitutes the delegation of authority to reach decisions autonomously, but supposedly predictably according to the intention of the law.

5   Human Rights and the Right to Protection

Basic to a human rights standard and a theory of rights are the notion of individual liberty and the corresponding absence of, and protection against, unlawful and arbitrary domination. This type of normative underpinning can be traced back to the classic liberal views especially of John Locke and Immanuel Kant. Both scholars promulgated a philosophy of individual freedom through constitutional protection, that is through rights, and with a strict impersonal principle of law especially underpinned by the principle stipulating the individual's equality before the law and non-discrimination. Operative expressions of constitutionalism carrying the ideas of Locke and Kant can be found in the preambles to the constitutions in both France and the USA. The principle of individual liberty rings heavily in modern nation-states and in efforts to implement, maintain and enforce human rights. In order for human rights to have any purposeful function, they need to be constitutional to other types of regulation and become universally applied to all who carry citizenships (see Chap. 3 for further elaboration). An important lesson from the liberal doctrine is that it constrains popular will and curbs the manner in which popular sovereignty works, what legal rules can pass, how public regulation and policy are performed and how public services are offered at street level through professional practice.

Particularly since the end of the Second World War, human rights have become embedded in state-constructs across the world, particularly where upholding the personal integrity of each individual person has become a hallmark. The development has firmly established the liberal constitutional democracy as an organizational norm which is optimal for introducing, maintaining and enforcing human rights. How such an organizational norm becomes operationalized, through what type of democracy and what type of constitutionality, nevertheless varies between nation-states.

Abiding by human rights, by enforcing a human rights standard that upholds the indivisibility of rights in all relevant matters, will have enormous consequences for the designs of activities in a nation-state, its regulations, organizations and use of knowledge. However, rights must actively be infused by lawmakers, bureaucrats and professionals through implementation and enforcement, in each and all actions relevant to collective problems-solving and coordination. In all relevant aspects of democratic rule-of-law, the respect of the integrity of each individual as a matter of human rights must be coherent and visible. By this way of thinking, modern state-constructs that lay claim to abide by human rights must let a system of rights become constitutive of any state activity in the sense that one can clearly trace the system of rights and explain how the state works by referring to rights.

6   Child Protection as a Public and Professional Service

Child protection is a public service aimed at protecting children against detrimental care, that is different types of maltreatment (Kriz and Skivenes 2014). Services are typically more rule-governed in the most intrusive cases where child protection services coercively remove children from their home. This means that on the one hand, the scope of what we above referred to as negative discretion, in cases involving coercion, is very narrow (see Burns et al. 2016). So-called in-house measures, on the other hand, where parents' and children's rights to privacy and family life are not infringed on in a significant manner, are typically less rule-governed. Through in-house measures, then, the case-worker has more scope to reach autonomous decisions, and has more responsibility to enforce the rights of the child. In areas where case-workers' autonomy is wide-ranging, their application of epistemic autonomy makes them more directly accountable.

However, both of types of interventions are structurally and epistemologically rule-governed practices of discretion. As the case-workers at street level meet families and children who need assistance or protection, the actions they can initiate are directly linked to the mandate they have through the delegation of authority. Once this area of discretion is structurally established through law-making, the decisional autonomy of the case-worker, or in Goodin's words, the 'lacuna in a system of rules', is the jurisdiction to which professions lay claim to provide the best-practice norms within the scope of negative discretion (Abbott 1988; Goodin 1986). It is in the lacuna of the system of rules that the case-workers of child protection take on the traits of what we have discussed earlier as the street-level 'Lady Justice'.

Although child protection services across modern nation-states are organized in different ways, many refer to the CRC as a legitimating force. In this way, the CRC becomes a legal framework to justify decision-making, policy development, organizational designs and regular law-making (see e.g. Skivenes and Sørsdal 2018: Chap. 4 in this book). The need for professionalization of child protection has grown out of the legislator's need to rely on knowledge-based practice within its services to fulfil its tasks in collective problem-solving and collective coordination. The push for increasing professionalization is driven by the development in knowledge about how best to protect children, but as well by more advanced professional educators and practitioners, those who receive services, and finally the democratic will embedded in the legislators pushing to provide certain types of protection and not others.

When children are subjected to varying degrees of maltreatment by their care-takers, they need protection. The state, as the only entity to exercise legitimate coercion, then has the legitimacy to intervene as long as it can be justified that the intervention is in the child's best interests (cf. CRC Art. 3).

In increasingly pluralistic and complex nation-state systems, adequate and knowledge-based interventions in child protection-cases cannot just be directed top-down, or decided on in advance, if the rights of the child are to be enforced. Thus, each decision needs to be made according to individual interests, needs and preferences. Case-workers needs to assess each particular child's care context, comprehend all relevant facets and act on the concrete distribution of resources to amend any maltreatment that the child is subjected to. Thus, each professional is delegated the authority and instructed to define what the problem at hand is, and then to give an independent evaluation of what is required to solve the particular problem (Goodin 1986).

7   Contents of the Book

In Chap. 2, Kirsten Sandberg explains and explores the right to protection as it is embedded in CRC Art. 19. The chapter provides a legal understanding of the child's right to protection against maltreatment by care-takers, and it also explores the obligations of states parties in implementing the right to protection in professional practice and in policy. The rights and obligations form the framework within which to exercise professional judgment in the area of child protection, and specifying their content is a prerequisite for rights to be realized. The focus is on the obligations to prevent and respond to maltreatment as well as on the best interests of the child.

In Chap. 3, Asgeir Falch-Eriksen explains what human rights entail for professional practice. The chapter elaborates theoretically and analytically using a counterfactual, namely that human rights, and in particular the CRC, is a standard point of reference for professional practitioners and practices within and across nation-state systems of child protection. The chapter elaborates on how rights challenge professional practice, and how to best answer some of these challenges. It especially focuses upon how to understand the child's right to liberty once adulthood kicks in, and how development must be carefully plotted out to maintain the integrity of the person through to adulthood.

In Chap. 4, Marit Skivenes and Line Marie Sørsdal discuss how the rights of the child are operative in legislation across nation-states. The chapter studies how governments have a range of steering mechanisms and incentives to guide and rein in professional use of discretion in decision-making. In their study, they examine how governments set a standard for decision-making about the best interests of the child in intrusive interventions. The empirical focus is the formulation of the principle of the child's best interest in child protection legislation in 14 countries.

In Chap. 5, Eileen Munro and Andrew Turnell illustrate the way the role of professionals is constructed within an organization, and how the design of such organizations helps or hinders them. They will use England as an example that illustrates the range of organizational change that has been needed both to allow and also to support rights-based practice.

In Chap. 6, Tarja Pösö discusses how Art. 12 of the CRC, which is the child's right to participation, is operative through organizations of predominantly children with experience from child protection services, so-called 'experts by experience'. The chapter discusses how their messages influence child welfare policy and practice. The focus is on one particular Finnish group of experts by experience, and its immense impact on policy and practice.

In Chap. 7, Anne-Dorthe Hestbæk examines the rights of young people in out-of-home care. The chapter utilizes five articles in CRC as a lever to critically assess whether or not they are operative in professional practice. The chapter highlights, for example, participation, protection against harm, and whether or not children feel cared for or loved. The chapter reaffirms the findings that young people being placed in institutional care seem to live under considerably more disadvantaged conditions than young people in foster care.

In Chap. 8, Elisabeth Gording-Stang problematizes practices of emergency cases in child protection, and how child protection services sometimes must intervene without traditional legal safeguards. She uses court decisions to shed light on how fundamental contradicting interests are being considered and balanced by the courts, and how professional practice at the street level may learn from it.

In Chap. 9, Bente Kojan and Graham Clifford discuss whether the avowed aim of a preventative approach in child protection, with strategies that set out to avoid the very large moral and economic costs of placement outside the family, is at all well served by the prevailing distribution of child protection assistance to families and children. They discuss how rights-based, professional child protection work might be of help.

In Chap. 10, Øivin Christiansen and Ragnhild Hollekim discuss how principles of the CRC inform and challenge the practices of professionals engaged in child welfare services' preventive in-home measures. The discussion centres on the threefold relationship between the child, the parents and the state. They question where to place the threshold for public intervention in family life, and how to realize children's rights to services when their parents do not give their consent. They further discuss reasons for and consequences following the fact that support to children is primarily strived for through targeting parents. Finally, the chapter problematizes three possible consequences: the homogenization of parenthood, reduction of complexity and the marginalization of children themselves.

In Chap. 11, Cecilie Basberg Neumann draws attention to the meaning of social workers' conduct of care practices with young children living in residential child protection institutions. She is interested in identifying what good care practices may be, and to discuss how these practices may be understood as realizations of CRC Art. 3, on the best interests of the child. Through observations and articulations of what social workers do when they provide care for children in residential institutions, she attempts to show that good care practices for young children have a lot to do with the social worker's willingness to engage in sensitive, responsible and embodied interactions with the children.

In Chap. 12, Elisabeth Backe-Hansen focuses on CRC Art. 12 as it pertains to foster children. In addition to participation rights that all children share, foster children have a set of administrative participation rights related to their case. Foster parents have to share their parental authority with persons of authority outside of the family. In contrast, she discusses children's participation in everyday decision-making as an integral part of family life, and what challenges may occur when foster children and other children with participatory rights must interact.

The concluding chapter summarizes the main findings and discusses their interconnection.

8 Conclusion

We are living in a time when systems of child protection across modern nation-states receive massive criticism both nationally and internationally. In particular, this pertains to out-of-home placements of children, against parents' expressed wishes. Voluntary in-house measures are mostly ignored in this context. Different nation-states' politicians, public officials, NGOs, professionals, scholars, the traditional and new media, all participate in these discussions, from various points of departure. Since child protection is characterized by controversy as well as being an academic field submerged in normative complexity and uncertainty, answers and heated discourses about what constitutes 'the best' type of protection abound.

However, rights are an equalizer, and children living in jurisdictions that claim to abide by rights should not experience widely different practices if said practices are supposed to abide by the same framework of legislation. Although there are widely different ways to perform child protection services, the CRC provides us for the time being a common goal.

References

Abbott, A. (1988). *The system of professions. An essay on the division of expert labor*. Chicago: University of Chicago Press.

Aristotle. (2014). Politics. In J. Barnes (Ed.), *The complete works of Aristotle: The revised Oxford translation, one-volume digital edition*. Princeton: Princeton University Press.

Burns, K., Pösö, T., & Skivenes, M. (2016). *Child welfare removals by the state. A cross-country analysis of decision-making systems*. New York: Oxford University Press.

Fox Harding, L. (2014). *Perspectives in child care policy*. London: Routledge.

Gilbert, N., Parton, N., & Skivenes, M. (2011). *Child protection systems: International trends and orientations*. New York: Oxford University Press.

Goodin, R. E. (1986). Welfare, rights and discretion. *Oxford Journal of Legal Studies, 6*(2), 232–261.

Kriz, K., & Skivenes, M. (2014). Street-level policy aims of child welfare workers in England, Norway and the United States: An exploratory study. *Children and Youth Services Review, 40*, 71–78.

Lipsky, M. (1980). *Street-level bureaucracy. Dilemmas of the individual in public services*. New York: Russell Sage Foundation.

Molander, A., Grimen, H., & Eriksen, E. O. (2012). Professional discretion and accountability in the welfare state. *Journal of Applied Philosophy, 29*(3), 214–230. https://doi.org/10.1111/j.1468-5930.2012.00564.x.

Rothstein, B. (1998). *Just institutions matter. The moral and political logic of the universal welfare state*. Cambridge: Cambridge University Press.

Skivenes, M., & Sørsdal, L. M. (2018). The child's best interest principle across child protection jurisdictions. In A. Falch-Eriksen & E. Backe-Hansen (Eds.), *Human rights in child protection. Implications for professional practice and policy*. London: Palgrave Macmillan.

Open Access This chapter is licensed under the terms of the Creative Commons Attribution 4.0 International License (http://creativecommons.org/licenses/by/4.0/), which permits use, sharing, adaptation, distribution and reproduction in any medium or format, as long as you give appropriate credit to the original author(s) and the source, provide a link to the Creative Commons license and indicate if changes were made.

The images or other third party material in this chapter are included in the chapter's Creative Commons license, unless indicated otherwise in a credit line to the material. If material is not included in the chapter's Creative Commons license and your intended use is not permitted by statutory regulation or exceeds the permitted use, you will need to obtain permission directly from the copyright holder.

2

Children's Right to Protection Under the CRC

Kirsten Sandberg

1 Introduction

The UN Convention on the Rights of the Child (CRC) recognizes children as rights holders and provides them with individual rights. The aim of this chapter is to provide the reader with a legal understanding of children's right to protection against maltreatment in their homes and the obligations of states parties in implementing this right in practice. The rights and obligations form the framework within which to exercise professional judgment in this area, and specifying their content is a prerequisite for rights to be realized.

Children's rights under the CRC are commonly divided into three categories, and protection rights are one of those, beside provision rights and participation rights (Hammarberg 1990, p. 100). However, children's rights are indivisible and holistic and should not be seen separately or in isolation from each other. This book is about child protection, but

---

K. Sandberg (✉)
University of Oslo, Oslo, Norway
e-mail: kirsten.sandberg@jus.uio.no

children cannot be properly protected without being provided with food, housing, care, health services and education or the opportunity to participate in decision-making regarding their own lives and in society. In protecting children, the interplay between the different types of rights is important.

Two of the articles in the Convention are central in obliging states parties to establish some form of child protection system. Under Article 19 children have the right to be protected from physical and mental violence, neglect, sexual abuse and exploitation, while they are in the care of parents or any other person. Article 3 para. 2 gives the child the right to such protection and care as is necessary for his or her well-being. The latter is formulated in a positive way, and especially the right to good care goes further than the right to be protected against various forms of maltreatment, which illustrates the blurred boundary between protection and provision.

In addition, Article 37 (a) contains a prohibition against torture and other cruel, inhuman or degrading treatment or punishment, similar to what applies to everybody under Article 7 of the International Covenant on Civil and Political Rights and Article 3 of the European Convention on Human Rights. However, CRC Article 19 is considered to be the core provision for addressing and eliminating all forms of violence against or maltreatment of children (GC No. 13, para. 7 a).

The primary position of the family in the upbringing of children is recognized by the Convention in its preamble:

Convinced that the family, as the fundamental group of society and the natural environment for the growth and well-being of all its members and particularly children, should be afforded the necessary protection and assistance so that it can fully assume its responsibilities within the community, ...

The child should primarily have the opportunity to grow up in its own family, and for that purpose assistance to the family may be necessary. However, the Convention also recognizes that children must be protected from violence, abuse and neglect and that separation from its parents may sometimes be necessary for the child's best interests (Art. 9, para. 1, GC No. 13, para. 7 a).

The Convention requires a child rights approach to child care and protection, meaning that the child should be viewed as a rights holder, not a beneficiary of adults' benevolence (GC No. 13, para 72 a). As explained by the UN Committee on the Rights of the Child (henceforth: the Committee):

> *In a child rights approach, the process of realizing children's rights is as important as the end result. A child rights approach ensures respect for the dignity, life, survival, well-being, health, development, participation and non-discrimination of the child as a rights holder.* (GC No. 21, para. 10)

In relation to child protection, the Committee underlines the connection between the child rights approach and the resources of the child itself and its surrounding social systems:

> *This child rights approach ... places emphasis on supporting the strengths and resources of the child him/herself and all social systems of which the child is a part: family, school, community, institutions, religious and cultural systems.* (GC No. 13, para. 59)

The Committee on the Rights of the Child is responsible for monitoring states parties' compliance with the CRC. It consists of 18 independent experts from various countries around the world, elected by the 196 states which have ratified the Convention (states parties)[1]; see Article 43. The states parties are under the obligation to report to the Committee every five years (Article 44). The Committee receives additional information from a variety of sources. Based on all of this the Committee holds a dialogue with a delegation from the country and subsequently produces its concluding observations with recommendations.

In addition to reviewing country reports, the Committee has developed 23 general comments (GCs). Since 2014 it also deals with individual complaints under the 3rd Optional protocol to the Convention on a communications procedure.[2]

This chapter will present children's rights in the context of child protection. The general principles of the Convention are introduced in Sect. 2. Section 3 presents Article 19, its interpretation and scope. In the following sections, the obligations of each state party are outlined. A major obligation is to do everything possible to prevent violence, abuse and neglect from occurring (Sect. 4). Once maltreatment of children has taken place, the states parties have the obligation to respond to it in various ways, with particular regard to protecting the child and fulfilling the child's right to rehabilitation under Art. 39 (Sect. 5). Considering the best interests of the child is crucial in all professional work in this area (Sect. 6). In the concluding Sect. 7 the threads are gathered.

2 General Principles

The Convention contains four general principles which are cross-cutting and thus relevant to child protection. One of them, the right to life, survival and development under Article 6, forms the very basis for the child's right to protection from all forms of maltreatment. The term 'development' should be interpreted in its broadest sense, to encompass the child's physical, mental, spiritual, moral and social development (CRC Article 27 para. 1, GC No. 13, para. 61).

The right to non-discrimination under Article 2 is an important safeguard against arbitrary treatment. While requiring that equal cases be treated equally, it also implies that differences and nuances between cases should lead to differential treatment. Thus, in child protection, where no case is equal, the idea of formal equality is not easily applicable to professional judgment. However, differences in treatment need valid reasons. If decisions are studied systematically certain patterns may appear which may give rise to the question of bias in the execution of professional discretion; for example with regard to ethnicity or social background.

The right of children under Article 3 para. 1 to have their best interests taken into account as a primary consideration in all actions concerning them is crucial for all decision-making. It requires precisely that each child is treated individually and is highly relevant for the child protection system (more in Sect. 6 below).

Children's rights under Article 12 to express their views in decision-making and have them given due weight is vital, both for their feeling of being involved in their own case and for the aim of reaching a good decision (GC No. 12). The child's view is also an important element in determining what is in his or her best interests.[3] Children's participation as well as their best interests are not only relevant for individual decisions affecting the child, but also in designing the system of decision-making.

3 Article 19: Interpretation and Scope

Article 19 contains the right to protection and reads as follows:

1. *States Parties shall take all appropriate legislative, administrative, social and educational measures to protect the child from all forms of physical or mental violence, injury or abuse, neglect or negligent treatment, maltreatment or exploitation, including sexual abuse, while in the care of parent(s), legal guardian(s) or any other person who has the care of the child.*
2. *Such protective measures should, as appropriate, include effective procedures for the establishment of social programmes to provide necessary support for the child and for those who have the care of the child, as well as for other forms of prevention and for identification, reporting, referral, investigation, treatment and follow-up of instances of child maltreatment described heretofore, and, as appropriate, for judicial involvement.*

The Committee has published a general comment on Article 19 (GC No. 13) on the right of the child to protection from all forms of violence, which is informative in explaining the content of this right and the obligations of states parties in this regard. Further guidelines for practice are found in the United Nations Alternative Care Guidelines and the handbook to these guidelines (Cantwell et al. 2012).

In its first paragraph, Article 19 lists all the various forms of maltreatment that the child shall be protected from. The Committee in GC No. 13 uses the term 'violence' to cover everything listed in Article 19 para. 1: all forms of physical or mental violence, injury or abuse, neglect or negligent treatment, maltreatment or exploitation, including sexual abuse.[4] The term 'all forms' indicates that there are no exceptions, which is deemed necessary as the slightest possibility of any form of acceptable maltreatment easily will be misused. Whether all instances of maltreatment should be prosecuted is another matter.

It is debatable whether using the term violence to cover all forms of maltreatment is useful in a child protection context. Even if it emphasizes that all the acts listed in Article 19 are harmful to children, the nuances disappear and thus the need to adapt the measures to the type of maltreatment in question. Instead, I will use the term 'maltreatment' below to make it clear that I do not only speak about physical or mental violence, but also neglect and sexual abuse.

Corporal punishment is unacceptable, however light (GC No. 13, para. 17, 22 (a) and 24, GC No. 8, paras. 2, 5, 8 and 11). Any excuse in law for parents, legal guardians or any other person to use physical punishment in the upbringing, such as 'reasonable chastisement', 'justifiable assault' or 'right to correct', must be abolished.[5] States parties are required by Article 19 para. 1 to take 'all appropriate legislative, administrative, social and educational measures' to protect the child from the above-mentioned acts. The measures are elaborated in para. 2 and further specified by the Committee in GC No. 13 (para. 11 b), including the need for judicial measures.

The objectives of GC No. 13 are to guide states parties in their efforts to understand their obligations under Article 19 and to outline necessary measures. Furthermore, the aim is to overcome isolated, fragmented and reactive initiatives to address child caregiving and protection, 'to promote a holistic approach to implementing Article 19 based on the Convention's overall perspective on securing children's rights' (para. 11 d), and to provide states parties and other stakeholders with a basis from which to develop a coordinating framework for eliminating maltreatment. In stressing these objectives, the Committee shows the necessity for states parties to develop an 'integrated, cohesive, interdisciplinary and coordinated' child protection system (para. 39). The system should consist of legislative, administrative, social and educational measures as mentioned in Article 19 para. 1 and cover all types of interventions mentioned in para. 2, that is various forms of prevention as well as identification, reporting, referral, investigation, treatment and follow-up of individual instances.

In short, the obligations of states parties are to prohibit, prevent and respond to all forms of violence as presented above. Prevention is at the very core of protecting children from violence. It has several aspects, and prohibition is a crucial part of it. I will come back to prevention in Sect. 4 below, after a few words about the system that needs to be in place.

Individual rights are of little value if the states parties do not have the structures in place to implement them, and children's right to protection cannot be upheld without a proper child protection system. That is why the Committee in its exchange with states parties pays a lot of attention to general measures of implementation (GC No. 5 2003). There must be legislation in place, a comprehensive policy and strategy, a coordinating body at the national level, and allocation of the resources necessary for the activities (GC No. 13 para. 72 and GC No. 19).[6] As a factual basis for formulating the law and policies, and for evaluating them, the states parties should have a comprehensive data collection system.[7] Knowledge of the Convention should be disseminated to the public and to children, and all professionals working with or for children need training on how to implement the Convention, including on best interests and how to have conversations with children.[8] To hold the government accountable, all states parties should have a fully independent national human rights institution (Paris Principles 1993; GC No. 2 2002), and the involvement of civil society should be supported.

4 Prevention of Maltreatment

4.1 Overview

The main way to protect children from all forms of violence as understood by Article 19 is to prevent it from occurring. In addition to social policy and educational measures being mentioned in Article 19 para. 1, prevention is specifically required by para. 2. The need for prevention is strongly emphasized by the Committee in GC No. 13 (para. 46). Prevention can take place at various levels. General prevention is aimed at combating the root causes of maltreatment of children, such as poverty as a stress factor in the daily lives of families or the status of persons with disabilities in a society. More specific preventive measures, but still at the general level, may be directed at supporting children and their families or at changing attitudes to children and the way they are treated. Individual prevention is necessary where a child is at risk.

Prohibition is an important part of prevention. It sends a clear message that violence against children is unacceptable, as well as, hopefully, deterring people from committing violence for fear of sanctions. Whether a prohibition should lead to reporting to the police in all instances will be discussed in Sect. 5.2 below.

Without coordination of the efforts of various sectors children may fall between the cracks and successful prevention may not be possible. Thus, GC No. 13 underlines that

> *[m]echanisms must be explicitly outlined to ensure effective coordination at central, regional and local levels, between different sectors and with civil society, including the empirical research community.* (Para. 72 (i))

More specifically, the Committee recommends that the links between mental health services, substance abuse treatment and child protection services be strengthened (GC No. 13, para. 47 [c] iii).

4.2 Social Policy Measures

Poverty makes it difficult for parents to take proper care of their children. Not only does it entail challenges in providing children with basic necessities such as food, clothing and shelter, it may also lead to various forms of parental behaviour that are detrimental to children. Parents may have to go away to find work in another part of the country or abroad, leaving their children behind without proper care ('I am Kuba' 2015; Sandberg 2018).[9] Where instead they stay at home, the stressful situation may lead to emotional neglect of the children and even physical violence or other forms of abusive behaviour. That is why poverty reduction strategies, including financial and social support to families at risk, as well as housing and employment policies, are important social policy measures to prevent violence against children from occurring (CRC, Art. 27, para. 3, GC No. 13, para. 43 [a], Alternative Care Guidelines 2010, para. 15).[10]

4.3 Social Programmes for Caregivers and Children

In general, the significance of the family as a favourable environment for children to grow up in is emphasized by the CRC, particularly in the preamble but also in provisions such as Article 18. Article 19 para. 2 requests that states parties establish social programmes to provide necessary support for the child and for those who have the care of the child. Support to the family in order to enable parents and other caregivers to take care of their children in an adequate way is high on the Committee's agenda.[11] Examples of social programmes to be established to provide optimal positive child-rearing are community-based mutual-help groups, welfare programmes, counselling support and therapeutic programmes for caregivers related to domestic violence, alcohol, drugs or mental health needs. Other measures are pre- and post-natal services and home visitation programmes. There should also be programmes directed at children themselves, such as childcare, early childhood development and after-school care programmes, child and youth groups and clubs, counselling support to children and 24-hour free helplines GC No. 13, paras 43 b and 47 c).

4.4 Educational Measures

Another type of prevention is educational measures to change attitudes in society to children and their upbringing, to violence in general and more specifically to violence and other harmful behaviour towards children. Educational measures are required by Article 19 para. 1 and further elaborated in GC No. 13. They should 'address attitudes, traditions, customs and behavioural practices which condone and promote violence against children' (para. 44). In particular, awareness campaigns should be conducted to promote positive child-rearing and combat negative societal attitudes, a recommendation which is repeatedly made to states parties in the Committee's concluding observations. More specifically parents and other caregivers should be educated in this regard.

Children's empowerment and participation under Article 12 are crucial aspects of the prevention of violence. Information should be provided which is accurate, accessible and age-appropriate. Training on life skills, self-protection and participation should be conducted. The Committee also underlines the need for all children to be registered in order to facilitate their access to services and redress procedures (GC No. 13, paras 44 and 47). Last but not least, training of professionals and others working with or for children is necessary for children's rights to be upheld. It should be carried out on a regular basis, as an ongoing process and not as a one-off event. The training must cover a child rights approach to Article 19 and its application in practice. Professionals and others should be able to guide parents and other caregivers on positive parenting and the importance of avoiding any kind of maltreatment in the upbringing. Groups mentioned in GC No. 13 are teachers at all levels of the educational system, social workers, medical doctors, nurses and other health professionals, psychologists, lawyers, judges, police, probation and prison officers, journalists, community workers, residential caregivers, civil servants and public officials, asylum officers and traditional and religious leaders (para. 44).

4.5 Individual Prevention: Identification and Intervention

Targeted prevention requires that children at risk are identified (see Article 19 para. 2). To prevent maltreatment from occurring, children must, according to GC No. 13, be given 'as many opportunities as possible to signal emerging problems before they reach a state of crisis' (para. 48). Adults that are in contact with a child should be able to recognize possible issues from the child's behaviour or what the child says, without the child explicitly asking for help. This is highly relevant for school and pre-school teachers who meet the child every day, as well as health professionals, social workers and police, but also for adults in the family or neighbourhood who meet the child in an informal setting. Identification requires that 'all who come in contact with children are aware of risk factors and indicators of all forms of violence, have received guidance on how to interpret such indicators, and have the necessary knowledge, willingness and ability to take appropriate action' (ibid.).

For those who see that a child may be at risk, there must be clear guidance as to how this can and should be reported to the child protection authorities. Such authorities should be present at community level and stand ready to deal with the issue swiftly, in order to prevent problems from escalating. Since the cases and situations may vary enormously, a number of measures should be available. Any intervention should be targeted at the situation of this individual child and selected according to his or her best interests (see Sect. 6 below). The government, civil society and professionals are encouraged to develop and implement community-based services. Assistance to the family should be provided

> *by adopting measures that promote family unity and ensure for children the full exercise and enjoyment of their rights in private settings, abstaining from unduly interfering in children's private and family relations, depending on circumstances.* (GC No. 13, para. 47)

The emphasis on family unity and the importance for the child of family relations is fully in line with the Convention, as mentioned above. A footnote to this quote in the GC refers to, among other items, a decision from the European Court of Human Rights from 1988 (Olsson) regarding the right to family life. Although that decision is still relevant, the European Court of Human Rights in recent years increasingly has made reference to the best interests of the child in determining the limits of parents' right to family life (see, among others, Jovanovic v. Sweden [2015], para. 77, and Chap. 4 in this book). There will always be the question of how far one should go in protecting family unity if a child is at risk. At the preventive stage, before the maltreatment has escalated, retaining family unity is the clear starting point and main rule. However, at a certain point it may not be possible to protect the child from maltreatment and uphold his or her best interests by preventive measures in the home only. It may be necessary to break family unity by removing the child or, as it may be, the perpetrator from the home.[12] A main purpose of separation is to prevent further maltreatment of the child. However, it is also necessary to respond in an adequate way to the maltreatment that has already happened (see the next section).

5 Responding to Violence, Abuse and Neglect

5.1 Reporting and Referral

The response to violence is outlined in Article 19 para. 2 as reporting, referral, investigation, treatment and follow-up. Before being reported or otherwise acted upon, maltreatment of children must be identified, which is further elaborated above. As an aspect of prevention, reporting of children at risk is important, but when maltreatment actually occurs there need to be stronger reporting mechanisms. The Committee strongly recommends that all states parties develop

> *safe, well-publicized, confidential and accessible support mechanisms for children, their representatives and others to report violence against children, including through the use of 24-hour toll-free hotlines and other ICTs.* (GC No. 13, para. 49)

The GC further states that reporting should at least be required of professionals working directly with children. The obligation to report should cover not only instances of violence, but also suspicion or risk (ibid.). To whom one should report is not elaborated in GC No. 13. It could be to a public agency with responsibility for child protection, but as apparent from the quote above it could also be for example to a helpline. The point is that whoever receives the report must have an obligation to act upon it and where necessary refer it to the relevant agency (see below).

The establishment of reporting mechanisms entails the need for providing training and support for personnel who receive the information on how to act upon it in a meaningful way. Related support services for children and families should be established, and they should be help-oriented, offering public health and social support, rather than triggering responses which are primarily punitive (GC No. 13, para. 49).

Closely related to reporting, which is expected of professionals dealing with a child, referral of the case to the appropriate agency is crucial for giving the child assistance according to his or her needs. The receiving agency should be the one in charge of coordinating the response, such as a child protection or child welfare agency. The child may be in need of services from various sectors, such as health care or specialized services for children with disabilities. Consequently, the Committee stresses the need for professionals in the child protection system to be trained in inter-agency cooperation and protocols for collaboration. According to GC No. 13, the process will involve:

(a) *a participatory, multi-disciplinary assessment of the short- and long-term needs of the child, caregivers and family, which invites and gives due weight to the child's views as well as those of the caregivers and family;*
(b) *sharing of the assessment results with the child, caregivers and family;*
(c) *referral of the child and family to a range of services to meet those needs; and*
(d) *follow-up and evaluation of the adequateness of the intervention.* (Para. 50)

5.2 Investigation and Prosecution

Investigation of a case of violence against children may take place within the child protection system, with the aim of providing assistance to the child and the family. It may also be conducted by the police with the aim of deciding whether to bring charges against the perpetrator. The two forms of investigation are not contradictory, and the one does not exclude the other. However, there are several challenges in the intersection between the child protection system in its narrow sense (as the system providing assistance to the child and family or making other interventions in the family) and the criminal justice system. Where prosecution may lead to a parent being sentenced to prison, this may not be in the best interests of the child. Additionally, if parents know that by admitting violence against their child they will be reported to the police, they may not be willing to admit such acts. Without the parents acknowledging what they are doing and the consequences for the child of being maltreated, it may on the other hand not be possible to provide them with the appropriate training, treatment or other measures to overcome the problems and so to maintain the unity of the family.

According to GC No. 13, 'extreme care must be taken to avoid subjecting the child to further harm through the process of the investigation' (para. 51), but it does not elaborate on how the various dilemmas may be dealt with. In GC No. 8 on corporal punishment, however, the Committee states,

> *While all reports of violence against children should be appropriately investigated and their protection from significant harm assured, the aim should be to stop parents from using violent or other cruel or degrading punishments through supportive and educational, not punitive, interventions.* (Para. 40)

The statement is directly related to violence used as a punishment in the upbringing, but it is just as relevant for other forms of parental behaviour which is detrimental to children. The main point of investigation should be to stop the violence, not to sanction the parents. Indeed, a prohibition and criminalization of violence against children may not be fully effective unless sometimes followed up by prosecution and sentencing to set an example. The Committee yet explicitly states that prosecuting parents is in most cases unlikely to be in their children's best interests. According to the Committee, a case should only be prosecuted where it is regarded as necessary to protect the child from significant harm and is in the best interests of the child, with due weight to the child's views (GC No. 8, para. 41). The prosecution authorities need training to carry out assessments of a child's best interests in such situations. However, it is not necessarily a good idea to leave this assessment to the prosecutor. In light of what is said above on the challenge of making parents cooperate with the child protection authorities if the case is reported to the police, it may not be in the child's best interest to do so. This should be assessed on a case-by-case basis by the child protection authorities.

5.3 Treatment and Follow-Up

In Article 19 the only reference to what kind of assistance should be provided to the child and/or the family is the term 'treatment'. A relevant provision in this respect is Article 39 on the child's right to rehabilitation, which requires the states parties to

> *take all appropriate measures to promote physical and psychological recovery and social reintegration of a child victim of: any form of neglect, exploitation, or abuse; ... Such recovery and reintegration shall take place in an environment which fosters the health, self-respect and dignity of the child.*

Effective access to redress, remedies and reparation to children when their rights are violated should be ensured by legislative provisions (Comment No. 13, para. 41 f and i). In individual cases of considering rehabilitation and reparation, attention must be given to hearing the child's views and giving them due weight under Article 12. The child's safety and the possible need for immediate safe placement are important considerations. Furthermore, as with all interventions in the child protection system, the 'predictable influences' of potential interventions on the child's long-term well-being, health and development must be taken into account (GC No. 13, para. 52). There is an unavoidable need in such cases to make predictions, and purely theoretical effects are not sufficient. Predictions should be based on empirical facts of the past and present, concerning the child and his or her situation and relationships. According to Art. 3 para. 1 the decision shall be made according to the child's best interests (see GC No. 14 and below).

As possible types of intervention GC No. 13 mentions medical, mental health, social and legal services and support, as well as longer-term follow-up services. A full range of services should be made available, including services and treatment for perpetrators of violence, especially child perpetrators. Family group conferencing and other similar decision-making practices are also mentioned (para. 52).

Separation of the child from its parents is not generally desirable and as a main rule shall not happen against their will (see Art. 9 para. 1 of the CRC). The same provision provides for an exception, but only in cases where it is necessary in the best interests of the child. Abuse and neglect are specifically mentioned as circumstances that may make separation necessary. If the child is placed outside the parental home, the child should be ensured contact with both parents under Article 9, para. 3, unless it is contrary to the best interests of the child (see GC No. 13, para. 53). Under Article 16 children also have a right to respect for their family life with the wider family, which whould be understood to include their siblings (see ECtHR, Moustaquim v. Belgium 1991, para. 36). Thus, the relationship of the child and his or her siblings should be taken into account in the professional judgment of what interventions to make.

The term 'follow-up' requires that it is made clear who has the responsibility for the child and the family through all the stages of a case and clarification of the aims of whatever actions are taken. Furthermore, it requires that deadlines are set for the implementation and that the duration of any intervention is made clear. Interventions should be subject to review, monitoring and evaluation, for which mechanisms and dates must be clarified in advance. There should be a case management process in order to secure continuity between stages of intervention (GC No. 13, para. 53). The child's right to development under Article 6, including its physical, mental, spiritual, moral and social development, is crucial and should be taken into account in all decisions (ibid., Art. 27, para. 1, GC No. 5, para. 12). Article 29 on the aims of education in its letter (a) presents the aspiration of the development of the child's personality, talents and mental and physical abilities to their fullest potential. The child also has the right under Article 25 to periodic review of treatment and placements.

5.4 Judicial Involvement

Article 19 does not require judicial involvement in all cases, only 'as appropriate'. With reference to the best interests of the child as the primary purpose of decision-making, the Committee stresses that regard should be given 'to the least intrusive intervention as warranted by the circumstances' (GC No. 13, para. 54). However, according to Article 9, para. 1 a decision to separate a child from its family should always be subject to judicial review. Administrative courts or court-resembling bodies[13] are included in this concept, provided they fulfil the requirements of independence and legal expertise.

In addition to juvenile or family court intervention, judicial intervention may consist of family group conferencing, alternative dispute-resolution mechanisms and restorative justice and kin agreements, provided that processes respect human rights and are accountable and managed by trained facilitators (para. 55).

Requirements for the judicial process include prompt and adequate information for the child and its parents. Wherever possible, the process should be of a preventive nature. The procedures have to be child-friendly throughout the process, taking into account the child's personal situation, needs, age, gender, disability and level of maturity, and fully respecting their physical, mental and moral integrity. Child-friendliness also implies that the process should be swift (para. 54 a–d, Alternative Care Guidelines, para. 57).

Where appropriate, juvenile or family specialized courts and criminal procedures should be established for child victims of violence, which could include specialized units within the police, the court and the prosecutor's office. Specific interdisciplinary training on the rights and needs of children should be provided to all professionals involved in such cases (para. 56).

6 Best Interests of the Child

In the implementation of the system, decisions and other actions have to be taken every day in relation to every child that needs protection. The best interests of the child are mentioned several times above in relation to various individual decisions that need to be made; they are relevant for any intervention made by the child protection authorities as well as the more specific decisions of separating the child from its parents, whether or not to prosecute parents, and so forth. Those who prepare and make decisions must use their professional judgment in looking for possible solutions and in choosing among the alternatives, and the best interests of the child should guide that judgment.

A main point of Article 3 para. 1 on the best interests of the child is that decisions have to be made according to the individual child and his or her situation. As emphasized by the Committee,

Assessing the child's best interests is a unique activity that should be undertaken in each individual case, in the light of the specific circumstances of each child or group of children or children in general. (GC No. 14, para. 48)

To guide the best interests assessment, the Committee in its GC No. 14 made a non-exhaustive list of elements to consider (para. 50).

The child's views are central in this respect, and the fact that the child is very young, has a disability, belongs to a minority group or is in any other vulnerable situation does not deprive him or her of the right to be heard nor reduce the weight to be given to the child's views. Another important element is the child's identity, including his or her personality and characteristics such as sex, sexual orientation, gender identity, religion and beliefs, and cultural identity. This demonstrates the need for diversity in assessing children's best interests. If the child is in a situation of vulnerability of some kind, such as having a disability, belonging to a minority group, being an asylum seeker, victim of abuse or living in a street situation, this situation should be taken into account. However, even children in such situations should be judged individually. Other elements in the best interests assessment are the possibility of providing care, protection and safety to the child, and preservation of the family environment and maintaining relations. These correspond with the rights emphasized above. The reason why they are also included as part of the best interests assessment is that this assessment has to be undertaken once the various rights do not point in a clear direction. The child's right to health and to education are also elements to be taken into account (GC No. 14, paras 53–79).

In deciding what measure to take in a child protection context, resilience and protective factors, as well as risk factors, should be taken into account. Protective factors include:

> *stable families; nurturing child-rearing by adults who meet the child's physical and psychosocial needs; positive non-violent discipline; secure attachment of the child to at least one adult; supportive relationships with peers and others (including teachers); a social environment that fosters pro-social, non-violent and non-discriminatory attitudes and behaviours; high levels of community social cohesion; and thriving social networks and neighbourhood connections.*
> (GC No. 13, para. 72e)

Once all the elements that are relevant for an individual child in his or her specific situation have been identified, examined and assessed, they have to be considered altogether for a best interests determination. If they all point in the same direction, it is clear what solution is in the child's best interests. Where, on the other hand, different elements point in different directions, they need to be balanced. This balancing exercise has to be performed with regard to the individual situation and needs of that child. For instance, where protection factors stand up against factors related to the autonomy of the child, the age and maturity of the child should guide the balancing. In assessing the maturity, the physical, emotional, cognitive and social development of the child should be taken into account (GC No. 14, paras 80–83). Interestingly, the GC adds that in the light of children's evolving capacities, decision-makers should consider measures that can be adjusted or revised accordingly, rather than irreversible solutions.

Where there are competing interests or rights of other people, Article 3 says that the best interests of the child should be 'a primary consideration'. They should have great weight, but Article 3 does not exclude the possibility of other rights or interests prevailing. In child protection cases, however, where the opposing interests are those of the parents that are responsible for the child, the best interests of the child should carry particularly great weight. The parents do not have the right to any action that may harm the child. This is the approach taken by the European Court of Human Rights, stating that 'in cases of this type (public care of children and contact restrictions) the child's interest must come before all other considerations' (Jovanovic v. Sweden 2015, para. 77).

7 Conclusion

In order to realize children's right to protection under Article 19 of the CRC, the state party has the obligation to make available all the preventive measures presented in Sect. 4 and have measures in place to respond to maltreatment of children as outlined in Sect. 5. At the individual level, child protection involves a choice of measures and other decisions for which Article 3 para. 1 requires that the best interests of the child 'shall be a primary consideration' (see Sect. 6). The best interests of the child give direction to the professional judgment to be exercised at all levels of these cases.

As Cantwell points out, it is essential that the reference to best interests does not divert attention away from the vital message of the Convention, that children have human rights.[14] At the outset, the best interests of the child is a paternalistic concept that should not override the idea of the child as a rights holder. However, the two are not necessarily contradictory. The child rights approach mentioned in the introduction to this chapter emphasizes the child as a rights holder, and the whole child protection system is to be based on the rights of the child. In exercising their professional judgment in individual cases, it is important that the professionals bear in mind their obligation to safeguard the child's right to protection, as well as the inter-connected rights such as the rights to health, rehabilitation and development. At the same time, they should seek to uphold, as far as possible, the right of the child to respect for its family life. In situations where the rights of the child point in different directions, or where there is a choice between measures to uphold the rights, the best interests of the individual child are a useful tool to guide the solution.

Last, but not least, the child's right to express its views and have them taken into account is vital in any decision-making. As demonstrated above, the child's views should be an essential element in the best interests assessment, making it less paternalistic. This right, however, does not imply that the adults can leave the decision to the child in the name of autonomy or for the sake of convenience. The responsibility for making decisions lies with the adults.

Notes

1. All nation-states in the world except the USA.
2. An optional protocol is an addition to the Convention, and states choose whether they want to ratify it. The two first optional protocols are on children in armed conflict and on the sale of children, child prostitution and child pornography.
3. See Peters (2018) for reflections on the voice, story and dignity of the child in relation to hearing children in child protection, Leviner (2018) on the need to rethink children's participation in the Swedish child

protection system, and Pösö and Enroos (2017) on the narrow representation and use of children's views in Finnish care orders.
4. In line with the Global Study on violence against children (2006), para. 8.
5. The first two terms are from common-law systems, the latter from countries influenced by French law.
6. The lack of a coordinating body in many South American countries is emphasized by Kamimura et al. (2017).
7. On the situation of data collection in some Latin American countries, see Kamimura et al. (2017), at pp. 848–853.
8. On the important role of professionals, see Cardol (2017), p. 891.
9. 'I am Kuba' (2015), Sandberg (2018).
10. The example of Mozambique is presented in Huijbregts and Chowdhury (2017).
11. Van den Boom (2017, pp. 810–811) calls for the Committee to become more explicit in its concluding observations to states parties about their duty to provide parent support services.
12. See Sandberg (2018) on the requirements for placing the child in alternative care.
13. Such as the Norwegian County Board.
14. Cantwell (2017), p. 62.

References

Cantwell, N. (2017). Are 'best interests' a pillar or a problem for implementing the human rights of children? In T. Liefaard & J. Sloth-Nielsen (Eds.), *The United Nations convention on the rights of the child: Taking stock after 25 years and looking ahead* (pp. 61–72). Leiden/Boston: Brill/Nijhoff.
Cantwell, N., Davidson, J., Elsley, S., Milligan, I., & Quinn, N. (2012). Moving forward: Implementing the 'Guidelines for the alternative care of children'. Glasgow: Centre for Excellence for Looked After Children in Scotland (CELCIS). Retrieved from http://www.alternativecareguidelines.org/Portals/46/Moving-forward/Moving-Forward-implementing-the-guidelines-for-web1.pdf
Cardol, G. (2017). Amendment of the Dutch child protection system: An improvement for children? In T. Liefaard & J. Sloth-Nielsen (Eds.), *The United Nations convention on the rights of the child: Taking stock after 25 years and looking ahead* (pp. 879–894). Leiden/Boston: Brill/Nijhoff.

Hammarberg, T. (1990). The UN convention on the rights of the child—And how to make it work. *Human Rights Quarterly, 12*(1), 97–105.
Huijbregts, M., & Chowdhury, S. (2017). Two for the price of one: Building a child protection system through social protection mechanisms. In T. Liefaard & J. Sloth-Nielsen (Eds.), *The United Nations convention on the rights of the child: Taking stock after 25 years and looking ahead* (pp. 814–834). Leiden/Boston: Brill/Nijhoff.
'I am Kuba'. (2015). Documentary film produced by Sant & Usant dokumentarfilm. Norway. www.iamkuba.no
Kamimura, A., Aragão Santos, V. O., & Ballesteros, P. R. (2017). Towards an effective system for child protection and prevention of violence against children in South America. In T. Liefaard & J. Sloth-Nielsen (Eds.), *The United Nations convention on the rights of the child: Taking stock after 25 years and looking ahead* (pp. 835–856). Leiden/Boston: Brill/Nijhoff.
Leviner, P. (2018). Child participation in the Swedish child protection system: Child-friendly focus but limited child influence on outcomes. *International Journal of Children's Rights, 26*(1), 136–158.
Peters, J. K. (2018). Seeking dignity, voice and story for children in our child protective systems. *International Journal of Children's Rights, 26*(1), 5–15.
Pösö, T., & Enroos, R. (2017). The representation of Children's views in Finnish court decisions regarding care orders. *International Journal of Children's Rights, 25*(3–4), 736–753.
Sandberg, K. (2018, forthcoming). Alternative care and children's rights. In U. Kilkelly & T. Liefaard (eds) International children's rights. Singapore: Springer Nature.
van den Boom, P. M. (2017). Advancing children's rights through parent support services. In T. Liefaard & J. Sloth-Nielsen (Eds.), *The United Nations convention on the rights of the child: Taking stock after 25 years and looking ahead* (pp. 801–812). Leiden/Boston: Brill/Nijhoff.

United Nations Documents

Alternative Care Guidelines. (2010). A/RES/64/142, Guidelines for the alternative care of children, resolution adopted by United Nations General Assembly 64/142, annex, 24 February 2010. Retrieved from https://www.unicef.org/protection/alternative_care_Guidelines-English.pdf

Global Study. (2006). Report of the independent expert for the United Nations study on violence against children, A61/299, P.S. Pinheiro. Retrieved from http://www.unviolencestudy.org/
Paris Principles. (1993). Principles relating to the status of National Institutions (The Paris Principles). Adopted by United Nations General Assembly resolution 48/134 of 20 December 1993. Retrieved from http://www.ohchr.org/EN/ProfessionalInterest/Pages/StatusOfNationalInstitutions.aspx

United Nations Committee on the Rights of the Child

GC (General Comment) No. 13. (2011). The right of the child to freedom from all forms of violence, CRC/C/GC/13.
GC No. 14. (2013). On the right of the child to have his or her best interests taken as a primary consideration (Art. 3, para. 1), CRC/C/GC/14.
GC No. 2. (2002). On the role of independent national human rights institutions in the promotion and protection of the rights of the child, CRC/GC/2002/2.
GC No. 21. (2017). On children in street situations, CRC/C/GC/21.
GC No. 5. (2003). On general measures of implementation of the convention on the rights of the child, CRC/GC/2003/5.
GC No. 8. (2006). The right of the child to protection from corporal punishment and other cruel or degrading forms of punishment (Arts 19; 28, para. 2; and 37, inter alia), CRC/C/GC/8.

European Court of Human Rights

Jovanovic v. Sweden. (2015). no. 10592/12, 22 October 2015.
Moustaquim v. Belgium. (1991). no. 12313/86, 18 February 1991.

Open Access This chapter is licensed under the terms of the Creative Commons Attribution 4.0 International License (http://creativecommons.org/licenses/by/4.0/), which permits use, sharing, adaptation, distribution and reproduction in any medium or format, as long as you give appropriate credit to the original author(s) and the source, provide a link to the Creative Commons license and indicate if changes were made.

The images or other third party material in this chapter are included in the chapter's Creative Commons license, unless indicated otherwise in a credit line to the material. If material is not included in the chapter's Creative Commons license and your intended use is not permitted by statutory regulation or exceeds the permitted use, you will need to obtain permission directly from the copyright holder.

3

Rights and Professional Practice: How to Understand Their Interconnection

Asgeir Falch-Eriksen

1 Introduction

The UN Convention on the Rights of the Child (CRC) is a catalogue of rights specifically aimed at protecting the integrity of each individual child.[1] By virtue of their humanity, children also carry other human rights, but the CRC is especially important to understand, given its sole purpose is to provide rights to children. The convention's potential lies within its global reach and its cosmopolitan human rights *ethos*. The human rights ethos is underpinned by the constitutional character of human rights, and the intention to safeguard and protect the rights-holder against different types of harm or to provide certain basic entitlements. A correct implementation and enforcement of the CRC would infuse the rights of the child in all areas of public regulation that affect children throughout childhood. Since so many nation-states claim to abide by the CRC, the CRC becomes increasingly important

A. Falch-Eriksen (✉)
Norwegian Social Research, Oslo Metropolitan University, Oslo, Norway
e-mail: asgeirer@oslomet.no

© The Author(s) 2018
A. Falch-Eriksen, E. Backe-Hansen (eds.), *Human Rights in Child Protection*,
https://doi.org/10.1007/978-3-319-94800-3_3

to understand and especially with regard to professional practice and policy development.

With respect to human rights, the signatories to the convention have *de facto*, but not always *de jure*, committed themselves to implement and enforce the public protection of children as a matter of a child's individual right (see Sandberg 2018: Chap. 2 in this book):

> *Art. 19.1. States Parties shall take all appropriate legislative, administrative, social and educational measures to protect the child from all forms of physical or mental violence…while in the care of parent(s)…*

Each signatory state must, in order to abide by the convention, operationalize the child's right to be protected as a positive entitlement. This can happen through budgets, through legal regulation, policy and professional decision-making on the street level (Goodin 1986; Lipsky 1980; Rothstein 1998).

When children become subjected to detrimental care, protection according to the CRC must not only abide by the formal-semantic intent of specific rights-provisions, but also positively enforce the CRC in accordance with the fundamental normative principle of human rights that underpins the convention itself. Such a fundamental human rights principle is conceptually prior to the specific rights-provisions of any human rights convention and can be referred to as a basic human rights standard. If we focus upon the CRC, we can argue in broad terms that such a standard constitutes a fundamental defence of the individual child's liberty and integrity against detrimental care or other illegitimate or unlawful treatment.[2]

The duty that each signatory state has taken on itself to enforce Art. 19.1 will in this chapter be referred to as the state's duty to implement and enforce rights-based child protection services. The convention's formal impact can hardly be understated. The rights of the child are to be infused and enforced 'in all matters concerning children' (ref. CRC Art. 3.1.). In order to accommodate the CRC throughout child protection services, that is its practices and through public policy, the CRC regulations and its human rights standard must actively become points of reference that set restrictions and demands and govern 'in all matters'.

Accordingly, interpretation and active enforcement and implementation of the CRC through decision-making and through policy development must be constitutive to professional practice.

If a government is to make sure that child protection services become rights-based, it *first* needs to develop legal rules complying with human rights, and a system of protection that maintains the ethos of a human rights standard. *Second*, it needs to be vigilant in making sure that *all* extra-legal activities comply with the CRC and the basic principle of human rights. This is especially relevant with regard to public policy and professionalism. Since the CRC must be integrated and enforced in 'all actions concerning children', *rights-based* child protection must actively be made a part of all aspects of protection if the claim to abide by the CRC is to hold any merit. If for instance practical solutions make shortcuts, and argue that you do not need to have rigid decision-making designs that maintain the human rights standard because they are costly, or if the intervention is small, or we argue 'we know best', in such cases services *de facto* and *de jure* violate the human rights of the child, albeit in varying degrees.

This chapter will lay out theoretical propositions that combined will propose a way to understand the link between rights-based child protection and professional practice. The overarching goal is to build a bridge between the sociology of the professions, pertaining especially to different versions of social work for children, and a theory of rights. In sum, it will constitute building-blocks for a new theory of professionalism specifically aimed at rights-based child protection. It will not be possible to do justice to the complexity of such a theory on the whole in one chapter, and so the propositions will need to be further elaborated elsewhere.

A general rights-based approach to professional practice in child protection will need to draw eclectically upon four different strands of theory in order to become both conceptually coherent and have a high amount of explanatory power. The *first* is a theory of rights. It will be argued that the legitimacy and moral acceptability of protection according to rights depend on the level of constitutionality of the CRC within each nation-state, and how the material intent of the rights of the child is implemented procedurally in parallel with practices and policies of child protection that abide materially by rights themselves.

The *second* is a theory of epistemology. It will serve as a backdrop to the type of knowledge that can and cannot feed into professional practice, provided it is supposed to be rights-based. Hence, the theory of epistemology is about limits to what can constitute knowledge. This does not mean a distinct epistemological theory for child protection, but that rights-based child protection defines certain challenges and restrictions on how to reach legitimate decisions based upon knowledge.

The *third* theoretical strand is drawn more directly from the sociology of the professions and is interlinked with a theory of epistemology. It revolves around professional practices being operative on street level and by a professional that is the final agent of implementation in the democratic chain of command.

The *fourth* strand is about rights-based childhood. It is a normative theory of what on the one hand constitutes childhood from the point of view of human rights, and on the other what the public system of government must do to make sure that children develop without being affected by any type of detriment to their individual integrity.

2 A Theory of Rights and the Right to Protection

Key to understanding the basic principle of human rights is the notion of individual liberty and the need for protecting individual liberty, that is the protection of freedoms of the individual against unlawful interference, barriers and domination as a matter of right (Alexy 2002; Locke 1823). Protections of these kinds rest on the individual negative right to liberty (Berlin 1958; Kant 1993). Adults can fully make use of their rights and act positively on them in all matters. Children, on the other hand, constitute *a special case*. Although they have the inherent right to all freedoms by virtue of their humanity, they are not always capable of adequately acting upon freedom, nor should they carry the burden of responsibility before they can be fit to make their own choices (Mill 1867; Rawls 1993).

We can thereby claim that although children have a negative right to individual liberty, children do not have the right to positively act upon freedoms (Mill 1867). Whenever needed, others must act on their behalf, either parents or others who are authorized *in loco parentis* (medical practitioners, teachers, child protection services etc.). Child protection as a right is a prohibition against causing harm through detrimental care of a child, that is care that constitutes ill-treatment. The child's right to protection is a matter of the public prohibiting *every* act of care that causes detriment to the child.

2.1 Basic Human Rights Standard: Negative Right to Liberty

Fundamental to a system of rights, of which the CRC is an operative expression, is the basic human rights standard. It can be more specifically referred to as the negative right to liberty. Isaiah Berlin explains what negative liberty entails:

> *I am normally said to be free to the degree to which no man or body of men interferes with my activity. Political liberty in this sense is simply the area within which a man can act unobstructed by others. If I am prevented by others from doing what I could otherwise do, I am to that degree unfree; and if this area is contracted by other men beyond a certain minimum, I can be described as being coerced, or, it may be, enslaved.* (Berlin 1958)

From such a foundation, we can either extrapolate other negative rights, that is rights that differentiate the general negative right to liberty (e.g. freedom of speech, religion, family-life, privacy etc.), or we can develop other rights that cannot be in conflict with the individual negative right to liberty (e.g. positive rights: welfare rights, right to care, to education). Once conflict arises, the fundamental negative right to liberty must prevail if human rights are supposed to work according to the intention of protecting individual integrity through rights.

Hence, a system of rights has the negative right to liberty as a basic demand to rights-based systems at the point of departure, and such a basic right can be deemed as fundamental. The next category of rights is membership rights (usually referred to as citizenship), the third category is the right to legal remedies. These three categories, the way they are ordered, and how they are interdependent and interconnected, constitute a constitutional guarantee of individual freedoms and protection of integrity and, 'in a word, there is no legitimate law without these three' categories being enforced simultaneously (Habermas 1996).[3]

Without the first three categories of rights infused in law, and distributed equally to all, there could not be any personal freedom or personal equality before the law to speak of. These three categories of rights 'neutralize' the legal order, that is make it non-discriminatory, and infuse a thin conception of liberal morality to rule-of-law and practices derived from it. Such a thin concept of morality does not infringe upon reasonable doctrines that individuals can choose from regarding how they would live out their lives in a pluralistic society (Rawls 1993).

If individual liberty is to be secured, any individual must also be able to control and make use of their liberty to choose whatever reasonable way of life they desire. 'Neutralize' therefore alludes to the fact that individual liberty demands a legal order that is morally compatible with reasonable pluralism among everyone carrying citizenship, and which allows for any individual to choose their own rational plan of life as long as it abides by the Kantian precept of such a choice being compatible with everyone else having the same choice.

2.2 The Child's Right to Liberty: The Special Case

Children constitute a special case for a system of rights. Negative rights, membership rights and the right to legal remedies are not automatically applicable to children as such rights are applicable to adults, although children do carry the right to liberty (Alexy 2002; Mill 1867). Although some rights can be bestowed on youth who are still not autonomous adults (e.g. religious liberty, right to expression), children and youth cannot act fully positively on their negative rights until adulthood and when they are granted full citizenship independent from their care-takers. Full membership and the right to act upon a basic negative right to liberty require adulthood: 'to bring a child into existence without a fair prospect of being able, not only to provide food for its body, but instruction and training for its mind, is a moral crime' (Mill 1867). The lead reasons, from a system of rights perspective, is that a child is formally not able to reach competent and reasonable judgements, and have no rational plan of life (cf. the two moral powers in Rawls 1993).

Lacking the ability to act upon liberty, or autonomy, is the lead normative and political reason for excluding children from carrying rights as fully fledged citizens. Hence, a child, it can be argued, has a prospective right to individual liberty in the sense that the child only receives access to the complete system of rights once it reaches adulthood. Until then, the child depends on others to act according to the child's best interests, that is maintaining the integrity of the individual child. The child's right to protection against detrimental care is the right a child has for the state to prohibit parents from providing detrimental care, while such care goes against the child's best interests. Child protection services thereby raises a claim on acting in the child's best interests, against the claims of parents acting in the child's best interests, and consequently a claim that child protection services manage the child's negative right to liberty better than parents. We will now discuss what such a prospective right entails.

2.3 The Prospective Right to Liberty

The prospective right to individual liberty points both to the immediate and distant future of the particular child—when the child reaches adulthood and must be accountable for his or her own choices. After such a formal transition, the child becomes treated as autonomous, and as if it acts freely according to rational self-interest. Normally, a young adult cannot rely on others to reach decisions that are in the adult's best interests. As a child, on the other hand, others must reach decisions as to what is in the child's best interests. This means first of all that carrying a full set of rights, and being able to manage liberty, must be an essential part of what a child develops into. Second, and most importantly, others, parents or someone *in loco parentis*, must take care of the child's negative right to liberty on behalf of the child as long as the child has not reached adulthood. In this way, the principle of the child's best interests, which is operative in all actions concerning children (cf. CRC Art. 3.1), becomes a substitute principle for the basic negative right to liberty during childhood. In this way, the individual child's negative right to liberty is maintained.

If a child receives detrimental care, his or her ability to live life according to its own best interests becomes impaired by parents (or others). We can then argue that the child's integrity is violated. Once the parents expose the child to detrimental care, they do not act according to the child's best interests. As detrimental care is consequential for the integrity of the child, this type of care threatens the child's prospective right to liberty during childhood. This dimension of a rights-based child protection is pressed forward by the basic negative right to liberty, that is the human rights standard, immanent to a system of rights. By approximating what a human rights standard would entail to child-protection, the liberty principle becomes especially important as it must be a reference point for rights-based practice. As already argued, there would not be legitimate law if a basic negative right to liberty was not operative. Any practices in child protection that threaten the child's negative right to liberty would thereby be illegitimate. Now, if the right to liberty is to be carried by children who later becomes adults, we can argue that the state must intervene and make sure the child is cared for in those cases where the integrity of the child is threatened, all the way until the child reaches adulthood.

If, however, the care-takers provide detrimental care, and thereby risk damaging the child's integrity, the care also constitutes a violation of the child's prospective right to liberty as their integrity shifted into a development trajectory that was not good for the child. Eventually, the child's ability to act upon liberty, as adulthood kicks in, has become violated. The child's need for care throughout childhood is thereby intrinsically linked to the child's basic negative right to liberty once adulthood kicks in.

2.4 Prospective Right to Liberty During Childhood

When parents violate the child's negative right to liberty, the state must intervene not only to make sure this does not continue to happen, but more importantly safeguard that the development of the child is returned to a developmental track in accordance with the child's own trajectory; hence repairing the damage to the child's integrity caused by detrimental care, so that the child eventually can act upon a basic negative right to liberty.

Such a prospective right to liberty not only has consequences for how a childhood should be protected with regard to the future adult, but also how childhood is in need of protection according to the current needs of the child. The current needs of a child are continuously what feed into the development of the child. Hence, it is imperative that the quality of care during childhood is not to the specific child's detriment.[4] If the child does not live a childhood free from detriment from moment to moment, the development will incrementally become stifled or skewed, and the individual child's ability to explore and develop as a person becomes impaired. The prospective right to liberty can thereby be a rights-based corrective for the role of child protection to push the child back on track so that development towards adulthood is what the child itself would want, that is according to the child's best interests.

3 Limits to Epistemology: The Indeterminacy of a Child's Best Interests

A bridge between rights and professional practice is based in an approach to epistemology, namely that knowledge and justified beliefs take a certain shape once the rights of the child are enforced. According to the CRC and the best-interests principle, professional practice must ensure that all actions that constitute child protection practice have the child's best interests as a primary consideration (Ref. CRC Art. 3.1.). What becomes challenging to the application of knowledge, and thus to the epistemology of rights-based professional child protection, is not only that every action, that is every decision, must have the child's best interests as a primary consideration, but also that a professional must know that such an aim is morally and factually indeterminate (Alston 1994; Elster 1987; Mnookin 1975; Mnookin 1985).

What is implied by indeterminacy is that a decision in the child's best interests is always a value judgment—it is a matter of locating one triumphant rational best interest of any child above all other interests of that particular child. The two problems with the principle of the child's best interests are called the prediction problem and the evaluation problem (Mnookin 1975). The prediction problem alludes to the problem of making decisions without knowing what can be the spectrum of interests that a child has or will pursue in the near and distant future. The evaluation problem is about the uncertainty of the normative key to discern what is the best interest from the second best.

In order to illustrate the massive implication that rights have for professional practice, based on the notion that the best-interests principle is indeterminate, we can point to a widespread practice within organizational designs. In many nation-states decisions are reached by a single person throughout the organization. Even if we had access to all possible evidence, and an all-things-considered decision-making process made upon the same material, but by two equally competent and reasonable case-workers, different decisions would most likely be made. They can both be wrong and also equally correct. Knowing that nobody can say that they alone know what is in a child's best interest, a decision must become qualified, one way or the other, by reaching a decision that can be defended across a multitude of disciplinary platforms, different professions and civic opinions.[5]

Due to the fact of indeterminacy, the best interests of any child can only be assumed. Professional practice becomes a matter of simulating the child's own rational choice as if that child was an adult, and as if the child could make such a choice. Although no one knows exactly what is in a child's best interests, qualified claims can be raised. As such, a final decision can only reach rational acceptability through a procedure of claims that culminate in a final and ultimate claim acceptable to all as the rational thing to do (Alexy 1989; Falch-Eriksen 2012).

In order to qualify a decision, the process of approximating the best interests of the child through arguments must open up for all relevant types of arguments, and be based on all relevant types of knowledge, that is a multitude of knowledge bases in order to achieve an exhaustive and fully ventilated argumentative procedure that tests all types of potential best interests of the child. This includes, inter alia, psychology, law, medicine and social work. Although this might seem like a big demand, it is alluding to the very ethos of rights-based professional practice. It is thereby not only an ethical obligation, but also a matter of methodological attitude in practice—namely developing methods that are dynamic and open enough to fit every potential child (see Munro and Turnell 2018: Chap. 5 in this book).

A decision can only be reached when it can withstand criticism and carry an embedded mutual understanding across qualified opinions (Falch-Eriksen 2012). In order to activate all qualified opinions, decision-making procedures must be open, and decisions must follow a formal procedural logic embedded into a rule of approximation. The rule of approximation stipulates that all relevant claims assists in qualifying what is in the best interests of the child, but without making a claim upon a decision *de facto* being in the child's best interests. Once mutual understanding is reached across a multitude of different opinions and relevant arguments, a decision can claim to be the best one. The decision involves what Robert Alexy refers to raising 'the claim to correctness': 'The claim to correctness involved in the assertion of any legal statement is the claim that … the assertion is rationally justifiable' (Alexy 1989). Only by infusing professional practice with some version of the approximation rule, so that decisions can be 'rationally justifiable', can a claim to correctness regarding what is in a child's best interests be raised.

4 Theory of Professionalism

A distinctive feature of modern nation-states is processes of professionalization and professionalism. Professionalism will in this regard be referred to as a combination of (1) the exercise of discretion when reaching decisions face to face with clients on street level, and (2) that the exercise of discretion is conducted according to some level of esoteric knowledge not easily nor conveniently accessible to a client, and (3) that practice choices are in accord with structural restrictions and the normative intent of the law (Abbott 2014; Goodin 1986; Lipsky 1980). Central to professionalization are both the increase of the use of discretionary decision-making based on knowledge, and also the advancement of knowledge development internal to a profession. In this sense, professionals also become the lead implementation and enforcement agents of the rights of the child.

4.1 The Formal Restriction

In the modern state-logic of delegating authority to professionals, the politicians also set restrictions and define the formal jurisdiction for the professions (Molander et al. 2012; Rothstein 1998). In this way, the knowledge base of the professions enters into a symbiotic relationship with the doctrine of nation-states and how they are governed through constitutional and democratic rule-of-law (Molander et al. 2012). Professionals are not only governed through regular law (where practices must be according to laws and policies), but they are also governed through settled and agreed-upon fundamental norms that are supposed to provide guidance as they distribute state resources according to their discretion. This is also where the human rights standard enters—as a fundamental guiding norm within the nation-state itself—which must pervade all relevant actions in the field of professional practice, also in the area where professionals are said to have discretion. The human rights standard, that is the basic negative right to liberty, is in its basic form constitutional, and provides guidance not only to politics, law-making and policy development, but also to professional practice on the street level.

Child protection systems have been delegated the authority to make decisions, that is perform professional discretion within a structure of laws, policies and rights. Provided that the parliament has decided that children's rights are to be enforced, the parliament will need to trust that every decision made by the child protection services enforces the principle of the child's best interests (Ref. CRC Art. 3.1). This also implies that professionals must be able to justify their actions according to the human rights standard, because the standard is a guiding norm, and thus a restrain on autonomy, on their decision-making (Molander et al. 2012).

If the professionals do not act in accordance with their delegated authority, which constitutes formal restrictions, and the discrepancy becomes too large between the democratic and constitutional ethos of the delegated authority and what the professional decides upon when acting upon discretion, the delegated authority must be revoked. Said differently, professionals that serve the role of gatekeepers within a nation-state must in all aspects of practice abide by laws, policies and fundamental norms to serve its purpose within the realm of rule-of-law. Hence, it is to be expected that professionals within child protection implement, enforce and maintain the rights of the child.

4.2 Rule of Approximation Embedded in Professional Practice

As we have already argued, there are many professional opinions as well as common-sense opinions about what constitutes non-detrimental care and the need for protection of children who are subjected to detrimental care. When arguments are offered about what action to proceed with, they are conditioned by the ability of professionals to solve practical problems. Furthermore, the human rights standard and the CRC set a distinct and real direction for what type of practice can be labelled as professional when applied to child protection.

Nobody has a monopoly upon what constitutes the best practice or best solution with regard to the best interests of the child. For instance, if a decision is reached only by a social worker, psychological knowledge will not be a substantial part of the deliberation, nor will law or medicine. If the decision were only conducted by laymen, then all scientific knowledge regarding children would be lost. It is no reason to either exclude any argument that might be deemed relevant, nor resort to only one set of arguments, although it might seem reasonable.

The rule of approximation implies that an optimal decision can only become established in an environment where all relevant arguments become sharpened through the resistance of open criticism. This does not mean that you always need a multitude of people sitting around a table, but that methods, practices, guidelines and so forth have the rule of approximation built into them.

In the attempt to approximate a decision that is in a child's best interests, and which sets restrictions on what can be deemed as professional practice, we have now touched upon three challenges. *First*, nobody holds the right answer to the practical problem of what to do with the child and his or her care. *Second*, every argument that is relevant must be included.[6] *Third*, a decision-making procedure must be able to extrapolate the relevant arguments in a fair manner. Due to these three challenges to each decision, the design of professional decision-making procedures approximating the child's best interests must on a fundamental level be formally rule-driven. To reach such an end, the approximation rule must abide by background principles underpinning general practical discourse, in which lies the potential of reaching decisions of mutual understanding.

Reaching a legitimate decision that rests upon mutual understanding can only be achieved if 'every rational being' becomes included to reach understanding (Kant 2002/1781). This precept is a limitation in the sense that in order to be regarded as a 'rational being' one must present relevant arguments, which implies being, at some level, affected or qualified by the goal of the decision. For instance: a parent is affected by the decision, whereby the medical practitioner affects the decision in a particularly qualified manner.Jürgen Habermas has formulated a discourse principle that incorporates the Kantian precept: 'valid for the will of every rational being'. It is a principle for the objective justification of norms in general:

> 'Only those norms are valid to which all affected persons could agree as participants in rational discourses' (Habermas 1996).

The discourse principle can thereby guide the rule of approximation as a design principle for an ideal standard of professional decision-making. By combining a rule of approximation to the discourse principle in decision-making designs, decision-making procedures will harbour the ability to reach mutual understanding through a rule-driven rational justification. Hence, mutual understanding ensures legitimate approximation of a child's best interests each time, that is a decision that upholds the child's prospective right to liberty. According to the discourse principle, legitimacy can only be reached through a discursive test that includes *all those affected*. Such a test can pragmatically be applied to decision-making designs in order qualify each decision. Hence, professionalism, with regard to ensuring the rights of the child in child protection, becomes a procedural concept in search of mutual understanding by approximating the best interests of the child.

By demanding that every relevant argument is to be raised and argued for before reaching a decision that holds the merits of rights-based professionalism, the discourse principle does not remove the need for determining the indeterminate of the best-interests principle, but it does strive for reaching a decision that can at least claim to be correct. This is what the ultimate goal must be since a valid or factually correct decision is impossible to reach. If the design of decision-making procedures attends the discourse principle during approximation, it could be assumed that an ultimate claim to correctness would arise at the intersections of arguments, where many different claims to correctness are raised and are potentially of equal strength.

5   A Theory of Childhood in the Face of Professional Practice

Any childhood is formative, significant and very complex, and the very right to protection is to protect against detrimental care during childhood. The purpose of this section is merely to present two circumstances of childhood that are important with regard to rights-based professional child protection. Any individual's right to personal liberty enables the carrier of such a right to freely choose how to live life as long as it does not restrain others from having the same opportunity. A consequence is that the social system where the individual resides will be in flux according to the aggregation of individual choices. Two main circumstances cause flux: reasonable pluralism (Rawls 1993), and the increasing complexity of modern societies (Giddens 1990). Flux influences how childhoods are conceived with regard to protection, what the different types are and what constitutes its nuts and bolts. Hence, flux challenges existing action norms of parents' reasonable choice of care, how children would want to live during childhood and how child protection services intervene.

The *first* circumstance is the magnitude of reasonable choices about how to live life, that is, the fact of reasonable pluralism (Rawls 1993). The gradual realization and implementation of the fact of reasonable pluralism have fragmented earlier common religious or sacred worldviews. It has in Weberian terms disenchanted the world and left it open for individuals to strive for whatever reasonable conception of good they want to choose (see Habermas 1996). By being confronted by an immense variety of childhoods and care-regimes, it becomes more apparent that service-design in child protection must embed a principle of equality of decision-making if professional practice is to emerge. Each type of childhood and each care-regime must be evaluated on its own merits, and whether or not care is sufficiently good must be decided upon in each case.

A child that receives detrimental care of the type that threatens their childhood and integrity needs protection on terms set by that child alone—that is according to the particular interests of the child. When a child's development is threatened to the extent that the child's integrity is in peril, those who intervene do it because it is a right of the child to have someone to take on the role of the parent and serve the best interests of the child.

Protection services must ensure that their care does not cause harm to the child's integrity and future ability to live a life he or she would want as an adult. If a type of care has caused harm to the child during childhood, the protection services must compensate or repair so that the child's integrity once again follows the track to which that particular child has a right.

6 Concluding Remarks: The World Is the Limit

In all relevant aspects of democratic rule-of-law, the respect of the integrity of each individual child must be coherent and visible. Modern state constructs that lay claim to abide by human rights must let a system of rights become constitutive of state-actions in the sense that you can trace the system of rights and explain how the state works by referring to a human rights standard. This is rarely the case. In most cases pragmatism kicks in, and we end up with practices that need to fit tight budgets, a varying degree of competence, varying decision-making designs and so forth. Ideal conditions are seldom present, but this is not an argument to stop reaching for it. Only by attempting to reach the ideal condition can we be certain to become better at the rights-based protection of children.

Nation-states' formal and informal commitment towards human rights can be treated as a counterfactual. This implies that, even if it is argued by nation-state politicians and public officials that child protection services of the nation-state uphold and maintain human rights (1) by taking such a position in public discourse, (2) by law-making assemblies making concessions within their legal orders towards such an end, (3) by developing practices within child protection towards such an end, (4) by providing organizational designs that harbour a rights-ethos, and (5) by bureaucratic decision-making that plainly refers to rights, all this does not mean that nation-states automatically respect human rights. Empirically, the dedication and conscious development towards human rights will obviously vary, and in many cases will even constitute practices in breach of human rights, although it is argued that nation-sates do in fact generally maintain human rights.

If we can argue that a nation-state is to *de facto* and *de jure* maintain and enforce the rights of the child, then we can critically discuss what such a dedication will imply for professional practice. This opens up a critical aim when discussing and assessing practices within child protection systems from the point of view of a basic human rights principle. For instance, if practices depart from human rights principles, then there is also something illegitimate with that practice, provided human rights are taken seriously. We can then go on to argue that if a nation-state claims to maintain and enforce the CRC, it cannot continue with practices that are in breach of the CRC's claim upon professionalism. Having such a focus, it is possible to critically assess and to unravel discrepancies between empirical practices that claim to maintain and enforce human rights on one hand and different theoretical propositions for practice that are founded upon a human rights principle on the other.

Every nation-state in for example Europe claims that they respect and uphold human rights while protecting children from detrimental care, and they do so often to legitimize politics and practices. If they claim to respect human rights, we can use such a claim as a counterfactual and move to the next step to discuss whether human rights are embedded in professional practices in child protection or not. Not forgetting that as long as the normative foundation of human rights is not an integrative force of social and political behaviour, it is to be expected that a society and a nation-state do not yet fully comply with human rights.

Notes

1. The concept of 'integrity' is complex and will not be discussed in this chapter. For this chapter it will suffice to argue that 'integrity' constitutes the quality of the person's character, especially infused by its interests, goals and well-being.
2. It will not be discussed here, but underpinning human rights is the defence of personal liberty from unlawful and illegitimate domination (see discussions from e.g. Berlin 1958; Dworkin 1977; Habermas 1996; Mill 1867; Rawls 1971).
3. There is also a fourth category referred to as political rights, and that secures the right to participation. The fifth category referred to is social welfare rights, or social rights. They are so-called positive rights and are usually implemented in order to safeguard a level of social justice and equality of opportunity. These categories of rights will not be problematized here.
4. The Universal Declaration of Human Rights is referenced in the CRC: 'children are entitled to special care and assistance'.
5. I will not discuss decision-making designs in this chapter. However, there are several ways to reach decisions that qualify arguments claiming to be in a child's best interests.
6. This holds true for any type of intervention, in-house interventions as well as out-of-home placements. However, the more severe the detriment, the more strict the demands towards decision-making must become.

References

Abbott, A. (2014). *The system of professions: An essay on the division of expert labor*. Chicago: University of Chicago Press.

Alexy, R. (1989). *A theory of legal argumentation: The theory of rational discourse as theory of legal justification*. Oxford: Oxford University Press.

Alexy, R. (2002). *A theory of constitutional rights*. Oxford/New York: Oxford University Press.

Alston, P. (1994). The best interests principle: Towards a reconciliation of culture and human rights. In P. Alston (Ed.), *The best interests of the child: Reconciling culture and human rights* (pp. 1–25). Oxford: Clarendon Press.

Berlin, I. (1958). *Two concepts of liberty: An inaugural lecture delivered before the University of Oxford on 31 October 1958*. Oxford: Clarendon.

Dworkin, R. (1977). *Taking rights seriously (new impression with a reply to critics. ed.)*. London: Duckworth.

Elster, J. (1987). Solomonic judgments—Against the best interest of the child. *University of Chicago Law Review, 54*(1), 1–45. https://doi.org/10.2307/1599714.

Falch-Eriksen, A. (2012). The promise of trust: An inquiry into the legal design of coercive decision-making in Norway. (2012 nr. 5), Høgskolen i Oslo og Akershus, Senter for profesjonsstudier, Oslo. Retrieved from http://hdl.handle.net/10642/1355

Giddens, A. (1990). *The consequences of modernity*. Cambridge: Polity Press.

Goodin, R. E. (1986). Welfare, rights and discretion. *Oxford Journal of Legal Studies, 6*(2), 232–261.

Habermas, J. (1996). Between facts and norms. Contributions to a discourse theory of law and democracy (W. Rehg, trans.). Cambridge, MA: The MIT Press.

Kant, I. (1993). *Grounding for the metaphysics of morals: On a supposed right to lie because of philanthropic concerns*. Indianapolis: Hackett.

Kant, I. (2002/1781). *Critique of pure reason*. Dent: Everyman.

Lipsky, M. (1980). *Street-level bureaucracy: Dilemmas of the individual in public services*. New York: Russell Sage Foundation.

Locke, J. (1823). *Two treatises of government* (Vol. 5). London: Thomas Tegg.

Mill, J. S. (1867). *On liberty*. London: Longmans, Green and Co.

Mnookin, R. H. (1975). Child-custody adjudication: Judicial functions in the face of indeterminacy. *Law and Contemporary Problems, 39*(3), 226–293.

Mnookin, R. H. (1985). *In the interest of children advocacy, law reform, and public policy*. New York: W. H. Freeman & Company.

Molander, A., Grimen, H., & Eriksen, E. O. (2012). Professional discretion and accountability in the welfare state. *Journal of Applied Philosophy, 29*(3), 214–230. https://doi.org/10.1111/j.1468-5930.2012.00564.x.

Munro, E., & Turnell, A. (2018). Re-designing organisations to facilitate rights-based practice in child protection. In A. Falch-Eriksen & E. Backe-Hansen (Eds.), *Human rights in child protection. Implications for professional practice and policy*. London: Palgrave Macmillan.

Rawls, J. (1971). *A theory of justice*. Cambridge, MA: The Belknap Press of Harvard University Press.

Rawls, J. (1993). *Political liberalism*. New York: Columbia University Press.

Rothstein, B. (1998). *Just institutions matter: The moral and political logic of the universal welfare state*. Cambridge: Cambridge University Press.

Sandberg, K. (2018). Children's right to protection under the CRC. In A. Falch-Eriksen & E. Backe-Hansen (Eds.), *Human rights in child protection. Implications for professional practice and policy*. London: Palgrave Macmillan.

Open Access This chapter is licensed under the terms of the Creative Commons Attribution 4.0 International License (http://creativecommons.org/licenses/by/4.0/), which permits use, sharing, adaptation, distribution and reproduction in any medium or format, as long as you give appropriate credit to the original author(s) and the source, provide a link to the Creative Commons license and indicate if changes were made.

The images or other third party material in this chapter are included in the chapter's Creative Commons license, unless indicated otherwise in a credit line to the material. If material is not included in the chapter's Creative Commons license and your intended use is not permitted by statutory regulation or exceeds the permitted use, you will need to obtain permission directly from the copyright holder.

4

The Child's Best Interest Principle across Child Protection Jurisdictions

Marit Skivenes and Line Marie Sørsdal

1 Introduction

In social science, a core challenge is to understand the uses of government power in professional practices in which exercise of discretion is essential. The aim of this chapter is to examine how governments in 14 high-income countries simultaneously interpret the vague and indeterminate principle of the best interest of the child in legislation and instruct professional decision-makers. Legislation is an important mechanism by which governments state their goals and ambitions and signal and instruct professionals on how they wish their goals to be implemented in the various institutions of a welfare state. Such signalling is typically followed by delegation of authority to exercise discretion, that is 'when someone is in general charged with making a decision subject to standards set by a particular authority' (Dworkin 1967, p. 32). The empirical focus of this

---

M. Skivenes (✉) • L. M. Sørsdal
Department of Administration and Organization Theory, University of Bergen, Bergen, Norway
e-mail: marit.skivenes@uib.no; line.sorsdal@uib.no

chapter is the state's responsibility for children that are at risk of harm and intrusive measures such as removing children into state care. Child protection is a surprisingly understudied area of the welfare state, given the power that is vested in the decision-makers in a very difficult and highly sensitive area of intrusive state interventions into individuals' private spheres (Burns et al. 2017). A key standard in this area is the Convention on the Rights of the Child (CRC) of 1989. This convention has almost universal, global support,[1] and several countries have made it national law. The CRC gives children strong rights, and a major article is the best interest principle that '*In all actions concerning children, whether undertaken by public or private, social welfare institutions, courts of law, administrative authorities or legislative bodies, the best interests of the child shall be a primary consideration*' (Article 3).[2]

The ratification of the CRC obligates countries to give the best interest principle primary consideration in decisions concerning individual children, and this entails a clear shift away from the traditional relationship between the family and the state (Gilbert et al. 2011; Skivenes 2002). However, the child's best interest principle as outlined in Article 3 in the CRC is ambiguous, and its application as a guideline for decision-making is not straightforward. It allows huge leeway for a variety of interpretations. Thus, an interesting and important question concerns how governments have applied this principle in their legislation. Do they fill the principle with material content or procedural directions? There are numerous dimensions in relation to a child's best interest that a decision-maker can (and must) consider, including expert knowledge about nutrition, attachment, education, brain development and the normative and cultural values for a good and meaningful life (cf. Skivenes and Pösö 2017). However, 'what is best for any child or even children in general is often indeterminate and speculative and requires a highly individualized choice between alternatives' (Mnookin and Szwed 1983, p. 8; see also Breen 2002; Elster 1989; Freeman 2005). In addition, these decisions involve complex predictions about the consequences of choices and future outcomes. Altogether, the best interest principle in its current state in the CRC offers little guidance for decision-makers; nonetheless, it is the guiding principle for decisions that have a tremendous impact on the lives of children and adults (Breen 2002; Elster 1989; Freeman 2007; Skivenes 2002).

We set out to examine how states formulate the best interest of the child in their child protection legislation in 14 high-income countries, and in this way, we examine how states interpret and implement the principle, whether they differ and how this may regulate, instruct and guide the discretionary authority delegated to decision-makers. The countries we examine in this chapter are Australia, Austria, Canada, Denmark, England, Estonia, Finland, Germany, Ireland, Norway, Spain, Sweden, Switzerland and the United States of America (USA).[3]

In the next section, we present the best interest principle and the concept of discretion, followed by an outline of the various countries' systems on child protection and law. Methods and then findings sections follow. We end with a discussion and a final section with concluding remarks.

2 The Principle of the Best Interest of the Child and Discretion

An overlooked part of discussions on democratic legitimacy is the role of implementation of policy goals, as political scientist Bo Rothstein (1998) points out in the book *Just Institutions Matter*. Professional decision-makers in child protection systems are obligated to make decisions according to national legislation and the CRC. Child protection interventions with families based on the best interests of the child and the legitimacy of decisions and interventions are regularly questioned in political and public debates, often in relation to terms such as 'draconian'.

Typically, discretion is categorized as weak or strong (Dworkin 1967). Strong discretion concerns decisions that are not 'bound by any standards set by an authority' (Schneider 1992, p. 33). The judges in the European Court of Human Rights can be classified as having strong discretion as they only use the European Convention of Human Rights as their standard for decision-making (Skivenes and Søvig 2016).[4] Weak discretion is when the authority to use judgement is limited by instructions to apply specified aspects or considerations, or to prioritize between different considerations (Dworkin 1967, p. 32; Archard and Skivenes 2009). Dworkin (1967, p. 32) uses an example of a sergeant that has been told to find five experienced people to execute a mission. If 'experienced' is the only criterion, it is clearly a broad instruction, and there is quite a wide array of options for discretion. However, if the sergeant has also been told how experience is defined, for example by criteria such as being over 50 years of age, having five years of practice and self-perceived calmness in stressful situations, the scope for selection is narrower and allows fewer choices. Furthermore, there may be detailed instructions in relation to understanding an order in terms of its material content and collecting information. Thus, in our analysis, a professional decision-maker will have strong discretion when given the authority to make decisions that are in the best interest of the child, that is Article 3 of the CRC. Professionals have weak discretion when instructions are given concerning the 'best interest principle', and with more instructions, their authority to exercise discretion is weaker. However, if instructions are contradictory, decision-makers must exercise discretion regarding which instruction to follow and how to weigh the instructions against each other, whereby seemingly weak discretion is stronger.

In summary, depending on the type of discretion that legislators set for professional decision-makers in child protection agencies and courts, there will be a continuum of strong to weak discretion for lawful interpretations of the best interest of the child. Before we move on to the broader background of the study, one important point to underscore is that this chapter focuses on legislation as a regulative mechanism, and we are well aware that governments have a range of steering mechanisms and incentives to guide and rein in decision-makers' exercise of discretion, such as guidelines, directives, organizational forms, auditing agencies and choice of profession to implement policy.

The criticism of child protection systems may be because of the strong discretion it gives professional decision-makers in determining the best interests of a child that needs protection. In May 2013, the Committee on the Rights of the Child published a comment on the best interest article (number 3) intended to accommodate the lack of common understanding of the principle (GC No. 14 2013). Part V, *Implementation: assessing and determining the child's best interests*, outlines seven elements that should be considered when a decision about the child's best interests is to be made (pp. 7ff.): (a) the child's views; (b) the child's identity; (c) preservation of the family environment and maintaining relations; (d) care, protection, and safety of the child; (e) situation of vulnerability; (f) the child's right to health, and (g) the child's right to education. Each of these elements is laid out in detail in the comment and should provide clear instructions for professionals across countries. However, because this principle covers all areas of a child's life, the comment also underscores that the principle remains ambiguous, and that these seven elements are not

> *relevant to every case, and different elements can be used in different ways in different cases. The content of each element will necessarily vary from child to child and from case to case, depending on the type of decision and the concrete circumstances, as will the importance of each element in the overall assessment.* (p. 9)

Our focus is on child protection care order decisions, and crudely speaking, the determination of the principle should consist of two parts (Skivenes and Pösö 2017). One part is based on the scientific knowledge of a child's development and needs. The empirical evidence and documentation provided by the research community establish the ground rules and the important arguments and considerations of valid determinations of what is best for the child. The other part involves normative ethical-cultural considerations about a good life and a good childhood. There is variation across cultures, religions and states, and between individuals and groups about meaningful and good ways of life (Rawls 1971; Shapiro 1999; Skivenes 2002). There are many competing and legitimate ways of bringing up children and as such defining what is good or best for them. Thus, there is not *one* 'best interest value' that can be expected to be valid and accepted as right for all children. For the former expert-based dimension, there is an argument based on the strength of the evidence and the validity of knowledge, and to some degree, there will be consensus on what has been established as solid knowledge and what is less solid. For the latter value-based dimension, by definition, when there is disagreement and plurality, ethical discussions and interpretations must consider what might be good for a particular individual, family or community. Thus, decisions about the best interests of a child cannot be based solely on expert evaluations, but also on values and norms that hold meaning for human beings. In this landscape, we analyse the instructions made by legislators in 14 countries as expressed in the formation of the best interest principle in child protection.

3 Child Protection Systems, Welfare States and Jurisdictions

The discretion and the standards that governments delegate to decision-makers are influenced by and dependent on factors such as type of child protection system, welfare state model, legal system and political order, and power in society. We do not have solid knowledge about the relationship between various system features and the child protection area. The countries differ in how they regulate and organize the institutional settings for child protection and decision-making processes (Burns et al. 2017; Gilbert et al. 2011; Hetherington et al. 1997). The prevailing typology of child protection systems distinguishes between risk-oriented and family service-oriented systems (Gilbert 1997; Gilbert et al. 2011). Risk-oriented systems are based on a high threshold for intervention in the private sphere and intervention when serious risk of harm to a child exists. These systems are focused on mitigating serious risks to children's health and safety (Gilbert et al. 2011). Family service-oriented systems have a low threshold for intervention and provide services for families based on a therapeutic view of rehabilitation, in which the state makes it possible for people to revise and improve their lifestyles and behaviour. The major differences between these two systems are their underlying ideologies, degree of solidarity and the ways in which they manage children at risk. This also includes variations between systems in how they regulate and set standards for children's upbringing and where they set the border between private and public responsibility for children in need of assistance. Our expectation is that risk-oriented systems will have a

Table 4.1 Child protection systems, child well-being rank, child rights index

Country	Child protection system	UNICEF's child well-being rank[a]	Child rights index[b]
Australia	Risk-oriented	–	27
Austria	Family-service-oriented	18	35
Canada	Risk-oriented	17	45
Denmark	Family-service-oriented	11	34
England	Risk-oriented[c]	16	156
Estonia	Risk-oriented	23	93
Finland	Family-service-oriented	4	18
Germany	Family-service-oriented	6	18
Ireland	Risk-oriented	10	41
Norway	Family-service-oriented	2	2
Spain	Family-service-oriented	19	5
Sweden	Family-service-oriented	5	7
Switzerland	Risk-oriented	8	3
USA	Risk-oriented	26	–

[a]UNICEF Child well-being rank (2013); Adamson (2013)
[b]Child rights index, 2017. Available online at: http://kidsrightsindex.org/
[c]England would often be characterized as a system that is in between the risk-oriented and family-service oriented systems

fact-based understanding of the principle, and with clear instructions on how to handle serious risk, whereas the family service-oriented systems will both include fact-based as well as diffuse values-based-needs instructions. Table 4.1 presents an overview of key characteristics of the 14 countries.[5] Our expectation is that countries scoring high on the child rights index and the child well-being index will also have engaged have included what is recommended by the CRC committee, GC 14.

4   Data and Methods

The data material for the study consist of the formulations of the best interest principle in child protection legislation in 14 high-income countries. These countries were strategically selected on the basis of prior research on child protection systems and a previous comparative analysis, as we had gained knowledge about these countries' child protection systems and established a network of national experts on child protection in each country. The countries in the study are Australia, Austria, Canada,

Denmark, England, Estonia, Finland, Germany, Ireland, Norway, Spain, Sweden, Switzerland and the USA. The various pieces of national legislation were collected by systematically examining the countries' chapters from previous book projects (Burns et al. 2017; Skivenes et al. 2015; Gilbert et al. 2011), reading the national CRC reports and doing specific literature searches. This material was collected in 2015–2016 with support and guidance from national experts.[6] To ensure that we had found the right child protection legislation used for care order removals, we asked child protection experts in each of the countries to inspect and confirm our selected law.

Of the 14 countries under study, five (Australia, Austria, Canada, Switzerland and the USA) have a two-layered structure with overarching legislation for the whole country (such as federal law) and then state legislation. In these countries, we first established an understanding of the relationship between the law on different levels, and then selected one state/canton/province/territory to represent the child protection legislation of the whole country in our analysis. We are clearly aware that this could not be regarded as representative of the whole country.[7] The states we selected in these countries were the state/canton/province/territory that our expert(s) were from in the Australian Capital Territory (Australia), the province of Ontario (Canada), the canton of Basel-Stadt (Switzerland) and the state of Massachusetts (USA). This way of selecting laws provided us with manageable material, and we had the advantage of our expert's knowledge of that specific child protection legislation. For simplicity, we use the term 'country/national legislation' even when we only have legislation from a state/canton/province/territory.

The data material for the analysis consisted of the sections of the laws that outline the best interest of the child. Typically, the legislation would have sections along the following lines: '*in deciding what is in the best interest of a child or a young person, a decision-maker must …*' (Australia: Children and Young People Act 2008). The length of the texts from each country varied, from a few lines in Switzerland to over a half page of law from Australia. Table 4.2 provides an overview of the title of the child protection law in the 14 countries included in the study, as well as the specific section that outlines the best interest of the child.[8]

Table 4.2 The child protection laws

Country	Legislation
Australia, Capital Territory	Children and Young People Act 2008 (Sec. 349)
Austria	Civil Code of Austria 2013 (Sec. 138)
Canada, Ontario	Child and Family Services Act, R.S.O. 1990, c. C.11 (Sec. 37 [3])
Denmark	Consolidation Act on Social Services 2011 (Sec. 46)
England	Children Act 1989 (Sec. 1)
Estonia	Child Protection Act 2016 (Sec. 21)
Finland	Child Welfare Act 2007 (Sec. 4)
Germany	German Civil Code 2002 (Sec. 1697a)
Ireland	Child Care Act 1991 (Sec. 24)
Norway	The Child Welfare Act 1992 (Sec. 4-1)
Spain	Organic Law 1/1996, of 15 January, on protection of minors, modification to the Civil Code and the Civil Procedure Act (Art. 2)
Sweden	Social Service Act 2001 (Sec. 2) and Swedish Children and Parents Code 2006
Switzerland, Basel-Stadt	Children and Young Persons Act 2015 (Sec. 3)
USA, Massachusetts	General law, Chapter 119 Protection and care of children, and proceedings against them (Sec. 1)

All texts we analysed were written in or translated into English. Five countries have English as the original language (Australia, Canada, England, Ireland and the USA) and five have an official English translation of the law (Denmark, Estonia, Finland, Germany and Norway). For Austria, Spain, Sweden and Switzerland we used a translation bureau to translate the laws into English. Translation is a critical process, as the English concepts and system terminology may not capture or be compatible with those of other countries' ways of organizing child protection systems. For the non-English-speaking countries, we checked the translations with the experts to make sure that the meaning was not lost in the translation process. The translation of the legal texts and the potential loss of meaning from or mismatch with the original language of the law is a validity problem for most cross-country studies.[9]

To analyse the laws, both researchers first read the texts and identified themes, and then discussed the themes and made a coding scheme of mutually exclusive codes (cf. Table 4.3). The analysis was driven by two questions: First, what is the material content of the best interest

Table 4.3 Codes for identifying themes in the texts

Code name	Code description and criteria for including or excluding text
Child's future	Includes factors concerning the future of the child and/or a long-term perspective for the child, including mentioning the situation of the child as an adult
Child's identity	Includes text that raises considerations of the child's individual characteristics, cultural inheritance or other aspects that may be important to the child's identity
Child's needs	Includes factors about the needs of the child, physical and emotional support and care, personal development, education, nutrition, stimulation and activation. This code *does not* include references to general terms of the child's well-being, such as best interests, the need for stability or the child's relationship with the parent/caregiver (covered by other codes)
Child's participation	Includes statements about participation for and/or involvement of children, including hearing the child's viewpoint, feelings, wishes, meaning and opinions
Child's relationship	Includes considerations of the child's relationship with a caregiver or a parent, and/or with the family or a wider network of relations. It also includes text concerning the 'biological principle' and/or the importance of the biological family
Parent's perspective	Includes text about the rights and/or capacity of parent(s) or caregiver(s) to take care of the child and/or their caregiving or parental skills, and/or their views or opinions
Protection	Includes factors about protection of the child against harm or risk of harm, and/or considerations of prior experiences of harm or potential future risk situations
Permanency	Includes text related to the importance of permanency or stability of the emotional and/or physical living conditions and upbringing of the child
Weight and procedures	Includes text that states how the best interests of the child should be weighed against other principles or rights, and/or how material factors should be ranked and/or whether a time frame is mentioned

principle, as formulated by the legislators? Second, what type of instructions and guidance does the legislation provide? The texts were coded manually by the researchers in several rounds, and then the reliability of the coding was tested by two project associates. In the few cases of discrepancies, the authors discussed the deviations and agreed upon a mutual interpretation.

4.1 Limitations

We have only looked at the formulation of the principle in the selective legislation for child protection; we have not examined other legislation or other mechanisms that may instruct professionals in the front-line services and the courts, such as political-administrative directives or case laws. We do not consider how the principle is actually applied and reasoned in courts or child protection agencies. The focus is solely on the legislative formulation of the best interest principle in the selected laws in these countries. The limitation with this approach is that owing to various ways of constructing legislation and their legal order, we cannot exclude the possibility that some countries include the general principles of their child protection systems within the best interest principle, whereas others have laid out principles and important considerations elsewhere in legislation and/or their administrative/legal systems.

5 Findings

The analysis of the legislation showed that the best interest principle is worded in various ways. Nine of the 14 countries used the term 'best interest' in the text, whereas England and Ireland used the wording 'the welfare of the child'. Similarly, Austria and Switzerland refer to 'the child's well-being' in a literal sense, and Finland uses the term 'the interest of the child'. Each country has chosen different strategies for approaching the principle, with eight of the 14 countries providing rather broad descriptions of the material content on how the principle is to be understood.

Overall, eight main material considerations are represented in the legislation analysed, as well as one category for the weight of the principle and procedural aspects. Table 4.4 presents an overview of the findings and shows how some themes are present in almost all legislation, whereas others are only of concern for a few countries.

Table 4.4 Main findings

Country	Child's participation	Child's needs	Permanency	Protection	Child's relationship	Child's identity	Parent's perspective	Child's future	Weight and procedures
SUM	12	10	9	9	8	6	4	3	14
Australia	1	1	1	1	1	1	1		1
Austria	1	1	1	1	1	1	1		1
Canada	1	1	1	1	1	1			1
Denmark	1	1	1	1	1				1
England	1	1	1			1		1	1
Estonia	1	1							
Finland	1	1	1	1	1	1			1
Germany		1		1	1		1	1	1
Ireland	1								1
Norway	1		1		1				1
Spain	1	1	1		1	1		1	1
Sweden	1	1		1	1				
Switzerland									1
USA	1			1					1

5.1 Child's Participation

Twelve of the 14 countries (the exceptions are Germany and Switzerland) require the child's view, opinion, wishes, feelings or meanings to be considered (cf. Table 4.4). The formulation in Australian law is illustrative:

> *(1) For the care and protection chapters, in deciding what is in the best interests of a child or young person, a decision-maker must consider each of the following matters that are relevant to the child or young person:*
>
> *… (b) any views or wishes expressed by the child or young person.* (#1.b)

The instructions in the legislation vary in both strength and content. Only Australia, Finland and Norway do not mention any caveats in relation to hearing the child's opinion. The others point out that the weight of the child's opinion depends on the child's age, understanding, abilities, maturity and/or competency. For example, '*5. the consideration of the child's opinion in accordance with his/her understanding and ability to form an opinion*' (Austria, #5). Only US legislation mentions age (12 years) as a presumption of competency. Denmark, Estonia and Spain have a broader approach to children's participation, including their resources and emotions, as in the Spanish legislation:

> *b) Consideration of the desires, feelings and opinions of the child, as well as their right to progressively participate, according to their age, development and personal development, in the process of determining their best interests.* (#2.b)

The law in Estonia stipulates that '*If the best interests of a child differ from the child's opinion or if a decision which does not coincide with the child's opinion is made on other grounds, the reasons for not taking the child's opinion into account must be explained to the child*' (#2.3).

5.2 The Child's Needs

Ten of the 14 countries include some wording regarding the needs of the child, whereas the legislation in Estonia, Ireland, Norway and Switzerland does not explicitly mention needs. The child's need is a contested concept. Although most of the considerations around best interest are directly or indirectly about the needs and care of the child in the wider sense, here we focus on direct mention of particular needs in relation to the child, such as physical, emotional, intellectual and educational needs. Thus, we do not include statements that focus on aspects such as the need for parental care or protection from harm, or any other consideration that is included in the other seven categories that we identified in the material.

Although the legislation from Australia, Austria, Canada, Denmark, England, Finland, Spain and the USA varies in its characterizations of needs, most of the countries cite both emotional and basic physical needs. Finland serves as an example of the latter, with an extensive description of needs on both general and specific levels:

> *(1) Child welfare must promote the favourable development and well-being of the child. ... 1) balanced development and well-being, and close and continuing human relationships; 2) the opportunity to be given understanding and affection, as well as supervision and care that accord with the child's age and level of development ...* (#1, 2.1, 2.2)

The USA and Denmark emphasize both care and affection as well as the impact of upbringing on the child's adult life: '*The health and safety of the child shall be of paramount concern, and shall include the long-term well-being of the child*' (USA #1, para. 3).

5.3 Permanency

Nine of the countries (Australia, Austria, Canada, Denmark England, Germany, Norway, Spain and the USA) cite factors related to the importance of permanency and stability of emotional and/or physical living conditions and the upbringing of the child. Permanence is essential for structure, strength and consistency to support children's development (Skivenes and Thoburn 2017), and in the US legislation it is formulated as follows: '*The department's considerations of appropriate services and placement decisions shall be made in a timely manner in order to facilitate permanency planning for the child*' (#1, para. 5).

Several of the countries have a focus on stability in relation to the birth family or a change to an established living arrangement. Australia, Denmark, Spain and the USA are all in this category: '*(d) the likely effect on the child or young person of changes to the child's or young person's circumstances, including separation from a parent or anyone else with whom the child has been living*' (Australia #1.d). Canada, England and Norway have chosen a neutral formulation of stability, here illustrated by Norway: '*When applying the provisions of this chapter, decisive importance shall be attached to finding measures which are in the child's best interests. This includes attaching importance to giving the child stable and good contact with adults and continuity in the care provided*' (4-1, para. 1).

5.4 Protection

Nine of the 14 countries include consideration of the child's safety or risk factors, and the five countries that do not explicitly mention this are Denmark, Estonia, Ireland, Norway and Switzerland. The focus is on two types of risk: (a) the potential harm unnecessary removal or intervention may have on the child, and/or (b) the risks of abuse, neglect or harm to the child if he or she remains in a potentially dangerous situation. The Austrian, Canadian and Swedish legislation includes both dimensions: '*In the assessment of what is best for the child, particular focus must be placed on—the risk of the child or other family member being subjected to abuse or the child being illegally removed or retained or otherwise treated badly*' (Sweden #2.a).

The legislation can reference protection broadly or be more detailed (but yet far-reaching), like the English legislation, which includes both past and present risks, in that '*(e) any harm which he (the child) has suffered or is at risk of suffering*' (#3.e). The legislation from Australia, Austria, Spain and the USA lists both physical and psychological (or emotional or spiritual) harm or abuse. Harm or violence against another family member is mentioned in the legislation from Australia, Austria, Canada and Sweden. The Austrian legislation highlights the negative impact a decision made against the child's wishes may have: '*6. the prevention of an adverse effect on the child due to the taking of action against his or her will*' (#6).

5.5 The Child's Relationships

The legislation in eight of the 14 countries includes various forms of consideration of the child's relationship with a caregiver or other significant others. The legislation in England, Estonia, Finland, Ireland, Switzerland and the USA does not refer to this consideration. This code does not include text that relates to the parent's or caregiver's care of the 'child's needs' intended to conserve 'permanency/stability' for the child. Amongst the eight countries that mention the child's relationships, most emphasize both the relationship to the caregivers or parents and the child's relationship with other family members. This is illustrated by the Canadian legislation, which expresses that the decision-maker shall take into consideration '*6. The child's relationships and emotional ties to a parent, sibling, relative, other member of the child's extended family or member of the child's community*' (#3.6). The legislation also emphasizes the child's place in the family and the importance of a positive relationship with a parent for development. Only the Swedish legislation in this sample defines the relationship with the natural parents: '*the child's need for close and good contact with both parents*' (#2.a).

5.6 The Child's Identity

Considerations that focus on the child's individuality in terms of cultural inheritance or other aspects important to the child's identity are mentioned in six of the 14 countries: Australia, Austria, Canada, England, Finland and Spain. The legislation that requires that the child's identity, individuality or culture be considered varies in the comprehensiveness and details of the wording/text. The Austrian, Canadian, English and Finnish legislation are brief, for example: '*7) the need to take account of the child's linguistic, cultural and religious background*' (Finland #2.7). By contrast, the Australian and Spanish legislation elaborates: '*d) Preservation of the identity, culture, religion, convictions, sexual orientation and identity of the minor, as well as non-discrimination against same for these reasons or any other conditions, including disability, guaranteeing the harmonious development of their personality*' (Spain #2.d).

The Australian legislation has a specific focus on Aboriginal or Torres Strait Islander children or young people, stating that it is a high priority to protect and promote the child's cultural and spiritual identity. '*[M]aintaining and building the child's or the young person's connections to the family, community and culture*' (#1.g) are also emphasized.

5.7   Parents' Perspective

Four countries mention the parents' or caregivers' capacity to care for the child, or their opinion about the child—that is, the legislation from Australia, Austria, England and Ireland. English law illustrates this, referring to '*(f) how capable each of his parents, and any other person in relation to whom the court considers the question to be relevant, is of meeting his needs*' (#1.f). The focus is on parents' abilities to meet the child's needs (Australia and England), their acceptance of the child (Austria) and the '*rights and duties of parents*' (Ireland).

5.8   Future

Three countries—Denmark, Finland and Spain—include considerations of the child's future life or adulthood, as the legislation from Spain illustrates: '*e) Preparation for transition to adulthood and independence, in accordance with their personal capacities and circumstances*' (#3.e).

5.9   Weight and Procedures

Although the interpretation of the best interest principle varies considerably, all 14 countries specify how factors should be ranked or the best interest principle weighted against other principles or mention a timeline. The role of the principle in relation to other principles and rights is foregrounded by eight countries—England, Estonia, Finland, Ireland, Norway, Sweden and Switzerland—and they include terms such as the best interest being paramount, a primary consideration or a priority. For example, '*the child's welfare shall be the court's paramount consideration*'

(England #1.b). Although many countries include specific material factors to be considered, as we have shown above, seven countries—Australia, Canada, Denmark, Estonia, Germany, Spain and the USA—have an unspecified caveat that '*any other fact or circumstance*' (Australia #2) considered relevant should be included in the decision-making process. Four countries—Australia, Canada, England and Finland—mention the importance of making the decision without delay, for example, in the English act '*any delay in determining the question is likely to prejudice the welfare of the child*' (#2).

5.10 Summary Findings

In sum, the findings show that there are different understandings between the 14 countries of the principle of the child's best interest, as well as differences in delegation by the government to the professional decision-maker of authority to exercise discretion. All countries have some reference to weighting, timelines and/or procedural requirements. Regarding the material content of the principle, we identify clear distinctions between the legislative interpretations of the child's best interest principle. It is clear that depending on the specific country, these considerations represent zero to seven material themes that professionals are instructed to consider. Ten of the 14 countries have four or more material themes reflected in the child's best interest principle, whereas the other four have zero to three material themes to consider. The principle's foundation as a right for children is evidently a right that is open to interpretation and degrees of implementation by the ratifying states.

6 Discussion

We learn that from an empirical view, there are eight factors that are important when a child's best interest is determined in child protection situations in these 14 states. This provides us with information about what is perceived to be important for children's upbringing and gives material content to the best interest standard. Some factors are more important than others: *Child's participation* is regarded as decisive by almost all of the countries (12 of the 14), which indicates that children have a prominent position in child protection legislation and that legislation accords with the fundamental principle of children's participation in the CRC (Art. 12; cf. GC 14 2013). There is also a large amount of the national legislation (in 10 of the 14 countries) that raises the issue of the *child's needs* as an important consideration. This is a basic premise for a healthy upbringing, and in child protection cases this is likely to have been a neglected factor in the lives of the concerned children. *Permanency* is also high on the list, and denotes the importance of continuity and the sense of belonging for a child. *Protection* of children from harm and neglect and providing them with a safe living environment are included by many of the countries (nine of the 14). Preservation of a *child's relationship*, be it to carers, parents or others in a wider sense, is included by eight of the 14 countries. These five factors centre around the child and his or her viewpoints, relationships, permanency, needs and risks. The remaining three considerations are included by fewer than half of the countries and can be regarded as factors that do not have the same relative importance: *child's identity* (six of 14); natural *parents' perspective* (four of 14) and the *future of the child* (three of 14).

Compared with GC 14, which refers to seven elements that should be considered, we find a strong overlap of four elements: (a) the child's views; (b) preservation of the family environment and maintaining relations; (c) care, protection and safety of the child, and (d) situation of vulnerability. However, it is interesting to note what is *not* overlapping. Only a few countries mention: (e) the child's identity; (f) the child's right to health and (g) the child's right to education. Most of the strong multicultural countries (in terms, e.g., of population constellation, indigenous people), such as Australia, Canada, England and Spain, have included the child's identity as a factor. However, neither Germany nor the USA mentions this factor, though both are multicultural countries that have received a large influx of migrants. The lack of focus in the legislation on education and health is surprising, as it is well established that these areas are extremely important for children's future adulthood, and to gain employment and independence from the state. Related to this is the curious lack of attention to the future well-being of the child, when the best interest of a child should be considered. Only three of the 14 countries in our sample mention this. The CRC committee does not include this element at all. We would expect the future of the child to be an important consideration for professional decision-makers with regard to measures such as a care order application. Furthermore, there is solid research from Adverse Childhood Experiences[10] studies on the negative consequences of neglect and abuse, and it makes sense for professional decision-makers to ensure that a child in need of protection can achieve a good adult life, as the Danish do.

We cannot identify a pattern between type of child protection system and understanding of the principle, nor between countries' ranking on indexes and the understanding of the principle nor in the form of an overlapping with the CRC committee's recommendations. This may be due to the countries involved, or it may be that the child protection 'typology' and index ranking are too broad and lack sufficient nuances.

All countries mention weighting of the material factors, time limits or relationships between rights or principles. An interesting point here is how the legislation draws upon a broader set of considerations if deemed necessary, just as the CRC committee recommends (cf. GC No. 14). The question of how much weight the decision-maker should attach to the child's best interest is also a way of regulating discretion. CRC Article 3 states that the best interest of the child shall be a primary consideration. A primary consideration does not have an 'absolute priority' over other considerations. 'Primary' means 'first', in that it should be a 'first consideration', but it does not necessarily determine the course of action (Freeman 2007).

7 Strong and Weak Discretion

Through legislation, governments set standards for decision-makers about interpreting and applying the best interest principle. A distinction between weak and strong discretion can be drawn, and in the material of the 14 countries, there are six where legislation provides decision-makers with *strong discretion*, including Estonia, Ireland, Norway and Switzerland. Strong discretion is evident, as in these countries. The legislators have only set a few requirements on the considerations that decision-makers must take into account when making the child's best interest decisions in child protection. At the opposite extreme is national legislation that provides decision-makers with weak discretion; the remaining eight countries are in this category. Here, a range of considerations are provided that the decision-makers should consider. For example, the Australian, English and Finnish legislation list seven considerations.

The category of strong discretion includes legislation or guidelines with few instructions concerning what professional decision-makers should consider (cf. Table 4.5 below). Of the four countries that we categorize as having strong discretion—Norway, Ireland, Estonia and Switzerland—the Swiss legislation is by far the most general, and professional decision-makers are vested with strong discretion: '*With all state action that affects children and young people, their welfare is to be given priority.*' Evident in this analysis is the complete lack of instructions to decision-makers on interpreting the best interest principle. This makes the decision-making situations vulnerable to contingency and personal perceptions and indicates a lack of standards to hold decision-makers accountable. We could have seen a procedural approach, evident in the Spanish and Estonian legislation, in which the decision-makers must collect all relevant information and hear all involved parties to ensure reasoned deliberation: '*3) assessing all the relevant circumstances in aggregate, to form a reasoned opinion concerning the best interests of the child with regard to the planned decision*' (Estonia #3). The Estonian legislation also displays a strong child-centrism by requiring that the situation and the person of the child are considered, and any decision that is contrary to the child's wishes must be explicitly justified. This child-centrism in the Estonian legislation may be explained by its recent enactment (2016), which is part of a trend of increasing child-centrism throughout Western countries (Gilbert et al. 2011; Skivenes and Søvig 2016).

The category of weak discretion is included in legislation in 10 of the 14 countries, and this category is characterized by substantial instructions for the decision-makers in the form of four or more instructions (cf. Table 4.6). The Australian legislation illustrates how the delegation of weak discretion takes form in practice: '*What is in the best interest of the child or young person? (1) For the care and protection chapters, in deciding*

Table 4.5 Strong discretion and material content

Country	Child's participation	Child's needs	Permanency	Protection	Child's relationship	Child's identity	Parent's perspective	Child's future
Norway	1		1					
Ireland	1				1			
Estonia	1						1	
Switzerland								

Table 4.6 Considerations in legislation that authorizes weak discretion

Country	Child's participation	Child's needs	Permanency	Protection	Child's relationship	Child's identity	Parent's perspective	Child's future	Number of factors
Australia	1	1	1	1	1	1	1		7
Austria	1	1	1	1	1	1	1		7
Spain	1	1	1	1	1	1	1		7
Canada	1	1	1	1	1	1		1	6
England	1	1	1	1	1	1	1		6
Denmark	1	1	1		1			1	5
Finland	1	1		1	1	1		1	5
Germany	1	1		1					4
Sweden	1	1		1	1				4
USA	1	1	1	1					4

what is in the best interests of a child or young person, a decision-maker must consider each of the following matters that are relevant to the child or young person:...' (#349, 1). This instruction is followed by a list of 11 separate considerations for a decision-maker. Australia, Austria and Spain authorize the weakest discretion, with Germany, Sweden and the USA at the other end of the weak discretion continuum. However, even for the countries that provide the weakest discretion, there are openings for considering additional elements that the situation and the decision-maker see fit, or the possibility to deviate from the considerations. Surely, it is sensible to have flexibility in these complex and sensitive cases and to let decision-makers use their professional competency to assess the situation and the specific child involved in the decision-making. However, as evident in the procedural approach in the Estonian legislation, it makes sense to recommend that whenever a consideration is deemed unnecessary, this should be explicitly explained.

8 Concluding Remarks

Although in this analysis, we have made bold statements about how 'countries' think about the child's best interest principle, we are also aware that child protection systems in most high-income countries are based on the same basic principles, including that the family/parents have the primary responsibility for their children, and the least intrusive principle, that removals should be temporary and that the welfare/best interest of the child should be considered (Burns et al. 2017). Nevertheless, the organization of systems and the removal proceedings differ between jurisdictions (Burns et al. 2017). Our analysis of national child protection legislation of the child's best interest principle shows distinct differences between countries in the interpretation of the principle of best interest. This indicates that what is deemed important for children across child protection systems differs, possibly because of cultural views. What is clearly evident is that the recommendations of the CRC committee are only partially included in child protection legislation that we have analysed; this may be attributable to the committee report only being published in 2013. Nevertheless, it is interesting that the overlap between the committee's recommendations and the countries' legislation is not more extensive as one should expect that standards for children's needs across countries would have included some of the same topics.

We should ask whether the indeterminacy and the ambiguity of the best interest principle demands that each individual be considered on his or her own terms, and that there should not be any material content guiding the decision because it can only be made in regard to the unique child it concerns. Following this line of reasoning, the very simple principle formulated in the Swiss child protection legislation may be consistent with this norm. However, this raises the fundamental problem with the exercise of discretion to which decision-makers are not bound by any standards, as Dworkin (1967) already had discussed. We believe that the emphasis on indeterminacy has led to an exaggerated belief in the differences between individuals at the expense of their commonalities. The established knowledge about common needs for people to lead a good life is valid for all children. Shapiro (1999) labels this basic need 'fact-based' and suggests that these should be distinguished from best interests (value-based considerations).

A striking finding is the variations in discretionary authority that are displayed. It is a broad continuum that extends from Switzerland at one end with strong discretion, and Australia at the other with weak discretion. An example of the force of clear instructions for professionals is shown in a study of child protection workers in England, California (USA) and Norway on the use of adoption as a child protection measure (Skivenes and Tefre 2012). Only Norway has given professionals strong discretionary authority over this matter. Presented with the same case, close to all staff in England and California (USA) recommended adoption for the child, whereas six out of ten of the Norwegians did the same. The empirical studies that should be pursued are whether and how the various prerogatives of professional decision-makers are exercised. We anticipate that in countries with weak discretion, there will be more similarities between decision-makers on important assessments such as care orders.

The implementation of children's rights across states still have a long way to go, and we are only witnessing an emerging child-centrism placing children on an equal footing to adults in modern societies. Providing instruction on the fact-based elements of the principle is in our opinion an important way to enhance children's position across societies, independent of ethical-cultural values and norms.

Notes

1. All states in the world, except the USA, have ratified the CRC as of 16 May 2017.
2. Cf. the recommendation by the CRC committee on the interpretation of the material content of the best interest principle (GC No. 14, 2013).
3. Although the USA has not ratified the CRC, we include it as several states use the principles from the CRC and the best interest principle in child protection, Gateway, C. W. I. 2016. *State statutes: Determining the best interests of the child* [online]. Available at: https://www.childwelfare. gov/topics/systemwide/laws-policies/statutes/best-interest/ (accessed 3 June 2016).
4. The Court is not without regulations, as only legal scholars can be judges, and decisions are made in accordance with legal methods and follow legal precedents.
5. For practical reasons, we use the country name in the text, even though for several countries, we only analyse the legislation of one state/canton/ province/territory.
6. We are very grateful for the expert knowledge, guidance and help received from: Morag McArthur (Australia), Katrin Kriz and Marianne Roth (Austria), Chris Walmsley and Nicholas Bala (Canada), Anemone Skårhøj (Denmark), Jonathan Dickens (England), Judit Strömpl (Estonia), Tarja Pösö (Finland), Monika Haug (Germany), Roberta Teresa Di Rosa (Italy), Kenneth Burns (Ireland), Gustav Svensson (Sweden), Stefan Schnurr (Switzerland) and Katrin Kriz (MA, USA).
7. It would have defeated the purpose of the comparison between countries to include, for example, child protection legislation for the entire USA.
8. An online appendix of all the laws included in the analysis is available on the project website: http://www.uib.no/sites/w3.uib.no/files/attachments/appendix_to_the_best_interests_of_the_child_in_child_protection.pdf. For the sake of simplicity, we reference only the country and the paragraph in the chapter.

9. Even in official translations, the wording of the principle may be different from that in the native tongue. For example, the expert from Estonia noted that the official English translation used the term 'best interest of the child', but the Estonian version uses the phrase 'child's interest'. The expert from Switzerland pointed out that the German word '*Kindeswohl*' entails more than the English translation of 'well-being of the child', although '*Kindeswohl*' might be understood as equivalent to the best interest of the child.
10. https://en.wikipedia.org/wiki/Adverse_Childhood_Experiences_Study.

References

Adamson, P. (2013). Child well-being in rich countries: A comparative overview (Innocenti report card no. 11). Florence: UNICEF Office of Research, Florence.

Archard, D., & Skivenes, M. (2009). Balancing a child's best interests and a child's views. *The International Journal of Childen's Rights, 17*(1), 1–21.

Breen, C. (2002). *The standard of the best interests of the child: A western tradition in international and comparative law* (Vol. 72). The Hague: Kluwer.

Burns, K., Pösö, T. & Skivenes, M. (2017). Child welfare removals by the state: A cross-country analysis of decision-making systems. New York: Oxford University Press.

Child Welfare Information Gateway (2016). State statutes: Determining the best interests of the child [online]. Available: https://www.childwelfare.gov/topics/systemwide/laws-policies/statutes/best-interest/. Accessed 3 June 2016.

Dworkin, R. M. (1967). The model of rules. *The University of Chicago Law Review, 35*(1), 14–46.

Elster, J. (1989). *Solomonic judgements: Studies in the limitations of rationality.* Cambridge: Cambridge University Press.

Freeman, M. (2005). Children's health and children's rights: An introduction. *The International Journal of Children's Rights, 13*(1–2), 1–10.

Freeman, M. (2007). Why it remains important to take children's rights seriously. *The International Journal of Children's Rights, 15*(1), 5–23.

Gilbert, N. (1997). *Combating child abuse: Comparative perspectives on reporting systems and placement trends.* New York: Oxford University Press.

Gilbert, N., Parton, N., & Skivenes, M. (2011). *Child protection systems: International trends and orientations*. New York: Oxford University Press.

Hetherington, R., Cooper, A., Smith, P., & Wilford, G. (1997). *Protecting children: Message from Europe*. Dorset: Russell House Publishing Ltd.

Mnookin, R. H., & Szwed, E. (1983). The best interest syndrome as the allocation of power in child care. In H. Geach & E. Szwed (Eds.), *Providing civil justice for the child* (pp. 7–20). London: Edward Arnold.

Rawls, J. (1971). *A theory of justice*. Cambridge, MA: The Belknap Press of Harvard University Press.

Rothstein, B. (1998). *Just institutions matter: The moral and political logic of the universal welfare state*. Cambridge: Cambridge University Press.

Schneider, V. (1992). The structure of policy network. *European Journal of Political Research, 21*(1–2), 109–129.

Shapiro, I. (1999). *Democratic justice*. New Haven: Yale University Press.

Skivenes, M. (2002). Lovgiving og legitimitet: En evaluering av lov om barneverntjenester av 1992 i et deliberativt perspektiv [Legislation and legitimacy: An evaluation of the Child Welfare Act of 1992]. Bergen: University, Department of Administration and Organization Theory, report number 79. PhD thesis (in Norwegian).

Skivenes, M., & Pösö, T. (2017). Best interest of the child. In A. Wenzel (Ed.), *The SAGE encyclopedia of abnormal and clinical psychology*. Thousand Oaks: SAGE Publications.

Skivenes, M., & Søvig, K. H. (2016). Judicial discretion and the child's best interest—The European Court of Human Rights on child protection adoptions. In E. Sutherland & L. Macfarlane (Eds.), *Implementing article 3 of the United Nations Convention on the Rights of the Child: Best interests, welfare and well-being*. Cambridge: Cambridge University Press.

Skivenes, M., & Tefre, Ø. S. (2012). Adoption in the child welfare system—A cross-country analysis of child welfare workers' recommendations for or against adoption. *Children and Youth Services Review, 34*, 2220–2228.

Skivenes, M., & Thoburn, J. (2017). Citizens' views in four jurisdictions on placement policies for maltreated children. *Child & Family Social Work, 22*(4), 1472–1479.

Skivenes, M., Barn, R., Kriz, K., & Pösö, T. (2015). *Child welfare systems and migrant children: A cross-country study of policies and practice*. Oxford: Oxford University Press.

Legislation and Conventions

Child and Family Service Act, R. S. O, c. C11. (1990). Canada. Available at: https://www.ontario.ca/laws/statute/90c11?_ga=1.16889017.1635595470.1 466670145 - BK2. Accessed 23 June 2016.

Child Care Act. (1991). Ireland. Available at: http://www.irishstatutebook.ie/eli/1991/act/17/enacted/en/html. Accessed 23 June 2016.

Child Protection Act. (2016). Estonia [Law in original language: Lastekaitseseadus]. Available at: https://www.riigiteataja.ee/en/eli/506052015001/consolide. Accessed 23 June 2016.

Child Welfare Act. (2007). Finland [Law in original language: Lastensuojelulaki, Barnskyddslag]. Available at: http://www.finlex.fi/en/laki/kaannokset/2007/en20070417?search%5Btype%5D=pika&search%5Bpika%5D=Child. Accessed 23 June 2016.

Children Act. (1989). England. Available at: http://www.legislation.gov.uk/ukpga/1989/41/section/1. Accessed 23 June 2016.

Children and Young People Act. (2008). Australia. Available at: http://www.legislation.act.gov.au/a/2008-19/current/pdf/2008–19.pdf. Accessed 14 June 2016.

Children and Young Persons Act. (2015). Switzerland [Law in original language: Gesetz betreffend Förder- und Hilfeleistungen für Kinder und Jugendliche (Kinder- und Jugendgesetz, KJG)]. Available at: http://www.gesetzessammlung.bs.ch/frontend/versions/3254. Accessed 14 June 2016.

Civil Code of Austria. (2013). Austria [Law in original language: Allgemeines bürgerliches Gesetzbuch]. Available at: https://www.ris.bka.gv.at/Dokument.wxe?Abfrage=Bundesnormen&Dokumentnummer=NOR40146725. Accessed 1 June 2016.

Consolidation Act on Social Services. (2011). Denmark [Law in original language: Lov om social service (Serviceloven)]. Available at: https://www.retsinformation.dk/Forms/R0710.aspx?id=173200-idcc44e087-df5d-42e4-a6c9-b82107b50646. Accessed 23 June 2016.

General Law Chapter 119 Protection and Care of Children and Proceedings against Them. United States of America, Massachusetts. Available at: https://malegislature.gov/Laws/GeneralLaws/PartI/TitleXVII/Chapter119/Section1. Accessed 14 June 2016.

German Civil Code. (2002). Germany [Law in original language: Bürgerlichen Gesetzbuches]. Available at: http://www.gesetze-im-internet.de/englisch_bgb/englisch_bgb.html-p5900. Accessed 30 May 2016.

Organic Law 1/1996, o. j., On Protection of Minors, Modification to the Civil Code and the Civil Procedure Act. (1996). Spain [Law in original language: Ley Orgánica 1/1996, de 15 de enero, de protección jurídica del menor, de modificación del Código Civil y de la Ley de Enjuiciamiento Civil]. Available at: http://noticias.juridicas.com/base_datos/Privado/lo1-1996.html. Accessed 30 May 2016.

Social Service Act. (2001). Sweden [Law in original language: Socialtjänstlag]. Available at: https://www.riksdagen.se/sv/dokument-lagar/dokument/svensk-forfattningssamling/socialtjanstlag-2001453_sfs-2001-453. Accessed 7 June 2017.

The Child Welfare Act. (1992). Norway [Law in original language: Barnevernloven]. Available at: https://www.regjeringen.no/en/dokumenter/the-child-welfare-act/id448398/. Accessed 23 June 2016.

United Nations Convention on the Rights of the Child. (1989).

United Nations, Convention on the Rights of the Child. (2013). GC No. 14, 2013 on the right of the child to have his or her best interest taken as a primary consideration.

Open Access This chapter is licensed under the terms of the Creative Commons Attribution 4.0 International License (http://creativecommons.org/licenses/by/4.0/), which permits use, sharing, adaptation, distribution and reproduction in any medium or format, as long as you give appropriate credit to the original author(s) and the source, provide a link to the Creative Commons license and indicate if changes were made.

The images or other third party material in this chapter are included in the chapter's Creative Commons license, unless indicated otherwise in a credit line to the material. If material is not included in the chapter's Creative Commons license and your intended use is not permitted by statutory regulation or exceeds the permitted use, you will need to obtain permission directly from the copyright holder.

5

Re-designing Organizations to Facilitate Rights-Based Practice in Child Protection

Eileen Munro and Andrew Turnell

1 Introduction

The actions of individual child protection workers are the final steps in how an organization promotes the realization of children's rights, with those actions being radically shaped in helpful and unhelpful ways by the organizational context. In many jurisdictions, managerialism has so constrained individual discretion and choice of action that rights-based practice is hard to achieve. Recent reforms in England aim to increase professional autonomy and decrease the top-down control mechanisms of managerialism such as proceduralization and key performance indicators that measure professional activity rather than outcomes for children. This chapter takes the example of implementing the Signs of Safety

---

E. Munro (✉)
London School of Economics, London, UK
e-mail: e.munro@lse.ac.uk

A. Turnell
Resolutions Consultancy, East Perth, WA, Australia
e-mail: andrew.turnell@resolutionsconsultancy.com

© The Author(s) 2018
A. Falch-Eriksen, E. Backe-Hansen (Eds.), *Human Rights in Child Protection*,
https://doi.org/10.1007/978-3-319-94800-3_5

practice framework in ten local authorities in England to illustrate how whole system reform is needed to support workers in achieving rights-based practice.

In England, widespread dissatisfaction with previous efforts to reform the child protection system led to the government establishing the *Munro Review of Child Protection* (2011). The review's analysis of the system of child protection identified how efforts to improve practice by providing greater guidance had combined with a blame culture and the introduction of managerialism's framework of procedures and key performance indicators to lead, over time, to a system focused on compliance with process, not on the impact on children and their families. Efforts to help professionals make sound judgments had slowly expanded guidance to the extent that judgment was increasingly replaced by rule-following, radically diminishing the professional role and leading to serious recruitment and retention problems. The system was so prescriptive that it could not readily adapt to the specific needs of individual children; practice was monitored by checking compliance with procedures, and not by seeing whether children had benefited from the service; keeping records up to date became more important than forming relationships with parents and children. One study reported that workers were spending up to 80% of their time in front of computers (White et al. 2010), and risk management was distorted by defensive practice where professionals sought to protect themselves from blame by sticking rigidly to procedures even when this led to choices that they did not consider were best for children. This is referred to as 'weak discretion', where autonomy is limited and decision-making in practice is predominantly routinized and controlled (see Skivenes and Sørsdal 2018: Chap. 4 in this book). Crucially such a system of rules fails to provide the 'requisite variety' (Ashby 1991) to meet the needs of individual children; skilled professionals are needed to use their judgment in applying general knowledge to the specific circumstances of a child.

While Signs of Safety is by no means the only practice framework that upholds and facilitates the rights of the child, the implementation of Signs of Safety is offered here as illustrative of the range of issues that shifting to a more rights-based approach raises (Turnell 2012). The work in England has highlighted the extent to which the organizational system can, possibly inadvertently, create obstacles to professionals' efforts to uphold, facilitate and ultimately respect children's rights.

Rights can be divided into three groups: provision, participation and protection rights. The focus here is mainly on the first two sets of rights since they had been more neglected in the former way of working in which risk management was central.

2 Provision Rights and Promoting Development

When family care poses a threat to children's healthy development, workers need to balance the dangers against the benefits that their intervention offers the child. In practice, there is considerable evidence that this is difficult to achieve. History in many jurisdictions reveals a fluctuating pattern of giving priority to child rescue or to family preservation (Parton 2009; Gilbert et al. 2011; Featherstone et al. 2013). Yet both dimensions are equally necessary when deciding what is in the best interests of children. Leaving children in potentially dangerous circumstances has obvious implications for whether a child realizes their survival and development rights, but so does removing them. Children who are removed lose intimate contact with their birth parents (and sometimes lose all contact). They also face the risk of their developmental needs not being adequately met—research on the outcomes for children raised in alternative care reveals how this is not a simple solution (Thoburn 2017).

A balanced assessment depends, in part, on having a practice approach that offers guidance on how to achieve the best possible balance between the benefits of interventions with non-intervention. In Signs of Safety, a balanced analysis is central to assessment (Table 5.1).

Table 5.1 Signs of safety assessment and planning framework

Signs of Safety Assessment and Planning Framework: Seven Analysis Categories (Professional Language)

What are we worried about?	What's working well?	What needs to happen?
HARM: Past hurt, injury or abuse to the child (likely) caused by adults. Also includes risk taking behaviour by children/teens that indicates harm and/or is harmful to them.	EXISTING STRENGTHS: People, plans and actions that contribute to a child's wellbeing and plans about how a child will be made safe when danger is present.	SAFETY GOALS: The behaviours and actions the child protection agency needs to see to be satisfied the child will be safe enough to close the case.
DANGER STATEMENTS: The harm or hurt that is believed likely to happen to the child(ren) if nothing in the family's situation changes.	EXISTING SAFETY: Actions taken by parents, caring adults and children to make sure the child is safe when the danger is present.	NEXT STEPS: The immediate next actions that will be taken to build future safety.
Complicating Factors: Actions and behaviors in and around the family and child and by professionals that make it more difficult to solve danger of future abuse.		

0 ◄———————————————————► 10

In a meeting between the social worker and family (sometimes with other professionals also present), the three columns are completed. After completion, both professionals and family members present are asked individually to answer a scaling question from zero to ten of how much danger they think there is. Conflicting scores lead to discussions of why people disagree or what would make them give a higher score.

Achieving a balanced assessment, however, requires significant organizational support based on a realistic understanding of how difficult the task is and giving greater weight to the importance of professional judgment and use of discretion in assessing a family. In England, the organizational obstacles we encountered were a mix of practical and cultural. One obstacle was relatively easy to deal with: revising guidance and forms to capture the principles, terminology and methods of the practice framework. Integrating the guidance into the IT system was more problematic in part because of the expense. The most difficult obstacles were cultural.

The key culture challenges were lessening the process-driven blame culture and changing priorities so workers had more time with families and more time for critical reflection (Munro et al. 2016).

A defensive blame culture was widespread. This can lead the individual worker (at whatever level of seniority) to place more weight on the option that offers minimum risk of blame to themselves or their agency than on the option that their professional assessment concludes is in the best interests of the child. In England, the influence of 'covering one's back' is vividly illustrated by the rise in applications for care orders to remove children whenever there is a high-profile death of a child from maltreatment (see, for example, Elsley 2010). Defensive practice was also apparent in the tendency to interpret guidance as fixed rules rather than as principles to inform professional judgment, which was their original purpose.

An alternative to a defensive culture is a just culture. Here, a just culture implies that professional case-workers can be confident that their work will always be judged according to reasonable standards even if a tragedy occurs. Hence, the focus of their decision-making can be on the protection of the child and not themselves or their agency. The two challenges to achieving this are agreeing on 'reasonable standards' and changing the culture.

On the first, there is a considerable literature from other high-risk areas of work to help in the effort to reduce defensive practices, for example in medicine (Department of Health 2001; Dekker 2007) and in policing (College of Policing 2009). The latter publication contains 'risk principles' which were produced by the College of Policing to tackle the problem of reducing defensive practice. These were used as a starting point for discussion within child protection of how to define reasonable standards and subsequently produce a version specific to this area of work.

Agreeing on reasonable standards is not sufficient. Senior managers need to show they endorse them and give a clear message that they will back their workforce if practice meets these criteria. In addition, all need to understand how powerfully and automatically hindsight distorts our judgment of past behaviour (Fischhoff 1975). Once we know what happened, it looks so obvious that this was the likely causal pathway that would ensue. In contrast, those involved at the time would have seen several plausible pathways down which events might unfold.

A just culture was also encouraged by reforming the quality assurance system. In the past, this had focused on checking whether records showed evidence of compliance with statutory requirements and tended to be experienced as punitive and anxiety-provoking by workers. The new quality-assurance system aims to be a collaborative learning process that seeks to understand not just what the worker did but why he or she took those actions, how he or she reasoned to reach that conclusion and what organizational factors influenced the process, providing managers with feedback on the realities of the practice environment. Only then is a judgment formed about the quality of the worker's practice.

Another necessary organizational change involved giving greater importance to critical reflection, supervision and group support. In short, encouraging what Kahneman (2011) describes as 'slow' thinking to review the 'fast' thinking that figures in so much direct work. While supervision is generally recognized as important, in practice it had become undervalued and often focused on checking compliance with case processing rather than being a forum for reviewing one's reasoning about a case (Rushton and Nathan 1996; O'Donoghue and Tsui 2013).

This chapter mainly talks about the child protection organizational system but this system is of course a subsystem of others. In England, they are part of a local authority and of the national political system. These wider systems are also major influences on what happens to children. Fundamental to all reforms is sufficient funding to be able to provide a high-quality service to children, undertaking the skilled work with families of assessing their strengths and dangers, helping the family to reduce the danger to children or providing good-quality alternative care when this cannot be achieved in a timespan that meets the child's needs. The GC on Article 19 (Unicef 2011) makes it clear that states parties have a duty to support families but the level of funding provided is influenced by political and economic factors. At present in England, as in many developed countries, the economic policy of austerity is a major complicating factor.

3 Respecting Participation Rights

Participation has been conceptualized as on a continuum and needs to take account of the evolving capacities of the child (Lansdown 2000), and this right is essential in a rights-based approach (see both Pösö 2018 and Sandberg 2018: Chaps. 6 and 2 in this book). Studies of child protection practice, however, have persistently reported failings in adequately respecting this right (Thomas 2015; Ferguson 2017). By practising Signs of Safety, the right to participation features in each step of the process, and with a focus not just on how this contributes to protecting the child, but also on how the whole experience of being involved in the child protection system can be managed in a way that minimizes distress and harm to the child.

3.1 Listening to Children

Children are clearly a major source of information about what is happening to them, how they are experiencing it and what they wish would happen. Even pre-verbal or disabled children can communicate their feelings. Their right to be heard is captured in Article 12 of the CRC. Social workers in England have been frequently criticized for not spending enough time with children and listening to their views (Research in Practice 2015). The Children's Rights Director for England sought feedback from fifty children about their experience of coming into care and found that more than half the children had not known they were coming into care until it actually happened and were not prepared for this radical change in their lives: 'Someone could have explained things so I could understand what was happening' (Morgan 2007).

The failure to spend time with children is often blamed on individual workers, with people ascribing it to deficiencies in practitioner skill or motivation. However, in the implementation of Signs of Safety, listening to children was an area where change was welcomed and very rapidly achieved, suggesting that organizational factors have played a stronger role than individual ones in omitting children from the conversation. Staff were enthusiastic in using My Three Houses[1] or similar methods to shape the conversation, but organizational changes were also important.

The My Three Houses tool can be used at any stage in a child's progress through child protection services and helps workers gain an understanding of the child's lived experience and their hopes and fears. A worker can simply use paper with pencils and crayons or use the My Three Houses app on their tablet (http://resolutionsconsultancy.com/app-support). The 'three houses' are the House of Worries, the House of Good Things (the present) and the House of Wishes (the future). Below is a worked example (anonymized) to illustrate the richness of the information gathered (Picture 5.1).

Picture 5.1 My three houses—photos in a series

Picture 5.1 (continued)

Picture 5.1 (continued)

Providing training and tools were not the most significant factors in achieving change: senior managers also changed their messages and actions. Besides saying that children needed to be listened to (a sentiment to which they would always have at least paid lip-service), they reinforced this message by asking to see and hear about children's views, expecting children's views to be available for case discussions, looking for them when auditing a case and praising workers for good practice.

Practical changes were also needed. A major problem was altering the IT software so that children's views, in whatever format, could be uploaded to be central to the case file. An interim solution was to attach them as an appendix but this risks their being overlooked or being seen as less important. The My Three Houses app that was developed required workers to have tablets with them when visiting children. Wherever possible interviews with children should be conducted where the child feels comfortable and familiar such as the child's home or the school, but if there is a need to conduct them in the agency offices then suitable room space is needed.

3.2 Involving Children in Creating and Implementing a Safety Plan

It might seem straightforward that listening to children more would lead to their information and opinions being used more in case planning, but we found that this was not always the case. The ongoing and pervading influence of the compliance culture showed its impact with some practitioners treating the task of listening to children as a discrete box to be ticked. When this happened, adult views and voices still tended to dominate case discussions and planning, and the child's rights were effectively set aside. To address this problem, it was important to train workers, supervisors and managers in how to integrate and use children's views within the entire trajectory of the case work and how to continue to involve children on an ongoing basis. Most critically, managers and supervisors need to lead for this broader involvement of the child and their views because creating the space where children genuinely contribute and participate is always challenging. The involvement of children is gradually improving as workers, supervisors and managers see more examples of good practice and understand the process changes required to facilitate children's participation. There are indications that the overall culture of the agency is becoming more sharply focused on children (Munro et al. 2016).

Planning how to keep children safe is a key task in children's services work. In Signs of Safety practice, this is done by formulating 'safety plans' with the family and, where appropriate, other professionals. Involving children in safety plans raises many issues, including how to manage different priorities and sensibilities between children and professionals about what is in the child's best interests. Respectful engagement with children means that their views should be taken seriously and considered though not necessarily acted upon—an issue for which there is no rule-based solution but requires case-by-case deliberation.

It was found that, in many instances, adults' reasons for overriding children's views stemmed from defensive practice. For example, in one case, Matilda, a 13-year-old girl living with her father, was only allowed contact with her mother in the community, not in the mother's home because of concerns that she would be exposed to violence and drug-taking there. Matilda kept going missing overnight but neither she nor her mother would admit she was staying there. Matilda made it clear that she was worried about her mother's well-being and wanted to visit her mother at home. The social worker decided to change the safety plan and seek to allow Matilda to visit her mother safely and Matilda then came up with her own safety plan.

> 'Mum and dad to arrange when I can go and see mum, this needs to happen quickly.'

> 'I want the flat to be clean and tidy, if it is not I want mum to take me out for dinner.'

> 'Mum to make sure she is not drinking any alcohol or take drugs while I am there'.

'Mum will agree that I will call dad if she has been drinking, if dad is not there I call will call mum's sister, if she is not there then I will call my Nan and someone will pick me up.'

'I do not want Jason to be there when I am seeing mum, if he comes then mum has to tell him to leave or i will go home'. 'If Jason is angry then mum will call the police, if this does not happen then I will not go to mum's house again.'

'Me and mum communicate with Dad and tell him when I get there and when I will be home.'

'Contact to be just for me and mum, if other people are there mum will tell them to come back later.'

Dad added an extra one: *'If I am worried that anything is wrong at mum's then mum will let me have a look around the house before Matilda comes. If dad can not do this Matilda won't go.'*

Once the plan was implemented, Matilda stopped going missing and her relationship with both parents improved.

In another example, three children devised a safety plan for being with their mother who was an alcoholic. Having listed what their mother needed to do to make them feel safe, they decided that she could not realistically achieve them and so they could not safely return home.

Bringing the child's views into planning meetings was found to have a significant impact on parents. In general, parents report that hearing and seeing their child's view about the effect of the parent's behaviour on them is a far more powerful motivator to change than being advised by a professional.

The Signs of Safety methods for planning safety provide specific means where children can not only contribute to the creation of the safety plan they can also take active roles in keeping themselves safe and communicate to adults that will make sure their concerns are dealt with. For example:

1. A child can have a 'safety object' and place it on the desk at school so that the teacher knows help is needed;

2. Specific people are identified within the naturally connected support network and given the specific job of being the child's safety person. He or she will spend time alone with the child regularly checking with them that everything is okay;
3. Specific people are identified within the safety network that the child can call (usually using a one-touch facility on a mobile phone) who will come immediately (even in the middle of the night) and sort out the child's worries.

For more detailed information about involving children in child protection safety planning using the Signs of Safety approach see (Turnell and Essex 2013).

3.3 Keeping Informed of What Is Happening and Why

An English judge, Lady Butler-Sloss, made a pertinent comment in a major review of child protection practice: 'a child is a person and not an object of concern' (Department of Health and HMSO 1988). Sadly, there is evidence that many children are treated more as 'objects of concern' than as people when it comes to keeping them informed of what is happening to them and why (Munro 2011, p. 42). A series of focus groups with 140 children reported that 'it was clear that looked after children were often denied key information, especially about their background' (Wood and Selwyn 2017, p. 29). Child psychiatrist Tilman Furniss (2013) observed that 'child abuse is a syndrome of secrecy'. All families tend to create dynamics where difficult issues are avoided to keep the peace and because it is very difficult to find words to talk about embarrassing issues. When the issues involve situations where children could be or are hurt, it is even harder to speak about and children very often don't know why the problems have happened and often start to blame themselves. As Alcoholics Anonymous members assert, 'You're only as sick as your secrets'.

While it is easy for professionals to pathologize families for not talking openly about their problems, professionals themselves find it very difficult to speak to children about maltreatment they have experienced. This can affect children's general development through causing anxiety and distress and their ability to exercise their right to contribute to decision-making. Signs of Safety places strong emphasis on providing explanations to children through doing 'Words and Pictures'—asking the parent(s) to write a story explaining events in language and pictures that the child can understand. This can be done even if the child is very young because it can be kept until such time as they are old enough. If abuse is a syndrome of secrecy, it follows that openness is the foundation of safety and healing. For the child, this means they have an absolute right to an explanation from their parents and their family about abuse they have suffered and the problems that has caused that harm. Moreover, to minimize the distress and trauma children experience when professionals remove them from their parents, children need this explanation at the time of removal.

The following brief excerpt is the work of child protection practitioner Pene Turnell and colleagues in Western Australia. This example was created with the parents 'Teresa' and 'Marcus' and presented to their five-year-old son 'Marcus' within 48 hours of the removal. The parents, extended family and support people are always present when the story is read to the child.

'A Words and Pictures story so Sammy knows why he is staying with the foster family and why he can't live with Mummy Teresa and Daddy Marcus right now':

* * *

'On Saturday the Police called child protection workers because Daddy Marcus was at the BP petrol station acting and talking in a very strange way, like he didn't know where he was or what he was doing. The Police were worried because they were told Daddy had been driving in a dangerous way and they were worried that Sammy could get scared and hurt. Police thought Daddy Marcus was using drugs. Daddy Marcus says he doesn't remember but that he was very tired (Picture 5.2).

Picture 5.2 A words and pictures story

Later on Saturday, more people were worried about Sammy because he was in the MacDonald's car park and no adults were watching him. Police say Mummy Teresa was in the toilet and they think she was using drugs. Mummy Teresa said the Police were wrong and that balloon man was watching Sammy while she went to the toilet and got an ice cream for Sammy (Picture 5.3).

Picture 5.3 A words and pictures story

Police told child protection workers about the problems and the workers were really worried so they went to the house. The workers told Mummy Teresa and Daddy Marcus that because of the worries Sammy would need to stay somewhere else while they talked with mum and dad about the problems. Mum Teresa helped workers by telling Sammy it was okay to go (Picture 5.4).

Picture 5.4 A words and pictures story

When they were in the car the workers asked Sammy about living with mum and dad. Sammy said that he likes it when mum and dad hug him but that he is scared when they cook glass and eat it and lose their minds. This made the workers more worried that mum and dad are using drugs even though they say they are not (Picture 5.5).

Picture 5.5 A words and pictures story

To talk about the worries, Mummy Teresa and her friend Brad came to a meeting with Patricia and Natasha and Natasha also spoke with Daddy Marcus on the phone. Mummy Teresa told Patricia that dad hits her a lot and that Sammy gets hit hard by Daddy Marcus too. Sammy told Darryl the social worker that dad had hit him across the face. Mummy Teresa said she knows that the hitting dad does and all the yelling at each other makes Sammy very scared (Picture 5.6).

Picture 5.6 A words and pictures story

Because the police and child protection workers are worried that Sammy is scared and could get hurt by the drugs, the hitting, the dangerous driving and being left on his own they will talk to a Judge about what should happen. The workers will ask the Judge for permission for Sammy to live with the foster family while Mummy Teresa and Daddy Marcus work with them to make plans to solve the problems (Picture 5.7).

Picture 5.7 A words and pictures story

While the meetings happen and plans are made, Sammy will live with the foster family who are caring for him. Mummy Teresa and Daddy Marcus love Sammy very much and the workers will make sure Sammy gets to see his mum and dad so he can play with them and tell them about what he has been doing.'

* * *

Creating an organizational appreciation of the importance of keeping children informed when they are removed from home was a major task that is not fully achieved yet. When removing a child, the worker has numerous legal and administrative documents to complete so that adding to the burden is a significant resource demand. However, time is always linked to priorities and the more that managers make it clear that they expect to see evidence of the child being informed, the higher it goes on the worker's list of priorities. Examples of completed 'Words and Pictures' help to convince people of how valuable they are.

4 Conclusion: How the Convention Can Guide Professional Practice

The experience of reforming child protection services to make them more focused on children as rights holders has highlighted the need for a whole-system approach. Signs of Safety is one practice framework that respects children's rights and contains a number of methods and tools to help the workforce treat children respectfully. On its own, however, it faces constant pressure from other organizational factors that make it hard for workers to keep a clear focus on children. The reforms required considerable alteration to organizational processes and documentation but the more important and harder change was in the culture: about what was important, how your work should be judged, and how the organization could support high-quality work with children and their families where workers were confident to exercise discretion, making judgments about what was best for this unique child instead of squeezing the child into a fixed set of categories and rules. One crucial change is in the way that practice is audited or quality assured. What gets measured, gets done, and so the measurements need to be of the quality of practice and the organizational culture within which workers are seeking to realize children's rights.

To end on a positive note, when given the opportunity to break away from an over-proceduralized style of work, people at all levels of seniority were very enthusiastic. They were also courageous in stepping out of their comfort zone into more child-focused work. Creating a culture that respects the rights of children is relatively easy in terms of gaining cooperation from the workforce but challenging in terms of the range of organizational factors that need to be changed to make it happen.

Notes

1. Building on work done by Nikki Weld, New Zealand.

References

Ashby, W. R. (1991). Principles of the self-organizing system. In G. J. Klir (Ed.), *Facets of systems science*. Boston: Springer.
College of Policing. (2009). *Risk*. London: College of Policing.
Dekker, S. (2007). *Just culture, balancing safety and accountability*. Aldershot: Ashgate.
Department of Health (2001). *Building a safer NHS for patients: Implementing an organisation with a memory*. London.
Department of Health and HMSO (1988). *Report of the inquiry into child abuse in Cleveland, 1987*. London.
Elsley, S. (2010). *Media coverage of child deaths in the UK: The impact of baby P: A case for influence*. Edinburgh: University of Edinburgh/NSPCC Child Protection Research Centre.
Featherstone, B., Morris, K., & White, S. (2013). A marriage made in hell: Early intervention meets child protection. *British Journal of Social Work, 44*, 1735–1749.

Ferguson, H. (2017). How children become invisible in child protection work: Findings from research into day-to-day social work practice. *The British Journal of Social Work, 47*(4), 1007–1023.

Fischhoff, B. (1975). Hindsight-foresight: The effect of outcome knowledge on judgment under uncertainty. *Journal of Experimental Psychology: Human Perception and Performance, 1*(3), 288–299.

Furniss, T. (2013). *The multiprofessional handbook of child sexual abuse: Integrated management, therapy, and legal intervention*. London: Routledge.

Gilbert, N., Parton, N., & Skiveness, M. (2011). *Child protection systems: International trends and orientations*. Oxford: Oxford University Press.

Kahneman, D. (2011). *Thinking fast and slow*. London: Allen Lane, the Penguin Press.

Lansdown, G. (2000). Implementing children's rights and health. *Archives of Disease in Childhood, 83*(4), 286–288.

Morgan, R. (2007). *Children and safeguarding*. London: Rights4me.

Munro, E. (2011). *Munro review of child protection, final report: A child-centred system*. London: Department for Education.

Munro, E., Turnell, A. & Murphy, T. (2016). *You can't grow roses in concrete* (Action research final report). Perth: Resolutions Consultancy.

O'Donoghue, K., & Tsui, M.-s. (2013). Social work supervision research (1970–2010): The way we were and the way ahead. *The British Journal of Social Work, 45*(2), 616–633.

Parton, N. (2009). Challenges to practice and knowledge in child welfare social work: From the 'social' to the 'informational'. *Children and Youth Services Review, 31*, 715–721.

Pösö, T. (2018). Experts by experience infusing professional practices in child protection. In A. Falch-Eriksen & E. Backe-Hansen (Eds.), *Human rights in child protection. Implications for professional practice and policy*. London: Palgrave Macmillan.

Research in Practice. (2015). *Voice of the child: Evidence review*. London: Research in Practice.

Rushton, A., & Nathan, J. (1996). The supervision of child protection work. *British Journal of Social Work, 26*, 357–374.

Sandberg, K. (2018). Children's right to protection under the CRC. In A. Falch-Eriksen & E. Backe-Hansen (Eds.), *Human rights in child protection. Implications for professional practice and policy*. London: Palgrave Macmillan.

Skivenes, M., & Sørsdal, L. M. (2018). The child's best interest principle across child protection jurisdictions. In A. Falch-Eriksen & E. Backe-Hansen (Eds.), *Human rights in child protection. Implications for professional practice and policy*. London: Palgrave Macmillan.

Thoburn, J. (2017). *Children in state care*. London: Routledge.

Thomas, N. (2015). The voice of the child in statutory work. In M. Ivory (Ed.), *Voice of the child*. London: Research in Practice.

Turnell, A. (2012). *The signs of safety* (Comprehensive briefing paper). Resolutions Consultancy.

Turnell, A., & Essex, S. (2013). It takes a village. In Broad, B., Young, S., Operario, D., Turnell, A., Gleeson, J., Cluver, L., Flegg, E., Wyke, J., Crehan, G., Kuo, C. and Gough, A., 2013. *Inside kinship care: Understanding family dynamics and providing effective support*. Jessica Kingsley Publishers.

Unicef. (2011). *General comment no. 13*. New York: United Nations.

White, S., Wastell, D., Broadhurst, K., & Hall, C. (2010). When policy o'erleaps itself: The 'tragic tale' of the integrated children's system. *Critical Social Policy, 30*(3), 405–429.

Wood, M., & Selwyn, J. (2017). Looked after children and young people's views on what matters to their subjective well-being. *Adoption and Fostering, 41*(1), 20–34.

Open Access This chapter is licensed under the terms of the Creative Commons Attribution 4.0 International License (http://creativecommons.org/licenses/by/4.0/), which permits use, sharing, adaptation, distribution and reproduction in any medium or format, as long as you give appropriate credit to the original author(s) and the source, provide a link to the Creative Commons license and indicate if changes were made.

The images or other third party material in this chapter are included in the chapter's Creative Commons license, unless indicated otherwise in a credit line to the material. If material is not included in the chapter's Creative Commons license and your intended use is not permitted by statutory regulation or exceeds the permitted use, you will need to obtain permission directly from the copyright holder.

6

Experts by Experience Infusing Professional Practices in Child Protection

Tarja Pösö

1 Introduction

In child protection, children's rights are embedded in the international conventions of human rights and, to a varying degree, in national legislation. In addition, they are also embedded in the ethical codes for social workers which guide their practice in child protection. Accordingly, social workers should respect human rights and human dignity, which is further specified to include the promotion of the right to participation. This is expressed by the International Federation of Social Workers as follows:

> Social workers should promote the full involvement and participation of people using their services in ways that enable them to be empowered in all aspects of decisions and actions affecting their lives. (International Federation of Social Workers 2017)

T. Pösö (✉)
Faculty of Social Sciences, University of Tampere, Tampere, Finland
e-mail: tarja.poso@uta.fi

More specifically, according to Article 12 of the Convention on the Rights of the Child (CRC), children are entitled to the right to express their views in all matters affecting them, and their views should be considered. In society, children should be heard not only as individuals regarding the decisions of their personal life but also as groups of children representing the interests and needs of children in general in public decision-making (Tisdall and Davis 2004; Tisdall 2008; Marshall et al. 2015). Despite the strong legal and ethical incentives, children's participation is not easily translated from principle into effective practice (Tisdall and Davis 2004).

A common obstacle mentioned in literature is the view that children have a limited capability to participate in their own child protection cases due to their low age or diminished competencies (Bijleveld et al. 2015). Nevertheless, groups of children and young people exist who have successfully made a platform for their views to be heard, and fought against the presumptions about their lack of skills and competences. These groups are referred to as 'experts by experience in child protection'.

In Finland and elsewhere, these experts by experience have gained a strong foothold in child protection as in other areas of social welfare and health care services as they present their views in the political arenas and operate for self-help purposes (Noorani 2013; Meriluoto 2016; Toikko 2016). This is reflected, among other things, in the review of the state of child protection by the Ministry of Social Affairs and Health in Finland. The first of the 54 recommendations states that the Child Welfare Act should be revised to include a paragraph about the experts by experience so that the municipalities, which are responsible for providing child protection services, should involve them to instruct their service-provision (Toimiva lastensuojelu 2013, p. 69). By such measures the experts by experience have indeed been put on the front line of developing child protection services and providing relevant knowledge. Consequently, the argument in this chapter is that the very position given to, and taken by, experts by experience is not only about involvement and the right for participation but about knowledge as well. The inclusion of the experts by experience is also about the very way we can *know* about child protection and children's rights. This chapter examines what kind of view on the right to participation the experts by experience promote and how their experiential knowledge influences child protection practice and related knowledge production.

The chapter will focus on one group of experts by experience, 'Selviytyjät', henceforth referred to by their English name of 'the Survivors'. There are two reasons for this: first, their long period of activism has grounded the Survivors' activities explicitly in children's right to participate; second, they have made their statements public in different forms—videos, publications and information sheets—which provide rich data for this essay. I will look at four of their documents and the ideas they present about children's right to participation in child protection. I will also track their influences on different arenas of child protection: national legislation and guidelines, policy documents as well as social work practice. The latter task is supported by my long involvement in Finnish child protection as a teacher and researcher as well as by being an observer and an occasional participant of the Survivors' activities. As will be demonstrated later, their input is, indeed, far from the tokenism which sometimes describes the superficial involvement of children in policy and practice (Tisdall and Davis 2004; Hart 1992). Their rationale will be presented after a short discussion of the definition of experts by experience.

2 Experts by Experience: Focus on Expert and Experiential Knowledge

The term 'experts by experience in child protection' (lastensuojelun kokemusasiantuntija) is widely used in child protection policy and practice although it does not have a fixed meaning in the Finnish context nor in international research literature (McLaughlin 2009). It generally refers to service-users of child protection services that share their experiences more or less publicly in order to inform and influence other service-users, service-providers, decision-makers, policymakers and other interested parties. They may be children who presently receive services or young adults who have left the child protection system. Experts by experience may function individually or in groups. There are no explicit criteria as to how much—or what kind of—insider experience one should have, but often the child protection experts by experience are children who have been taken into care and thereby have substantial experience.

As a term, 'experts by experience' differs from 'service users'. This difference is important to acknowledge because the terms define and construct identities, relationships, roles and positions in the welfare system (Hübner 2014). The focus on *knowledge and expertise* differentiates the term 'expert by experience' from that of a 'service-user' in which the *use* of services and the binary positions of service-user and service-provider are emphasized. The term 'experts by experience' 'makes a claim for specialist knowledge base rooted in an individual's experience of using services' as stated by McLaughlin (2009); thus, in order to become an expert by experience, one needs to have service-user experiences (Toikko 2016). The term defines the nature of expertise to be based on experience and thereby differentiates it from expertise gained otherwise (through formal education for example). It does not state that this expertise is less or more valuable than 'formal' expertise; it is just a quality of expertise cherishing a postmodern view on expert knowledge in which the authority of professionals as experts is challenged (Scourfield 2010). Rather it suggests 'a relationship of equals whereby one expert's position has been gained through their training and practice and the other through their experience' (McLaughlin 2009) and that 'experiential authority' exists in addition to 'traditional authority' (Noorani 2013).

As in any form of user-involvement in social and health care, the expertise of experts by experience is by its nature experiential knowledge (e.g. Beresford and Croft 2001). Experiential knowledge is a distinctive form of particularizing knowledge. It emphasizes everyday life and is sometimes addressed as a 'science of everyday life' (Gubrium 2016). Although experiential knowledge has been recognized before in the literature of social work knowledge, what is new is that experiential knowledge has become strongly incorporated into policymaking and its implementation, especially as a result of the user-involvement movement (Gubrium 2016; Beresford and Croft 2001). It has moral bearings of its own: it emphasizes the experiences of an individual, and challenges—and even contests—knowledge from formal education, qualifications and research. Indeed, the very positions of experts, formal knowledge and professional problem constructions are challenged by experiential knowledge (Beresford 2013; Järvinen 2016; Alm Andreassen 2016; Meriluoto 2016).

Child protection practice, on the other hand, aims to strengthen its evidence base, to be informed by research and related 'formal' knowledge (Shlonsky and Benbenishty 2014). In addition, formal qualifications are expected from people who carry out tasks in statutory child protection. Finnish social workers should be licensed to have the right to work in child protection. In order to gain the licence, they must have completed five years of university studies, including social work studies, culminating in a master's degree. The base for formal knowledge is further guided by legislation which, among many other issues, defines the rights entitled to children and the obligations for social workers and municipalities. Consequently, the experiential knowledge of experts by experience is practised in conjunction with the requirements for formal knowledge in statutory child protection.

3 The Expert Views from Inside: Survivors' Messages

The distinctive period of experts by experience in child protection goes back as far as the mid-2000s in Finland. A particular landmark occurred in 2008 when one NGO, Pesäpuu ry, organized a group of young people experiencing care to inform practitioners about the key issues in child protection as experienced from inside. This group of 10 young women was called 'Selviytyjät'. Later it expanded considerably and similar groups were established in different parts of Finland. At the end of 2016, these groups of children and young people, estimated to be about 20 in number, formed a national network to inform and support each other and to work collectively in their activities to influence and develop child protection policy and practice (Barkman et al. 2017). Some groups involve young children—between the ages of 3 and 8—but the majority of the groups involve teenagers or young adults.

Over the years, the experts by experience have created a distinctive social forum for the recognition of personal experiences of children in care. The messages of the Survivors are listened to in many arenas—national and local child protection conferences, government programmes and steering groups, legislative initiatives and the media. In 2017, the count of public talks was 611,000 and the number of published statements was 50,000 since the establishment of the Survivors (Barkman et al. 2017, p. 12). The volume of their public statements is considerable in a country of 5.4 million inhabitants. In addition to these public activities, the Survivors have small peer-group meetings, sharing intimately personal experiences as well as larger meetings with the aim of formulating the shared messages based on their insider experiences, and projects with specific tasks (such as preparing interview tools for practitioners for interacting with teenagers). In order to learn about the contents of the messages of the Survivors, I will look more closely at four of their key documents.

3.1 Listen to Children in Care

The first of these is a web-based publication summarizing the key messages of children, the outcome of the first national gatherings of children in care under the umbrella of expertise by experience in 2010. Most attention is given here to *dreams*—that children in care have the right to dream about their future and things which are important to them. It is also stated that the professionals should listen to the child and meet her with time and dedication—a message similar to research literature on children's views on professionals (e.g. Hill 1999). It also summarizes the aim for their activities in the following way (a translation of the original text):

> *The more adults listen to the experiences of young people and see their eagerness to make a change, the more responsible adults are in promoting the issues relevant to young people. That is why politicians and decision-makers should also listen to children in care.* (Minä selviydyn 2010)

The publication states that the more adults—social workers, politicians and decision-makers—hear children's insider views and see their interest in making an impact, the more responsibly adults would act. It is stated elsewhere in the publication that the involvement of the experts by experience follows the principles of the United Nations Convention on the Rights of the Child (CRC). In this way, the experts by experience position themselves as a group influencing policy, service-development, practice and legislation. This formulation is a strong statement about the public nature of the insider views and experiences (e.g. McNeish 1999).

3.2 Know Your Rights and Responsibilities

The second public statement to present here is a booklet, 'We believe in you—so should you', which was published in 2010, first in Finnish and later in Swedish and English. It was written 'to children in care from children in care' as stated in the document. It included information about children's rights and child protection. Its task is described as follows:

The title of this book was inspired by our experiences: when we were placed in substitute care, we did not believe in ourselves. We badly needed someone to believe in us. We hope this book will help you to understand your life situation better and to make it through the days to come!
This book is your personal guide to the world of child welfare. There is lots to read here. Read one page at a time and reflect on it. Take some time to digest what you have read. Make notes, tick the boxes and answer the questions. If you feel like it, ask a grown-up to help you. Ask him or her for advice and for more information on things you don't understand.
Know your rights and responsibilities and act according to them.[1]

There is a strong empowerment element in this description: it opens a rights-based approach to being in care. Shared experiences are described as being a shared strength—that is 'why we trust in you'.

3.3 'We-Talk' as an Ethical Choice

The third document, the code of ethics for participation, was published in 2014 (Hipp and Palsanen 2014). The focus is widely on children's and young people's participation in developing services for children and young people. The code includes ten principles of ethical awareness. It also points out that children and young people might need to be protected from the media and other public arenas. Therefore, the Survivors' introduced 'we-talk', which is primarily about 'us' instead of 'me'. The selection of the 'we'-messages is typically done in groups: the individual and unique experiences are selected, thematically grouped, reworded and presented as collective experiences to outsiders (Barkman et al. 2017, pp. 27, 44).

3.4 Changing the View from Problems to Strengths

The fourth document was published in 2017: the book 'Muutosvoimaa' (Barkman et al. 2017) summarizes the experiences gained during the years of expertise by experience in child protection and instructs professionals and policymakers how to include experts by experience in their practice. It is also written for children and young people who are thinking of becoming experts by experience (ibid.). Although the book with its 63 pages covers many topics, the underlying message is that children's involvement can make a change in child protection and such involvement has already started making a change. It states that when children have been involved and when they have been listened to, the view on children has shifted from being problem-focused to strengths-based in policy and practice.

The published materials and the documents presented above total only a small fraction of the activities of the Survivors as the majority of activities take place in face-to-face interaction among themselves as well as with practitioners and policymakers. Nevertheless, in sum, when reading the documents, the overarching message is that children and young people want to—and need to—be heard, trusted and involved based on their experiences of child protection, and that they should be seen as individual human beings instead of abstract clients or service-users. Their translation of Article 12 of the CRC into practice is thus *see me/us, hear me/us, learn to know me/us and trust me/us*.

4 Experiential Knowledge on Rights: Influences and Contradictions

The experiential knowledge of experts by experience is grounded in individual experiences and people's—children or young people who have experienced care—willingness to talk about their lives. This is embedded in present society, which Plummer (2001, p. 79) describes as being an 'auto/biographical society'. According to him, life stories are everywhere and they 'come in many forms, shifting across time and space' (Plummer 2001, p. 79). He also states that sometimes stories are silenced and other times they speak volumes: thus storytelling as well as listening to the stories are selective. Individualization in its typical form for late modernity emphasizes the self-realization of its members, including children, and a decline in the authority of expert knowledge (Prout 2000). When 'telling a life' includes face-to-face interaction, either directly or via the media, the likelihood increases that the stories will be listened to; this is also the case for the stories based on experiences of child protection (Marshall et al. 2015, p. 377). Hearing the views directly from children brings an individual and human element to the topics policymakers and practitioners are dealing with (ibid.).

4.1 Experiential Knowledge Influencing Policy and Legislation

The very characteristic of the experiential knowledge of being human and presented directly, and thus highly valued and prioritized in auto/biographical society, was vividly demonstrated in the seminar organized by the Finnish Ministry of Social Welfare and Health in 2016. The seminar issued the state's apology for the historic abuse which had taken place in substitute care during the years of the first Child Welfare Act (1936–1983). The apology followed a research report exploring the maltreatment experiences of people placed in residential and foster care during that period of time (Hytönen et al. 2016). The report itself and the ensuing interest in the quality of substitute care was unique in the Finnish history of child protection. After the study had been presented, including 300 interviewees, two sessions with experts by experience were a part of the programme. This event thus comprised two different views on the experiences of child protection: the experiences gathered by a research team and its scientific rationale including the reflection of selection biases, validity and generalizability, and the face-to-face experiences by the experts by experience. In addition to the knowledge of historic abuse, the message of the programme was that, first, the direct experiences of experts are important in the public arena of child protection, and second, the knowledge gained through research is not sufficient on its own to inform about historic abuse and suggest the ways ahead. The third and more hidden message was that the knowledge of the previous or present practitioners is not needed to inform—and to make sense of—the extent and nature of historic abuse.

This event could be seen as a gesture to bring children's and young people's views into policymaking with regard to a delicate topic (Tisdall and Davis 2004). The experts by experience contributed to the seminar despite the difficulties of voicing experiences that are shadowed by taboos, losses or private emotions as well as structural violence (e.g. Farmer et al. 2013). The tragedy is, however, that what seems to follow from the recognition of historic abuse is rather contradictory in policy and practice as the plans to monitor the quality of substitute care tend to decrease the obligations for the public agencies in this regard. As a result, in November 2017, a group of experts by experience in child protection, including the Survivors, contacted the Ministry of Social Welfare and Health to ask for more statutory and systematic monitoring of substitute care services. In their public statement (Kannanotto … 2017) their view was that the plans to increase in-house monitoring and decrease the monitoring duties of child protection authorities would be against the rights of children in care, and in fact, against the findings and recommendations of the report of historic abuse, and would further threaten children's safety in care. They do suggest that they could be involved in monitoring the quality of substitute care as peer-reviewers but that this should not diminish the duties of the public authorities.

This contradictory outcome of the official apology makes one wonder how the messages by the experts by experience have been received in child protection practice and policy as, on the one hand, the experts are given the floor in most important events, and on the other, the service-users' claims for protection in care are somewhat neglected.

There is no straightforward measure to capture these influences. Finland changed its child protection legislation in 2007 so that children's rights, especially participatory rights, were included in legislation, and consequently, on the legislative level, the Finnish child protection system has been and can be described as being orientated towards child-centrism in cross-country comparisons (Gilbert et al. 2011). In this context, the Survivors and other experts by experience have actively influenced policy programmes and even legislative changes: their experiential knowledge has indeed informed recent policy and legislation. The request for being met as a person ('see me, listen to me, trust me') by a social worker, for example, was reflected in the Child Welfare Act which introduced a new paragraph in 2013 stating that the social worker should meet the child in person often enough and that the meetings should be recorded in the case files to demonstrate that they have taken place (§ 29). This change in legislation is supported in the planning stages by the references to the statements given by the experts by experience saying that they have too few opportunities to meet their social workers (e.g. HE 130/2013).

In addition, when the national quality recommendations for child protection were introduced by the Ministry of Social Affairs and Health in 2014, they emphasized the importance of involving children individually in any part of the process of child protection as well as involving children to develop the services at the local level (Lastensuojelun laatusuositus 2014). The latter recommendation is the same as suggested by the committee established by the Ministry of Social Affairs and Health to review the state of child protection (Toimiva lastensuojelu 2013). However, the gap between legislation and the front-line practice of child protection regarding children's rights to have their views heard has been noted by research: practice does not in every respect include children in the same way as the legislation requires (e.g. de Godzinsky 2014; Toivonen 2017; Pösö and Enroos 2017). In this contradictory context, the Survivors and other experts by experience have merged together the general principles of the CRC, and Article 12 in particular, as well as their own wishes and needs, with more diffuse influences on the practice than on the policy level.

4.2 The Inclusion of Children's Views in Front-Line Practice

The front-line practice of child protection is currently influenced not only by the CRC but also by the cost-awareness of public expenditure and the privatization of child protection services. This creates an obvious tension, widely experienced by social workers, between the wishes and needs of the experts by experience, the CRC, the norms towards human child protection and the ethical principles of the profession to respect human rights and dignity (Alhanen 2014). Social workers have expressed their concerns about their working conditions: heavy caseloads, lack of qualified staff and resources as well as lack of support in the organizations, all of which hinder them from working in the manner which would meet the ethical and professional standards of good social work (van der Mänttäri-van der Kuip 2016). In the six largest Finnish towns, social workers are estimated individually to work with 59 children on average (Ahlgren-Leinvuo 2016, 33); according to anecdotal knowledge the number may occasionally exceed more than 100 children. This is to say that the working conditions in child protection are not suited to support social work in the manner suggested by the experts by experience. Finnish social workers experience moral conflicts and distress as they cannot do their work in a morally sustainable way (Mänttäri-van der Kuip 2016). Social workers' knowledge of the fulfilment of children's rights—or a lack thereof—is, however, not highly valued in the public arenas of child protection (Alhanen 2014; Mänttäri-van der Kuip 2016).

Indeed, if the ideas of experts by experience are taken seriously, they would challenge the fundamental rationale and organizational design of child protection services. Cecilie Basberg Neuman (2016) writes about the request for love, expressed by the experts by experience in child protection in the Norwegian context, and how it challenges the foundations of professionalism and welfare state services. She argues, very wisely, that

> ... an unproblematised requirement that child protection workers must provide children with parent-like love may intersect with a current neoliberal international tendency towards de-professionalisation, that may

have problematic consequences for both providers and recipients of care in the child protection services. (Basberg Neuman 2016)

Instead of asking social workers to love, in her view, it would be important to secure training, supervision and the emotional well-being of social workers so that they could provide children with good professional care (Basberg Neuman 2016). The claims and wishes of experts by experience should be transformed into practices which recognize the conditions of professional work provided by the state to improve the good quality of social work instead of de-professionalising it. This implies that there might be a need to critically reflect the implications drawn from the experiential knowledge of children's rights.

The experiential knowledge of children about the fulfilment of their rights is, by its very nature, individualistic, human and 'particularizing knowledge' (Gubrium 2016) and thereby selective. It does not concern itself with the social conditions and structures in which the experiences are embedded and rights practised. The risk in following *only* the knowledge given by the experts by experience is that the social conditions supporting or hindering the fulfilment of the rights are ignored. Human rights in child protection are, after all, materialized in social practices (Ife 2001; Clark 2002).

5   Summing Up

We have seen above that the recognition of children's rights, views and wishes owes a lot to the experts by experience in child protection. They have shaped the overall way of addressing child protection issues so that Article 12 of the CRC and the experiences of children are paid more attention to. This is especially obvious in the public arenas of policymaking whereas the impact on the front-line child protection practices is more diffuse. The social workers do widely share the mission of the experts by experience based on their ethical principles and legislation that guide their work. We have, as well, seen above that the implementation of rights-based practice is not straightforward as practice is influenced by many other factors as well—such as the very organization of the services and its resources.

What the Finnish case demonstrates is that more than the inclusion of experts by experience is required to make a change for better implementation of the CRC in child protection. We also need to focus on the overall social and moral conditions in which child protection takes place and the very notion of knowledge. The analysis above suggests that even more than before, there is a need *also* for formal and research-based knowledge in child protection as the experts by experience have highlighted the extreme complexity in putting children's rights into practice. The challenge is how to recognize, balance and value the different types of expertise and experts in child protection, and to put them into practice wisely with regard to the CRC.

Notes

1. http://www.pesapuu.fi/media/uploads/dokumentit/nuoret/we_believe_in_you_so_should_you.pdf

References

Ahlgren-Leinvuo, H. (2016). Kuuden suurimman kaupungin lastensuojelun palvelujen ja kustannusten vertailu vuonna 2015 [The comparison of child welfare services and costs in 2015 among the six largests towns]. Kuusikkotyöryhmä. Retrieved from http://www.kuusikkokunnat.fi/SIRA_Files/downloads/Lastensuojelu2015_06102016.pdf

Alhanen, K. (2014). Vaarantunut suojeluvalta—Tutkimus lastensuojelujärjestelmän uhkatekijöistä [Compromised power of protection—A study of threats to the child welfare service system] (Report 24). Helsinki: Terveyden ja hyvinvoinnin laitos.

Alm Andreassen, T. (2016). Professional intervention from a service user perspective. In J. Gubrium, T. Andreassen, & P. K. Solvan (Eds.), *Reimagining the human service relationships* (pp. 34–58). New York: Columbia University Press.

Barkman, J., Inkinen, H., Isoniemi, S., & Vario, P. (2017). Muutosvoimaa! Kohti nuorten kokemusasiantuntijuutta lastensuojelussa [Change power! Towards the expertise of young people in child welfare] (Opas- ja käsikirja 3). Jyväskylä: Pesäpuu ry.

Basberg Neuman, C. (2016). Children's quest for love and professional child protection work: The case of Norway. *Scottish Journal of Residential Child Care, 15*(3), 103–123.

Beresford, P. (2013). From 'other' to involved: User involvement in research: An emerging paradigm. *Nordic Social Work Research, 3*(2), 139–148.

Beresford, P., & Croft, S. (2001). Service users' knowledges and the social construction of social work. *Journal of Social Work, 2*(1), 295–316.

Bijleveld, G., Dedding, C., & Bunders-Aelen, J. (2015). Children's and young people's participation within child welfare and child protection services: A state-of-the-art review. *Child & Family Social Work, 20*, 129–138.

Clark, C. (2002). Identity, individual rights and social justice. In R. Adams, L. Dominelli, & M. Payne (Eds.), *Critical practice in social work* (pp. 38–45). Basingstoke: Palgrave Macmillan.

De Godzinsky, V. (2014). Lapsen etu ja osallisuus hallinto-oikeuksien päätöksissä [The child's best interest and participation in administrative court decisions] (Report 267). Helsinki: Oikeuspoliittinen tutkimuslaitos.

Farmer, E., Selwyn, J., & Meakings, S. (2013). 'Other children say you're not normal because you don't live with your parents'. Children's views of living with informal kinship carers: Social networks, stigma and attachment to carers. *Child & Family Social Work, 18*(1), 25–34.

Gilbert, N., Parton, N., & Skivenes, M. (Eds.). (2011). *Child protection systems. International trends and orientations*. New York: Oxford University Press.

Gubrium, J. (2016). From the iron cage to everyday life. In J. Gubrium, T. Andreassen, & P. Solvan (Eds.), *Reimagining the human service relationships* (pp. 3–32). New York: Columbia University Press.

Hart, R. (1992). Children's participation: From tokenism to citizenship. Florence: UNICEF. Retrieved from http://www.unicef-irc.org/publications/100

HE 130/2013. Hallituksen esitys eduskunnalle laiksi lastensuojelulain 28 §:n muuttamisesta [Government Proposal concerning the the change of the paragraph 28 in Child Welfare Act]. Retrieved 7 December 2017, from http://www.finlex.fi/fi/esitykset/he/2013/20130130

Hill, M. (1999). What's the problem? Who can help? The perspectives of children and young people on their well-being and on helping professionals. *Journal of Social Work Practice, 13*(2), 135–145.

Hipp, T., & Palsanen, K. (2014). Lasten osallistumisen etiikka—Lapset ja nuoret palveluiden kehittäjinä [The ethics of children's participation—Children and young people as developers of services]. Helsinki: Lastensuojelun keskusliitto. Retrieved on 15 March 2017, from https://www.lskl.fi/materiaali/lastensuojelun-keskusliitto/Lasten_osallistumisen_etiikka1.pdf

Hübner, L. (2014). Constructing relations in social work: Client, customer and service user? The application and relevance of the term user in social work discourse. *Nordic Social Work Research, 4*(2), 87–98.

Hytönen, K., Malinen, A., Salenius, P., Haikari, J., Markkola, P., Kuronen M., & Koivisto, J. (2016). Lastensuojelun sijaishuollon epäkohdat ja lasten kaltoinkohtelu 1937–1983 [The failures and abuse of children in substitute care 1937–1983] (Report 22). Helsinki: Sosiaali- ja terveysministeriö.

Ife, J. (2001). *Human rights and social work. Towards rights-based practice.* New York: Cambridge University Press.

International Federation of Social Workers (2017). Statement of ethical principles. Retrieved from: http://ifsw.org/policies/statement-of-ethical-principles/ on 10 December 2017.

Järvinen, M. (2016). Expertise and ambivalence in user-focused human service work. In J. Gubrium, T. Andreassen, & P. Solvan (Eds.), *Reimagining the human service relationships* (pp. 59–78). New York: Columbia University Press.

Kannanotto sijaishuollon valvonnan säilyttämiseksi (2017). A claim to keep the monitoring of substitute care. Retrieved 14 December 2017, from http://pesapuu.fi/media/uploads/dokumentit/kannanotto_sijaishuollon_valvonnan_s%C3%A4ilymiseksi.pdf

Lastensuojelun laatusuositus [Quality recommendations for child welfare]. 2014. Report 4. Helsinki: Sosiaali- ja terveysministeriö.

Mänttäri-van der Kuip, M. (2016). Moral distress among social workers: The role of insufficient resources. *International Journal of Social Welfare, 25*(1), 86–97.

Marshall, C., Byrne, B., & Lundy, L. (2015). Children and young people's right to participate in public decision-making. In T. Gal & B. Duramy (Eds.), *International perspectives and empirical findings on child participation* (pp. 357–380). New York: Oxford University Press.

McLaughlin, H. (2009). What's in a name: 'Client', 'patient', 'customer', 'consumer', 'expert by experience', 'service-user'—What's next? *British Journal of Social Work, 38*(6), 1101–1117.

McNeish, D. (1999). Promoting participation for children and young people: Some key questions for health and social welfare organisations. *Journal of Social Work Practice, 12*(2), 191–203.

Meriluoto, T. (2016). Kokemusasiantuntijuus ohjaavana ja voimaannuttavana hallintana [Expertise by experience as a form of ruling and empowering governance). In M. Nousiainen & K. Kulovaara (eds), Hallinnan ja osallistamisen politiikat [The policies of governance and involvement] (pp. 65–96). Jyväskylä: Sophi.

Minä selviydyn. Nuoret Nuorille sijaishuollon foorumi Jyväskylä 17.11.2010. [I survive. From young people to young people]. Retrieved 14 June 2017, from http://pesapuu.fi/media/uploads/dokumentit/nuoret/nf2010.pdf

Noorani, T. (2013). Service user involvement, authority and the 'expert-by-experience' in mental health. *Journal of Political Power, 6*(1), 49–68.

Plummer, K. (2001). *Documents of life 2. An invitation to a critical humanism.* London: Sage.

Pösö, T., & Enroos, R. (2017). The representation of children's views in the Finnish court decisions of care orders. *International Journal of Children's Rights, 25*(3–4), 736–753.

Prout, A. (2000). Children's participation: Control and self-realisation in British late modernity. *Children & Society, 14*(4), 304–315.

Scourfield, P. (2010). A critical reflection on the involvement of 'experts by experience' in inspections. *British Journal of Social Work, 40*(1), 1890–1907.

Shlonsky, A., & Benbenishty, R. (2014). *From evidence to outcomes in child welfare.* New York: Oxford University Press.

Tisdall, K. (2008). Is the honeymoon over? Children and young people's participation in public decision-making. *International Journal of Children's Rights, 16*(3), 419–429.

Tisdall, K., & Davis, J. (2004). Making a difference? Bringing children's and young people's views into policy-making. *Children & Society, 18*(2), 131–142.

Toikko, T. (2016). Becoming an expert by experience: An analysis of service users' learning process. *Social Work in Mental Health, 14*(3), 292–312.

Toimiva lastensuojelu. (2013). Selvitysryhmän loppuraportti [Functioning child welfare. The final report] 2013 (Raportteja ja muistioita 2013:19). Helsinki: Sosiaali- ja terveysministeriö.

Toivonen, V.-M. (2017). Lapsen oikeudet ja oikeusturva. Lastensuojeluasiat hallintotuomioistuimissa [Children's rights and legal safety—Child welfare cases in administrative courts]. Helsinki: Alma Talent.

We believe in you—So should you. Retrieved 16 January 2017, from http://www.pesapuu.fi/media/uploads/dokumentit/nuoret/we_believe_in_you_so_should_you.pdf

Open Access This chapter is licensed under the terms of the Creative Commons Attribution 4.0 International License (http://creativecommons.org/licenses/by/4.0/), which permits use, sharing, adaptation, distribution and reproduction in any medium or format, as long as you give appropriate credit to the original author(s) and the source, provide a link to the Creative Commons license and indicate if changes were made.

The images or other third party material in this chapter are included in the chapter's Creative Commons license, unless indicated otherwise in a credit line to the material. If material is not included in the chapter's Creative Commons license and your intended use is not permitted by statutory regulation or exceeds the permitted use, you will need to obtain permission directly from the copyright holder.

7

The Rights of Children Placed in Out-of-Home Care

Anne-Dorthe Hestbæk

1 Introduction

The aim of this chapter is to shed light on how children's rights in out-of-home care are met, exemplified through a study on 11- to 17-year-olds living in out-of-home care. For practical reasons the group is labelled 'young people' throughout the chapter.

Being placed in out-of-home care interferes with fundamental elements of a young person's life—relationship to parents, peers, siblings, as well as with schooling, leisure, health, and educational planning. On a more general level, placement of young people by the child protection services (CPS) interferes with the development of a young person's identity.

According to the Convention on the Rights of the Child (CRC), any child must be credited certain rights, whether in care or not. Furthermore, the child is entitled to protection and a secure base for development. But

---

A.-D. Hestbæk (✉)
VIVE—The Danish Centre for Social Science Research,
Copenhagen, Denmark
e-mail: adh@vive.dk

is it at all possible to implement the intentions of the CRC, given the structural conditions of public care? In this chapter, the implementation of CRC in everyday life in care will be exemplified in the context of unique data from a study of young people in out-of-home care (Lausten and Jørgensen 2017; Ottosen et al. 2015). According to this study, young people in care, on average, feel loved by the parents they are removed from. A great many of them also feel that they are placed with the right foster family or at the right institution[1]—the two main archetypes of placement milieus in many welfare states.

In general, young people placed in residential care often display more serious problems than those referred to foster care, which is why they are referred to professional care in institutions. However, Danish data finds serious challenges since the experiences of young people in residential homes and group care homes differ negatively from those in foster care. Significantly more often, they do not feel heard, do not feel safe where they are living, and do not feel loved by the adults around them to the same extent as do other young people in care. Last, but not least, only a third consider their residential home a very good place to grow up. To what extent are these findings in accordance with the intentions of providing children with rights through the CRC? In this chapter, Denmark serves as an example of a probably more general welfare state challenge in child protection, rather than a specific country with a specific problem to be studied.

Both from a rights perspective and a social investment perspective, it is questionable whether the relatively low level of well-being and satisfaction is acceptable. In most Western countries, 24-hour care in residential and group care homes is very costly, which of course renders expectations of high-quality interventions, with a high degree of user satisfaction, and with positive developmental perspectives. It is well documented in research that growing up in out-of-home care is itself a risk factor. Young adults who were in care earlier in life are significantly worse off than other young adults who had similar social problems in childhood but who did not enter care (Backe-Hansen et al. 2014; Egelund and Hestbæk 2003; Hestbæk and Henze-Pedersen 2017; Olsen et al. 2011).

Thus, research provides evidence that raising discussions on how we can improve residential 24-hour care for young people from a rights-based perspective is important.

2 Background: The Danish Out-of-Home Care Landscape

The share of children in out-of-home care in Denmark has during the last four decades been close to around 1 per cent of the 0- to 17-year-old child population, with a slightly downward trend in the past few years (0.917 per cent at the end of 2016). During the same decades, there has been a significant increase in the use of preventive measures, reflecting a slowly but steadily changing intervention prioritization. Research evidence on the importance of family-like settings on the one hand, and heavy budget cuts on the other hand has encouraged local governments to limit the number of children in residential care. Therefore, in line with international trends, foster care now plays a dominant role in the out-of-home care landscape, while several residential homes have been shut down due to decreasing demand. Ten years ago, 47 per cent of all children 0 to 17 years old in care were placed in, respectively, foster care and residential settings. Today, foster care represents more than 65 per cent of all children 0 to 17 years old in care, mirrored by a corresponding decrease in residential care.

During the same period of time, child protection social work in Denmark has faced large reforms (Hestbæk 2011). From an overall perspective, these reforms have quite a few aspirations in common with the CRC. First of all, there has been a predominant focus on *continuity for the child*, with a stronger child protection perspective. The parents' right to take home a child placed with consent has been restricted. The local government may decide that a child in foster care must stay in the foster family for up to three years—or for the entire adolescence, if the child has developed a close attachment to a foster family—without the consent of the parents, even if the criteria for using forcible measures are not fulfilled (Karmsteen et al. 2018).[2] Another focal point in the latest child protection reforms is the aim of a stronger involvement of the child and the parents. Young people are a party to their own case from age 15. Furthermore, they must be heard as early as possible, but at a minimum from the age of 12.

3 The CRC as a Standard

The CRC has not been fully incorporated as Danish law. However, children's rights and the child's perspective were strengthened significantly when the provision from the CRC on *the best interests of the child* was incorporated in the Consolidation Act on Social Services in 2001 (Hestbæk 2011). The concept of 'the best interests of the child' is pretty abstract, however, and the political discourses in Denmark mainly focused on *continuity* as mentioned above, on the *participation* of children and young people, and on the *involvement* of the child's close network (Hestbæk et al. 2006). The overall aim of safeguarding the well-being, health, and development of the child or young person was not that visible in Denmark. The incorporation of the Convention is done with a varying focus and to a varying degree across countries, and Denmark is no exception to that.

Articles 3 and 6 in the CRC establish the fundamental requirement for protection and development, framed in, for example, the principles governing the best interests of the child, the overall aim of protection and well-being, and that institutions responsible for the care of children must meet certain standards for development. In this chapter I will restrict the focus to five articles of relevance to young people in out-of-home care (Articles 12, 19, 20, 25, and 27) listed in Table 7.1.

The billion-dollar question is to what extent governments succeed in establishing conditions for children and young people in care that, from an overall perspective, seem to meet these CRC's requirements. To shed light on this, we will explore a study in the next section that has collected a huge amount of data in this field, discussing the five articles with this project as our context.

4 Growing Up in Out-of-Home Care: Methods and Data

The analysis will mainly rely on data of children and young people in publicly subsidized out-of-home care in Denmark, yielding a huge amount of survey data, giving a unique opportunity for insight into a

Table 7.1 CRC articles and out-of-home care

Articles from the UN CRC of relevance to problems in out-of-home care targeted in this chapter

Article	Main content
12	States Parties shall assure the child's right to express his or her own views freely. The child's views must be given due weight in accordance with the age and maturity of the child. The child shall be heard in any, for example, judicial and administrative proceedings affecting the child.
19	States Parties shall take all appropriate measures to protect the child from all forms of violence, injury or abuse, neglect or negligent treatment, maltreatment, or exploitation, including sexual abuse, no matter who takes care of the child.
20	A child deprived of his or her family environment, or in whose own best interests cannot be allowed to remain in that environment, shall be entitled to special protection and assistance provided by the State. States Parties shall ensure alternative care.
25	The child placed for the purposes of care has the right to protection, treatment, and to periodic review of the treatment and all other circumstances relevant to the placement.
27	The child has the right to a standard of living ensuring adequate for the child's physical, mental, spiritual, moral, and social development.

field with scarce evidence. It is a plausible hypothesis that the study mirrors dilemmas and challenges of relevance to many countries.

The TABU study[3] was conducted among young people placed in out-of-home care. The respondents' age span (11, 13, 15 and 17 years) implies that they should obviously have been included considerably in the decision on where to live while in care, in the organization of their everyday life and in other important aspects. In 2014 and 2016, more than half of young people 11 to 17 years old in out-of-home care (a sample of c.2500 out of a population on 4600 young people) were invited to take part in the nationwide survey. Children 11 and 13 years old were interviewed personally in their care facility by a trained interviewer. Young people 15 and 17 years old were invited to participate in a web-based survey. In case they did not respond, they were contacted again and offered a face-to-face interview, which was accepted by a third of the eldest informants (Lausten and Jørgensen 2017; Ottosen et al. 2015).

The questionnaire was pretty long (interviews lasted about 45 minutes) and was centred around everyday life in the care facility, well-being, health and leisure, contact with family, network and peers, schooling, risk behaviour and delinquency, and the involvement of the young people themselves.

5 Rights of Young People in Out-of-Home Care

In the following sections, the CRC articles in Table 7.1 will be used as the basis for a discussion of data about the living conditions of young people in out-of-home care, in order to shed light on the extent to which the CRC's aspirations seem to be realized.

5.1 Participation: Giving the Child's Views 'Due Weight'

CRC Article 12 describes the child's right to express his or her views freely, and that the views of the child *must* be given so-called 'due weight' in accordance with his or her age and maturity. Furthermore, in judicial or administrative proceedings affecting the child, the child must be provided the opportunity to be heard.

As mentioned, the participation of children and parents has been a specific aim in several Danish child protection reforms. The Consolidation Act on Social Services of 2017 (CASS) states that the child or young person must always be involved adequately in accordance with age and maturity (§ 46.3). Before any decision of importance to the child, the caseworker must talk closely with the child or young person and explain what is going to happen, facilitating a dialogue about his or her opinion on the issue as a matter of professional practice (CASS § 48).

Does this legal demand for a dialogue with the child ensure that the child's view is given due weight as prescribed by the CRC? When we ask young people in out-of-home care to what extent they have been involved, the results are not overwhelmingly positive. Regarding the decision on where to live when placed in out-of-home care, only around *a third* (35 per cent) felt that they were consulted. The majority (55 per cent) did not feel involved or consulted. However, the older they were, the more involvement they experienced, which is a common finding in this kind of study. Even among young people placed during the last year, whom you might expect to remember the level of involvement rather precisely, less than 60 per cent felt involved in the decision (Lausten and Jørgensen 2017).

A report based on qualitative interviews with impartial assessors involved in cases with children being placed in care found that the child's perspective was given far too little attention (Child Helpline 2017). However, it is interesting to note that, when social workers were asked the reverse question in another study, more than 90 per cent found that they *did actually involve* the child in the hearing process following the decision on out-of-home care. And 80 per cent found that they talked with children across all age groups specifically about the placement. Only for a very limited number of cases was this talk not obtainable due to, for example, the age of the child or severe disability (Christoffersen et al. 2005). It is plausible to hypothesize that *both* perspectives are true. In most cases, a representative from the local authorities *has actually talked* with the child. And in most cases, the child or young person does not experience this as involvement or participation—an unsolved paradox.

5.2 Protection from, for example, Violence, Abuse, Neglect

The state must take all appropriate legislative, administrative, social and educational measures to protect the child against all forms of physical and mental violent behaviour (cf. Article 19). Further, a child that cannot remain at home shall be entitled to special protection and alternative, suitable care (Article 20). While Article 19 is mainly directed towards violence, abuse and neglect at home, in the present context we examine protection whenever young persons are in custody of child protection authorities.

On average, 80 per cent of the 11 to 17 year olds in care feel safe where they are living. However, the differences depending on type of care are obvious. More than 50 per cent of the young people in residential care agree fully on feeling safe—for young people in foster care, it is almost 95 per cent (Ottosen et al. 2015). Conversely, around 10 per cent of young people in residential care do not at all feel safe where they live. This is only true for 1 per cent in foster care. The results about foster care are very positive—but we are left with a challenge concerning safety when in residential care, where the most vulnerable young people live.

The young people were also asked about whether they have experienced any kind of violation from peers or adults while in care. In general, the prevalence of violence is low. Almost 90 per cent have never experienced any kind of violence from peers where they live. While about 1 per cent in foster care have been exposed to violence or sexual assaults from peers one or more times while in care, this is true for 12 per cent of the youngsters in residential settings. If we look at violence from adults, we find a somewhat lower level. In total, 7 per cent have experienced some form of violence exerted by adults, where the young person lives. This accounts for more than 13 per cent of the youngsters in residential care and for 3 per cent of those in foster care. However, data does not allow us to distinguish between inappropriate violent behaviour from adults on one hand, and what the young person may experience as violence, but which—from a professional point of view—might also reflect a need to protect either the young person or his or her surroundings on the other hand.

All in all, it seems that we face a challenge of how to make residential care a safe place to live for young people placed in these types of caring milieus. It is quite a *paradox* that public, strictly professionalized institutions, with regular inspections, that work *in loco parentis* in order to provide the most vulnerable young people a safe and sound environment for upbringing, in some cases do not succeed in fostering basic security for all residents.

5.3 Risk Factors Characterizing Young People in Care

Articles 25 and 27 both touch upon the overall requirements for high living standards that are adequate for physical, mental, spiritual, moral and social development. From former research we know that young people who have been placed in out-of-home care differ from other young people as concerns health and risk behaviour (Hestbæk and Henze-Pedersen 2017). As is evident from Table 7.2, young people 15/18 years old in care are significantly more often exposed to risk indicators. While 54 per cent of the young people in care had had sexual intercourse at the age of 15, this is true for 31 per cent of other 15 year olds. The relatively early sexual debut is reflected in a significantly higher level of abortions (18 per cent of 18-year-old women previously in care have had abortions, compared to 4 per cent in general).

Further, 39 per cent of young people with out-of-home care experiences had tried hashish, compared to 12 per cent in general, and 39 per cent of the young people in care had been involved in different types of delinquent behaviour, which is true for 10 per cent of 15 year olds in general.

Another risk indicator concerns the extent to which young people in care have been exposed to rape. This applied to 34 per cent of the young people interviewed (mostly young women), compared to only 6 per cent of young persons in general. Lastly, it is sad to note that *more than every*

Table 7.2 Risk indicators in out-of-home care

Risk indicators with 15/18 years old, in out-of-home care and never in care (percentage)		
Indicator of health and risk behaviour	Teenagers in care	Teenagers never in care
Sexual intercourse (15 years old)	54	31
Had an abortion (18 years old)	18	4
Tried hashish (15 years old)	39	12
Delinquency (15 years old)	39	10
Exposed to rape (18 years old)	34	6
Tried to commit suicide (18 years old)	28	5

Sources: Lausten et al. (2013), Olsen and Lausten (2017), Ottosen et al. (2015)

fourth young person (28 per cent) previously in care at the age of 18 had tried to commit suicide. Suicidal behaviour accounts for 5 per cent of other youngsters at the age of 18. Young people who have primarily been placed in residential care have an even higher rate of suicide attempts (*c.*45 per cent) than those with mainly foster care experiences (18–26 per cent; cf. Olsen and Lausten 2017).

We know that children and young people in residential care, on average, belong to the most vulnerable groups in the youth population, having been exposed to intensive risk factors during adolescence and exerting predominant risk behaviour themselves—which is part of the reasons for being in residential care. But even so the data might direct our attention towards how we can develop caring environments that both compensate the young person for consequences of insufficient or harmful care during his or her upbringing, and simultaneously constitute protective living conditions that are 'adequate for the child's physical, mental, spiritual, moral and social development', as mentioned in Article 27.

5.4 Everyday Life in Care and Life Satisfaction

While Sects. 5.1 and 5.2 focused on the right to participation and the right to protection, this section concerns the right to a development-oriented living standard. Here we will discuss the factors related to young persons' rights in everyday life when placed in out-of-home care. The young persons were posed questions that touch upon this aspect in a wider perspective.

Regarding the overall satisfaction with the care home where they are living, almost two thirds consider it to be a very good place to live. However, the discrepancy between foster care and residential care is striking. While only 34 per cent of the young people in institutions agree that it is a good place to live, this applies to 77 per cent in foster care. Some 40 per cent of the young people in residential care consider the place where they live to be only tolerable or even not so good. Are these figures inevitable due to structural barriers, or is it possible to achieve positive changes?

The same trend can be seen when we look at freedom to decide. Almost two thirds (62 per cent) feel free to decide how to live their life. While 70 per cent of the young people in foster care agree, the same pertains to 51 per cent in residential care, and, conversely, 24 per cent in residential care disagree or disagree fully.

One of the basic conditions for healthy development is to be loved—that a child or young person actively experiences being loved. As mentioned initially, almost 90 per cent of the young persons in out-of-home care always or often feel loved by the foster parents or by the professionals or in the residential unit. For young people in foster care, as many as 95 per cent always or often feel loved by the foster family, while 72 per cent of the young people in institutions feel loved. On the one hand, there is quite a difference between the two groups. On the other hand, is this what is realistic to expect given the group of very vulnerable young persons and given the conditions of residential care?

In this respect, it is also very interesting to note that more than 90 per cent of all young persons in care feel loved by their parents no matter the problems they have been exposed to (Ottosen et al. 2015). This finding underlines the importance of supporting a continuous relationship between young people in care and their parents, as is also one of the aims of the CRC (Article 9).

The last statement from the Danish study to be included here is a question designed to measure overall life satisfaction on a scale from 0 to 10. On average, more than half of the young people 11 to 17 years old in care (53 per cent) answered in the range 8–10, interpreted as a high life satisfaction score. This is true for 37 per cent of the young persons in residential care and 64 per cent of the young people in foster care—almost twice the rate.

It is also interesting to look at the lower part of the scale. The amount of young people with very low life satisfaction (0–3) is three times higher in residential care (15 per cent) than in foster care (5 per cent; cf. Table 7.3). Even though the figures for the most negative scores are relatively low, it is sad to conclude that 15 per cent of the participants in the study of all young people in residential care consider their life satisfaction that low. When CRC recommends states to strive for high living standards and environments that should create adequate conditions for the child's physical, mental, spiritual, moral and social development, based on the findings in Table 7.3 we have to confess that there is still quite a potential for improvement. In this regard it is important to mention that

Table 7.3 Satisfaction with life in out-of-home care

How satisfied are you with your life on a scale from 0–10? (0 expresses the worst life possible, 10 the best life possible)			
	Foster care	Institution	Total
Low score (0–3)	5	15	8
Medium score (4–7)	32	49	39
High score (8–10)	64	37	53
Total	101	101	100

Source: TABU study (Ottosen et al. 2015)

CRC signals an implicit priority to foster care as the first-mentioned alternative to growing up in the family environment, while residential care is mentioned as the last alternative: 'or if necessary placement in suitable institutions for the care of children' (Article 20).

6 Challenges in Measuring CRC Rights Enforcement

From a rights-based perspective, the analysis gives rise to reflections about to what extent we provide satisfactory conditions for adolescents in publicly financed residential care. And we are left with many questions, of which two will be discussed here: First, from a methodological perspective is it at all possible to measure quality of life in out-of-home care in the context of CRC through surveys? Second, how can we, from a rights-based perspective, improve processes around care and life satisfaction in residential 24-hour care?

6.1 Measuring Life Satisfaction and Implementation of Rights in Out-of-Home Care

Acknowledging the quite critical views on residential out-of-home care revealed in this chapter, it is interesting to question to what extent it is possible to examine, how basic rights are met in care through standardized survey questions.

First, it is not possible to establish an average cut-off, a simple measure or threshold, distinguishing satisfactory rights-based conditions from unsatisfactory conditions. Most of the figures presented in this chapter may be subject to discretion and discussion, while only a few results point directly to an acceptable versus an unacceptable level of rights. For example, we find a surprisingly large group of young people who do not feel involved in the process when entering care. This is even true among 60 per cent of those who had entered care within the last year. We do not need academic analyses to conclude that this is unacceptable and not at all in alignment with the intentions of participation in the CRC, and that this result calls for action. Munro suggests (see Munro and Turnell 2018: Chap. 5 in this book) that we develop the processes around child protection enabling a better and 'deeper' involvement of young people on young people's grounds.

Second, we must acknowledge that it is not reasonable to strive for 100 per cent 'consumer satisfaction' with young people, neither in residential care nor in families in general. This is partly because young people in care come from highly disadvantaged backgrounds that leave mental scars that may not disappear fully, even after long-term placement, and partly because we know that teenagers in general become more and more critical as they come of age, being in care or not. The older the teenagers, the more they dislike their everyday life, the more critical they are of their surroundings—parents and carers included—and the lower they rate their health, life satisfaction and so on. But how do we then set a threshold for adequate satisfaction with rights-based conditions when living in out-of-home care?

A basic methodological reflection concerns what kind of knowledge we may expect to find when using standardized survey questions to shed light on complex conditions, such as life satisfaction or the feeling of being loved. The survey data used for this analysis are of a high quality and collected by professional interviewers among a relatively large sample. However, as any survey data the data used here lack the more complex narratives behind the simplified figures. What do young persons mean when they answer that they have been subject to violations from peers? What made them feel uninvolved, when most social workers find that they always talk with a child before deciding on care? We cannot answer these questions precisely from survey data; in these matters qualitative in-depth studies could yield a significant contribution.

Finally we acknowledge that the data used for analysis in this chapter are generated in a Danish context. It is plausible to assume that some of the problems revealed also are relevant in residential settings in other welfare states. However, the data only allows for Danish generalizations.

6.2 Pathways for Strengthening the Rights Perspective

Research shows unequivocally that, on average, growing up in care itself reinforces the stigmatizing process that children and young people from the most vulnerable families are exposed to throughout adolescence. Therefore, during the last decades, great effort has been directed towards how to compensate disadvantaged children better and how to develop and target interventions in order to achieve better outcomes. However, we still lack evidence. In many—perhaps most—respects, we cannot point out exactly which intervention and which type of care will contribute to which effects for a given child.

The analysis in this chapter reveals quite a few discouraging results as concerns the rights of young people in care, the processes around care and their self-reported satisfaction in selected domains. Also, some young people in residential care seem to live with 'impaired' life conditions. It seems quite *paradoxical* that professional residential units acting *in loco parentis*, and aiming at providing the most vulnerable young people with a protective and sound environment for upbringing, do not succeed in implementing basic rights.

An important question is *why* the living conditions and life satisfaction of young people in care in the areas mentioned appear so relatively poor. Would rights be improved if we transformed all placements into foster care? Most likely it would be an inadequate—perhaps even a detrimental—strategy to let foster care fully replace residential units for the eldest teenagers and the most complex cases. There is an obvious need for the competences and overall treatment facilities in residential settings (Whittaker et al. 2016).

However, the analysis indicates that the rights perspective may not be given adequate priority, neither in the child protection agencies, nor in the residential milieus. From a rights-based perspective it is necessary to examine the most important barriers and potentials. Which steps could be taken and which procedures and specific criteria might contribute significantly to establish a stronger environment that, to a greater extent, will support the rights of young people, especially in residential care?

7 Conclusion

Participation seems to be a field where there is considerable room for improvement. Listening to the messages from this chapter, we first and foremost need to establish procedures and methods that put more emphasis on involving children and young people and giving their voices due weight in accordance with age and maturity. This is true for both the social work processes, but also for everyday life in residential care.

As concerns the *social work processes*, central organizational changes might be needed. Municipal autonomy leaves room for large variations in services. A Danish study found that 45 per cent of the local authorities did not have any systematic guidelines for how to involve children and young people. Further, the local governments were not that concerned about it, and only a few local Governments had regular reports about the statutory participation of children (Hestbæk et al. 2006). Thus, an example of a rights-based request is that there are adequate mandatory processes for participation and the monitoring hereof, supervised by management, and that social workers in the child protection agencies become even more skilled in practicing involvement, performing more responsive processes.

Involvement is also crucial in *everyday life in residential settings*. Despite the fact that most institutions have skilled staff, such as social pedagogues and psychologists, many of the young people in residential care do not feel adequately seen, heard and respected. Through data we get an impression that rights are not always adequately respected, and quite a few do not develop their full potential. Presumably, changes require both development of pedagogical and treatment methods; it requires training and supervision of professionals; and it requires a striving for new relations between carers and the young people being cared for, characterized by the involvement, protection and personal development and integrity of the young individual.

Notes

1. 'Institution' includes residential homes, residential treatment facilities, group care homes and other types of 24-hour residential care. Foster care includes common foster care, kinship care, network care etc.
2. We know from research that the implementation of these measures is pretty rare; however, see Baviskar et al. (2016) and Karmsteen et al. (2018).
3. TABU is an acronym for Trivsel hos Anbragte Børn og Unge, meaning the well-being of children and young people in out-of-home care. The study was conducted by VIVE, the Danish National Centre for Welfare Research and Analysis, and financed by the Ministry of Children and Social Affairs.

References

Backe-Hansen, E., Madsen, C., Kristofersen, L. B., & Hvinden, B. (2014). *Barnevern i Norge 1990–2010. En longitudinell studie.* Oslo: Nova Rapport 9/14.

Baviskar, S., Christoffersen, M. N., Karmsteen, K., Hansen, H., Leth-Espensen, M., Christensen, A., & Brauner, J. (2016). *Kontinuitet i anbringelser. Evaluering af lovændringer under barnets reform. Delrapport I.* Copenhagen: SFI—The Danish National Centre for Social Research.

Christoffersen, M. N., Hestbæk, A.-D., Lindemann, A., & Nielsen, V. L. (2005). *Nye regler for udsatte børn og unge.* Copenhagen: SFI—The Danish National Centre for Social Research.

Egelund, T., & Hestbæk, A.-D. (2003). *Anbringelse af børn og unge uden for hjemmet. En forskningsoversigt.* Copenhagen: SFI—The Danish National Centre for Social Research.

Child Helpline. (2017). *Ret til inddragelse.* Copenhagen: Child Helpline (Børns Vilkår).

Hestbæk, A.-D. (2011). A child welfare system under reframing. In N. Gilbert, N. Parton, & M. Skivenes (Eds.), *Child protection systems: international trends and orientations* (pp. 131–153). Oxford: Oxford University Press.

Hestbæk, A.-D., & Henze-Pedersen, S. (2017). Anbragt. Udfordringer fra barndommen ind i voksenlivet. In N. Ploug (Ed.), *Social arv og social ulighed* (pp. 93–121). Copenhagen: Hans Reitzel.

Hestbæk, A.-D., Lindemann, A., Nielsen, V. L., & Christoffersen, M. N. (2006). *Nye regler—ny praksis*. Copenhagen: SFI—The Danish National Centre for Social Research.

Karmsteen, K., Frederiksen, S., Mørch, F. H., & Hestbæk, A.-D. (2018). *Kontinuitet i anbringelser. Delrapport II: Når forældre og forvaltning mødes.* Copenhagen: VIVE—The Danish Center for Applied Social Science Research.

Lausten, M., & Jørgensen, T. (2017). *Anbragte børn og unge trivsel 2016.* Copenhagen: SFI—The Danish National Centre for Social Research.

Lausten, M., Frederiks en, S., Olsen, R. F., Nielsen, A. A., & Bengtsson, T. T. (2013). *Anbragte 15-åriges hverdagsliv og udfordringer.* Copenhagen: SFI—The Danish National Centre for Social Research.

Ministry for Children and Social Affairs. (2017). *Consolidation Act on Social Services.* Copenhagen.

Munro, E., & Turnell, A. (2018). Re-designing organisations to facilitate rights-based practice in child protection. In A. Falch-Eriksen & E. Backe-Hansen (Eds.), *Human rights in child protection. Implications for professional practice and policy.* London: Palgrave Macmillan.

Olsen, R. F., & Lausten, M. (2017). *Anbragte unges udsathed.* Copenhagen: SFI—The Danish National Centre for Social Research.

Olsen, R. F., Egelund, T., & Lausten, M. (2011). *Tidligere anbragte unge som voksne.* Copenhagen: SFI—The Danish National Centre for Social Research.

Ottosen, M. H., Lausten, M., Frederiksen, S., & Andersen, D. (2015). *Anbragte børns og unge trivsel 2014.* Copenhagen: SFI—The Danish National Centre for Social Research.

United Nations. (1989). *Convention on the Rights of the Child.* Geneva: Office of the High Commissioner, United Nations Human Rights.

Whittaker, J. K., Holmes, L., del Valle, J. F., Ainsworth, F., Andreassen, T., Anglin, J.,…Zeira, A. (2016). Therapeutic residential care for children and youth: A consensus statement of the international work group on therapeutic residential care. *Residential Treatment for Children & Youth, 33*(2), 89–106.

Open Access This chapter is licensed under the terms of the Creative Commons Attribution 4.0 International License (http://creativecommons.org/licenses/by/4.0/), which permits use, sharing, adaptation, distribution and reproduction in any medium or format, as long as you give appropriate credit to the original author(s) and the source, provide a link to the Creative Commons license and indicate if changes were made.

The images or other third party material in this chapter are included in the chapter's Creative Commons license, unless indicated otherwise in a credit line to the material. If material is not included in the chapter's Creative Commons license and your intended use is not permitted by statutory regulation or exceeds the permitted use, you will need to obtain permission directly from the copyright holder.

8

Emergency Placements: Human Rights Limits and Lessons

Elisabeth Gording-Stang

1 Introduction

Children living in situations of risk because of violence, severe drug abuse, sexual abuse or other forms of serious neglect from their care persons depend on an efficient public system of emergency intervention to safeguard their right to care and protection. The administrative, legal and practical design of such an emergency system differs between countries. The thresholds of intervention might differ as well. Most Western countries have established some kind of emergency institution, although a variety of organizational affiliations of emergency bodies are possible (see e.g. Gilbert et al. 2011). Most common are the social welfare services/ Child Protection Services (CPS), the police or a combination of those two institutions.

Safeguarding the rights of children in emergency situations is an obligation that follows from the UN Convention on the Rights of the

---

E. Gording-Stang, LL.D. (✉)
Department of Social Work, Child Welfare and Social Policy, Oslo Metropolitan University, Oslo, Norway
e-mail: elisst@oslomet.no

Child (CRC) Article 19 and the European Convention of Human Rights (ECHR) Articles 3 and 8, (Gilbert et al. 2011; see Sandberg, Chap. 2 in this book). In this chapter, ten decisions from seven Norwegian district courts[1] will serve as examples of how human rights and legal criteria are relevant to professional practice in emergency cases. It will be discussed whether there is something to learn for professionals working in child protection from the way the courts argue and justify their decisions.[2]

Emergency decisions have to be made within a short period of time, based on alarming, although limited, information about the child's care situation resulting in an urgent need for the child to be protected. It follows from the nature of such placements that they do not meet the normal standards of the rule of law. The right to information, contradiction, careful pre-investigation and collection of all relevant data, informing and hearing the child, are in many cases not possible to comply with. These decisions shed light on how fundamental contradicting interests are being considered and balanced by the courts. How to safeguard the parent's procedural rights and the right to proportionate measures on the one hand, and at the same time secure the child's needs and right to effective protection against violence, abuse and other forms of neglect on the other, are crucial in these cases (see Baugerud and Melinder 2012; Melinder et al. 2013; Storhaug and Kojan 2017).

Human rights and national regulations limit the discretionary power of child protection workers, judges and other decision-making professionals by formulating legal standards, criteria, principals and other kinds of provisions that on the one hand cannot be violated, but on the other hand can be subject to interpretation. This chapter will show and discuss how human rights interact with legal criteria in national law and case facts in child protection emergency cases. The ten cases analysed here are selected from seven Norwegian district courts. In law research, case law can serve both as a relevant legal source of interpretation, and as empirical material. I will use it in both ways, to reveal how discretionary power is performed within the borders of the law, and how professional practice can be guided by fundamental human rights principles.

2 The Relevance of Human Rights to Professional Practice in Emergency Cases

As the Committee of the Rights of the Child is not empowered to make legally binding decisions for the member states, we must turn to the European Court of Human Rights (henceforth 'European Court') to study relevant case law which imposes legal obligations on local social welfare authorities in Europe. In the decisions from the European Court, the Court now regularly refers to the CRC in serious cases of child abuse and neglect, strengthening a child rights perspective and the position of the CRC in its own case law.

The European Convention on Human Rights (ECHR) Article 8(1) states that everyone has the right to respect for his private life and family life. In connection with child abuse and maltreatment, the European Court has developed an extensive case law during the last 20 years. Many of the cases have been initiated by parents claiming their right to *family life* violated by care order decisions, forced adoption or denial of visitation rights. Some of the cases have been brought into court by the (now adult) children, claiming their right to protection and *private life* has been violated by non-intervention during their childhood, despite public authorities' knowledge of ongoing child abuse and neglect in their families. The European Court has developed a dynamic interpretation of the term *private life* in ECHR Article 8, often in conjunction with Article 3 which protects against torture and inhuman and degrading treatment. According to the case law, the notion of private life contents the obligation to secure the child's right to protection of his or her *moral and physical integrity*.

ECHR Article 8(2) regulates the criteria for intervention in private and family life. *First*, interference in private or family life can only take place in accordance with the law, which reflects *the principle of legality*[3]; the need for a specific legal basis in law for the interfering measure. *Second*, interference can only take place if it is *necessary* in a democratic society for the protection of the rights and freedoms of others, that is, in this case: the protection of children's life, health and development. This reflects *the principle of proportionality*. Alternative and less intrusive measures must have been considered or carried out.

The ECHR case law reveals the fine balance between the child's and his or her parent's mutual interest in protecting their family life, and the specific interests of the child to be protected from a *harmful* family life when necessary. As stated in the case Adele Johansen vs Norway 1996, parents 'cannot be entitled under Article 8 of the Convention to have such measures taken as would harm the child's health and development' (see Stang 2015).

In cases concerning child abuse and neglect, the European Court repeatedly underlines the obligations of public authorities to secure effective protection of children, or other vulnerable persons, who are exposed to such ill-treatment committed by parents or other care persons.[4] It follows from ECHR Article 8 case law, and CRC Article 19, that public authorities must ensure that, upon a discovery of child abuse or neglect, *immediate steps* will be taken to protect the health and welfare of the abused or neglected child as well as that of any other child under the same care who may be in danger of abuse or neglect (Detrick 1999; Sandberg, Chap. 2 in this book).[5] Emergency placement is one of the relevant measures that meets the obligation set forward in Article 19.[6]

3 National Regulation of Interim Orders in Emergencies

The Norwegian Child Welfare Act (CWA) of 1992 has a specific provision for emergency cases. Section 4–6 (2) states that if there is a risk that a child will suffer material harm by remaining at home, the head of the child welfare administration or the prosecuting authority may immediately make an interim care order without the consent of the parents.[7] The emergency order must immediately after execution be sent to the County Board for judicial control (see note 6). The order must be approved by the Board Chair as soon as possible, and preferably within 48 hours after receipt. Brief grounds shall be given for the decision. The decision from the County Board might be appealed to the District Court for review.

Section 4–6 represents an exception from the main legal proceedings in cases of coercive child protection measures. Ordinary proceedings such as a careful three-month investigation, implementing of home-based preventive measures, voluntary measures, hearing the child and documenting the child's own viewpoints, hearing the parents and witness examinations will not be systematically implemented in emergency situations. In these cases, the Parliament has taken a stand by prioritizing the child's right to protection against serious harm over the procedural rights of the parents and the child. The provision of emergency orders is designed in a way that 'downscales' the ordinary safeguarding rule-of-law procedures to facilitate immediate action to protect the child. The European Court has accepted that standpoint in emergency cases. In K. and T. vs Finland 1994, the Court stated that

> when an emergency care order has to be made, it may not always be possible, because of the urgency of the situation, to associate in the decision-making process those having custody of the child. Nor … may it even be desirable, even if possible, to do so if those having custody of the child are seen as the source of an immediate threat to the child, since giving them prior warning would be liable to deprive the measure of its effectiveness.[8]

In the K. and T. vs Finland decision the European Court supports the similar principles and child rights-based approach as expressed in CRC Article 19 and in the CRC Committee's General Comment on protection from corporal punishment (cf. Sandberg, Chap. 2 in this book).

However, the fact that the child will suffer harm does not qualify for emergency interventions if the harm does not reach a certain level (material; serious) and the risk situation is urgent. This follows from ECHR Article 8(2): The intervention must be absolutely necessary. General neglect will, as such, normally not qualify for emergency placements. As stated in K. and T. vs Finland, 'The authorities had known about the forthcoming birth for months in advance and were well aware of K.'s mental problems [schizophrenia, psychosis], so that the situation was not an emergency in the sense of being unforeseen.'[9]

4 Court Review of County Board Decisions in Emergency Cases

In Norway, there has been a remarkable increase in all kinds of County Board decisions brought to court through appeal (Viblemo et al. 2015).[10] The share of emergency decisions has increased from 5 per cent in 2008 to 16 per cent in 2013. Quite a large portion of the County Board emergency decisions are being *approved* by the courts, however, for instance 75 per cent in 2013.

Below, I will describe the kind of situations that lead to emergency placements, and discuss how legal criteria, human rights principles and case facts interact. I will use Norwegian case law as an example of challenges and practices that are most likely to be found in other countries as well. Despite the relatively short presentation of the facts in the Court decisions, they give important information. I will present the cases from the following categories of what emerges as main reasons for the emergency placements: violence, sexual abuse, drug abuse, psychological disorders, risk of abduction and other forms of neglect. In several cases more than one of these factors are present.[11]

4.1 Violence

The first case is from Romerike District Court in 2011, concerning three children aged ten, eight and six. The CPS had been in contact with the family since the first child was born. The father had custody for the children because of the mother's mental problems. The eldest boy told CPS that he was beaten by his father each time he did something wrong, and expressed that he was scared of his father. The boy had told his mother that he wanted to kill himself. The mother went to their father's place, a conflict situation developed, and an emergency placement was carried out. All three children were placed in family foster homes with their aunts and their families, and they all seemed to settle down well there. The Court assessed whether the children would suffer serious harm by living with their father, and concluded that such a risk was clearly present. The

Court also stressed that preventive, voluntary measures had been tried out for a long time, without any significant effect on the children.

In a case from Oslo District Court in 2013 the Court concluded that the criteria for emergency placement of an eight-year-old boy were not met, despite descriptions of neglect and violence from their mother, given by his sister. She had explained that her mother was pulling her hair, beating her, threatening and verbally harassing her. She had told CPS that she spent much time alone at evenings and nights, caring for her younger brother. She also mentioned that her mother took her shoplifting. The younger brother had been witnessing his mother exposing his sister to violence. CPS describe the boy as a vulnerable and insecure child who struggled at school, socially as well as educationally, and showed antisocial behaviour.

The Court underlined the legal criterium 'suffer material harm'; that there is a high threshold for taking a child out-of-home by an emergency placement. Long-lasting neglect is not enough; in such a case ordinary proceedings for a care order would be the proper choice. The boy himself stated, through his spokesperson, that he still would like to live with his mother, that he was fine with her, and if he could not live with her, he wanted to see her Friday, Saturday, Sunday and Monday. Thus the Court could not find that the boy would be exposed to serious harm by staying at home, and that the emergency decision should cease.

These two cases illustrate how long-lasting neglect would typically not reach the level of an emergency unless a situation occurs where the child is proven to be in risk of serious harm, as it did in the first case. There is reason to believe that in the last case, the boy's own and clear views had a major impact on the decision as well. But there is a limit to how serious the long-lasting situation can be before immediate action is required. Where children are living with ongoing, severe maltreatment, sexual abuse or severe drug abuse, public authorities have a clear duty to protect the child immediately and prevent both the actual child and other family members from being exposed to serious risk and harm, by reporting the case to the police, the CPS or otherwise. That duty follows both from CRC Article 19 and ECHR case law, as well as from national regulation on the duty of disclosure.[12]

4.2 Sexual Abuse

A decision from Eiker, Modum and Sigdal District Court from 2013 concerned an eight-year-old boy. The parents had a custody conflict going on, and the Court of Appeals had awarded custody to the father three years before the District Court decision. The mother had access rights under supervision. Despite detailed descriptions of sexual abuse over time, none of the psychological experts appointed by the District Court nor the Appeals Court had been able to conclude as to any present risk of sexual abuse. Instead, they were of the opinion that it was the mother's strong focus on the issue of abuse that enabled the boy to maintain the story over time. At several occasions, over several years, the boy had told both his mother, the police and CPS about sexual abuse from his father. The police had dismissed the case. Psychological experts had proposed alternative theories to explain the boy's allegations of abuse. After having watched a film with his class at school about sexual abuse, the boy told a teacher 'daddy is doing to me what we saw in the film', and said that he did not want to go home, that he was scared of his dad. CPS effected an emergency placement on the same day, and moved the boy to his mother. Before the Court, CPS referred to the human rights principle of the best interests of the child, and to the principle of proportionality. In its decision, the Court underlined the strict legal criteria in the CWA, and stressed the principle of proportionality as well. Nevertheless, the Court did not agree with earlier court decisions that the boy's statements of sexual abuse derived from his mother's manipulation, and found the boy credible. The Court stated that there was a qualified risk that the boy actually was exposed to abuse from his father, and upheld the emergency care order.

This case is an example of how hard it often is to prove sufficient probability of sexual abuse. This might also be one of the reasons why CPS rarely argue solely with sexual abuse in cases with ordinary care orders. CPS rather tend to prove general neglect, with abuse as a part of this. In cases of physical violence, there might often be other witnesses or supplementing information to the child's own testimony. It is characteristic for sexual abuse that there is a total lack of other evidence than the child's own statement, which also underlines the importance of child interviews being carried out according to the law, the ethical guidelines and professional conduct for such conversations. The time pressure in emergency situations does not always permit such interviews.

4.3 Drug Abuse

In a case from Sarpsborg District Court 2008, a three-year-old boy was taken into emergency care after the mother was arrested twice and taken into custody because of retention of a large quantum of amphetamine. Both parents were long-time drug abusers, but the mother had managed to maintain a job and keep the abuse hidden from family and working colleagues. The mother temporarily placed the boy with his two uncles and their wives. Just before the mother was released from custody, CPS decided to place the boy in a foster home. Despite the preventive measures that had already been tried, the mother did not prove able to cut contact with the criminal environment of which she was a part, and thus was not able to protect her son from being exposed to criminals and drug abusers who came to their home. In this case, and despite the huge challenges faced by the mother and the negative consequences for her son, the Court concluded that the emergency provision did not apply. The Court agreed with CPS that the care situation could lead to a risk of harming the boy, but not as seriously as required in the law. The boy was described as a well-functioning three year old with a strong and close attachment to his mother. The Court also considered the risk of harm by breaking these bonds. The Court upheld that voluntary preventive measures were likely to minimize the risk of harm to an acceptable level.

The Court did not discuss what an 'acceptable level of risk' actually implies, but this case too shows the importance of a present incident or a more critical situation that clearly differs from more general long-lasting neglect, to meet the criteria for emergency placement instead of an ordinary care order. The fact that the boy was well functioning with a close attachment to his mother was probably important, in the light of the consequences of emergency placements often lasting for a longer period of time with very little or no contact between the child and his or her parents. The best-interest principle turned into a 'principle of minor harm'.

4.4 Psychological Disorders

In a case from Alstahaug District Court 2011, the emergency order was refused because the criteria in the CWA were not met. The nine-year-old boy in this case had special medical and educational needs. He had shown challenging behaviour at school as well, and his temper was described as 'explosive'. His mother was exhausted and depressed, and could not manage ordinary tasks in the household like washing, dishwashing and cleaning, nor the upbringing of her son who required special attention and care. In a meeting at the CPS office, the mother got so upset she left the meeting. That incident motivated CPS to carry out an emergency placement.

In line with case law, the Court underlines the high threshold and strict criteria for emergency orders. The Court decided not to uphold the order, as it had not been proven that the boy would suffer serious harm by staying at home until the ordinary care order proceedings could start. The Court noted that CPS had failed to make new assessments of the mother's care abilities, nor offered any preventive measures during the period from the emergency placement to the beginning of the Court proceedings.

In a case from Oslo District Court 2009 a seven-year-old girl was taken into emergency care because of the mother's severe psychological problems (acute psychosis) and general neglect. The Court underlined the strict criteria for emergency placements, and that the situation for the child had to be critical. The Court found that there was a serious risk for the child if she was to stay with her mother, and moved the child to a secret address. The mother believed that her daughter was exposed to sexual abuse by the father and by people at school, but the allegations were viewed by the medical experts and the Court as false—as expressions of paranoid delusions—despite the child's descriptions of her father 'using the finger' on her, in the police interview. The Court further concluded that preventive, voluntary measures would not be sufficient to secure the child the care she needed, and would not protect the child from the mother's serious delusions.

As with the two cases of violence, these two cases of psychological problems represent the demarcation line between emergency situations due to the level of harm, and 'ordinary' neglect that is harmful, but not *that* harmful. If a child's care situation makes it acceptable to wait for ordinary care order proceedings, which would take a couple of more weeks, maybe months, to prepare, that would be preferable in the light of the rule-of-law principles; proper investigation, hearing the child and the parents, mapping the child's and parent's network and capacities, and trying out assisting measures.

4.5 Risk of Abduction

In some cases, the risk of abduction or harming the child might constitute a legal basis for an emergency placement. In a case from Gjøvik District Court 2009 that was the issue, but the Court overruled the County Board decision. Three children of eight, seven and five were placed at a secret address. One of the children had told a teacher that the family was to move to another country during the autumn vacation 'because then we will get rid of Child Protection Services'. There had been a concern for the care situation during a long period of time, and several notifications had reached the CPS from different professionals. However, the Court did not find that CPS had sufficiently proven that there was a current, concrete and obvious risk of the mother taking the children out of the country.

In another case, from Bergen District Court 2014, the risk for abduction led to an emergency care order decision for three children aged nine, six and two. The father had taken the two oldest children to Sri Lanka, and returned alone two months later. The children came back to Norway after 11 months, and told about violent experiences, sexual abuse, threats and physical punishment while staying with their aunt and uncle in Sri Lanka. The Court, though, concluded that it did not find a real risk for abduction at the time of the Court proceedings. The Court did, in opposite to the County Board, not find it proven that the children had been traumatized or had changed behaviour after their stay in Sri Lanka. There were no reports stating that as a fact, or alleging other forms of maltreatment or serious neglect. The children were described as happy and secure during the visitation time with their father, and they had also expressed a wish to see their father. The Court did not share the views of CPS that the mother was incapable of protecting her children, and underlined that the mother had handled the conflicts between the parents in a good manner and with regard to the best interests of the children. The Court concluded that no elements of immediate harm were to be identified in the case, and that the emergency decision had to cease.

These two cases show how CPS have a challenge proving that the risk criteria are met by the facts of the cases, when the Court makes a here-and-now assessment of the risk involved. In the last case, the Court highlighted the children's behaviour towards their father, and that they expressed a wish to see him.

4.6 Neglect of Newborn Babies

The case from Gjøvik District Court 2012 concerns the care situation for a baby boy. The baby had been taken to hospital by the parents because he was dehydrated and had lost weight since birth, and needed immediate medical aid. The hospital delivered a notification of concern to CPS, on the basis of lack of fundamental parental abilities. The father was described as passive towards the child; the mother as over-focused on her own situation and health problems. She was later diagnosed with psychosis and transferred to the emergency medical ward. Parental assistance and guidance were offered by CPS, but the situation for the baby was considered to be so serious that an emergency placement was carried out. The District Court found that the baby had been exposed to serious neglect the two first weeks of his life to such a degree that the CPS leader was not sure it would be possible to drive him from one place to another after the care-order decision, due to his state of health. The Court concluded that the boy would face serious harm if he was not immediately placed elsewhere.

In a case from Sarpsborg District Court 2011 a premature baby boy was placed immediately after birth. Concern for the baby was already expressed during his mother's pregnancy, as the parents did not seem to fully understand their future responsibility as parents, and showed little insight into a newborn child's mental, emotional or physical needs. Further, they did not seem to understand how to act in order to protect the baby from physical harm and accidents. After one month at a family centre, the parents wanted to end the counselling and leave the centre. As CPS feared for the baby's life and health, and considered that the baby needed 24 hours' supervision, the CPS made an emergency decision to prevent the parents from taking the baby with them when they left the family centre. The Court accepted the decision and argued that the baby's special needs as premature and particular vulnerability made special demands on the parents. The Court agreed that the terms 'serious' and 'risk' must be interpreted with regard to the child's young age and vulnerability. The Court underlined that other, less interfering measures had been considered and rejected as not sufficient to safeguard the child's health and development.

The first case shows how fundamental and serious neglect and emotional maltreatment can be life-threatening towards a baby and rather quickly turn into an emergency situation. In this case, there was no time to wait for ordinary care-order proceedings. In both cases, the child's very young age and state of health had an important impact on the risk assessment and might have lowered the threshold for an emergency order. On the other hand, taking a baby into emergency care is a harsh measure towards the parents, but the child's health condition makes the measure proportional. The latter is important in the light of the right to family life. In K. and T. vs Finland, the European Court outlines that

> when such a drastic measure for the mother, depriving her totally of her new-born child immediately on birth, was contemplated, it was incumbent on the competent national authorities to examine whether some less intrusive interference into family life, at such a critical point in the lives of the parents and child, was not possible.[13]

5 Lessons Learned from Norwegian Case Law

The case law discussed here shows that the children involved are often finding themselves in *very serious situations*, as they risk being exposed to their parents' violence, drug abuse, psychological problems, sexual abuse, abduction or other forms of neglect and maltreatment. The case facts give a picture of emergency measures being used first and foremost in cases of grave neglect and abuse. This is an important perspective to consider. In some of the cases, it might even be difficult to see an obvious explanation for letting the child remain in a clearly harmful home situation, only to wait for ordinary care-order proceedings to be exercised. What level of harm or neglect is acceptable for a child to live with for another couple of weeks or months? The quite brief presentations of the facts and assessments in the Court decisions do not give necessary and complementary information to sufficiently review the assessments of the child's best interests, but it still is an important, and quite uncomfortable, question to ask.

In several of the cases, the *risk assessments* seem inadequate and incomplete according to general quality standards, but do not follow any common national protocol. The wide margin of discretion in these cases combined with the lack of time to make thorough investigations, may increase the risk of making wrong decisions. That may be a necessary price to pay for being able to intervene on short notice to protect the child involved.

The case law shows that the criteria in the CWA are being *strictly interpreted*: there must exist a real, present risk for the child's health and development, if emergency placements are to be judged the right measure. If the situation is harmful, but has not yet developed into critical, the child and the family might still be better taken care of through ordinary care-order proceedings. In some cases even voluntary measures like family counselling might work to solve the main problems.

One interesting aspect of the Court decisions is the *lack of a broader best-interest assessment* in several decisions. The Court's assessments seem to focus mainly on the judicial control of legal criteria, like the level of risk and harm, whether the situation is an emergency, and whether assisting and less intrusive measures have been tried out. Only a few of the court decisions contain a thorough assessment of the best interests of the child, which is a professional duty according to the CWA, the CRC and ECHR case law as well as the Norwegian Constitution. On the other hand, the child's own views are being highlighted in many of the cases, and given due, and sometimes decisive, weight.

Another aspect with the court decisions is the tendency to consider or carry out *family placements* in emergency cases. Family- or network-based placements would in some cases reduce the stress for both the child and the parents, and enable the maintenance of bonds between the child and family members other than the parents.

As follows from the review of case law, several types of *mistakes* might cause disapproval in the Court, whether this is in the child's best interests or not. CPS might not be able to argue sufficiently well for the necessity of the placement, or that preventive measures have been proven insufficient. CPS might have interpreted or used the CWA provision in a wrong way/on wrong terms, or is not able to prove that the child is living in a situation of real, present, qualified risk.

One lesson learned from the case law may be that child protection workers have to pay due attention to the *legal criteria* for coercive measures and interventions. They need to convince the County Board or the courts why and how the child's situation corresponds to the risk level in the relevant emergency provision. Child welfare workers also need to explain why less intrusive measures would not be sufficient to prevent serious harm to the child, and consider the positive and negative impact of emergency placement on the parents' and the child's situation. Thorough and well-founded best-interests assessments are supposed to be developed and carried out, and risk assessments should be improved, including how the child's age, vulnerability, own viewpoints and state of health influence the risk level.

Nevertheless, the considerations and interpretations of legal criteria, assessments of facts, the guiding principles and human rights, all involve elements of professional discretion. A variety of relevant aspects are to be carefully balanced; judicial, psychological, cultural and medical aspects for instance. The case law reveals a blurred borderline between 'serious' and 'less serious' harm; between 'critical' and 'not so critical' neglect. The most complex assessment is that of the best interests of the child, or rather of the least detrimental alternative. The individual traits of the case and the needs of the child involved will be crucial.

6 How Human Rights Can Guide Professional Practice in Emergency Cases

Emergency placements represent an extreme intervention into the right of family life. The national authorities—the CPS, the County Board and the courts—must not exceed their margin of appreciation. National authorities must exercise their discretionary power within the borders of the law. The CPS and the County Boards have to prove why and how the emergency placement is *necessary* to prevent the child from being exposed to serious harm. The European Court underlined in K. and T. vs Finland that national authorities must 'establish that a careful assessment of the impact of the proposed care measure on the [parents] and the children, as well as the possible alternatives to taking the children into public care' are carried out prior to the implementation of such a measure.[14] The European Court sets an ambitious standard here, in the light of the nature of emergency situations and the need for quick action, that does not fit completely well with the Court's own case law, highlighting the duty of the member states to effectively protect children living with serious neglect and abuse.

As a main rule, less interfering alternatives should be considered or tried out prior to an emergency placement, or at least as a part of the judicial control. Important questions are when and for how long preventive measures and network-based interventions should be tried out without risking further harm to the child's health and development. The human rights obligations to effectively protect children exposed to real, present risk for serious harm because of violence, sexual abuse or other forms of serious neglect, must be implemented as well. A thorough assessment of the child's best interests should provide an answer in each case.

Human rights conventions represent the external, judicial limits for the local authorities' investigations, measures, proceedings, and for how they balance the different interests of the parties involved, as well as the single elements of the case facts, while exercising their discretionary power. Like any other public authority, social and child protection services must manage their professional power within the framework of human rights legislation, national law and fundamental principles.

7 Conclusion

The complex tension between the strong interventional nature and stressful character of emergency placements and the necessity of legal regulations which enable such placements to secure effective protection for children at risk, reflects contradicting human rights. The right to respect for family life, the principle of proportionality, the best-interest principle and the right for the individual child to immediate protection from serious and present risks to the child's health and development, do all apply in emergency cases. In balancing all these rights and interests, it follows from the CRC and the ECHR case law that the best interests of the child shall be a paramount consideration, and that public authorities hold a duty to protect children and other vulnerable individuals against harmful experiences that threaten their private life, their physical and psychological integrity, or that expose them to inhuman or degrading treatment. For children in particular, serious violations of their integrity impose a threat to their fundamental right to life and development.

Notes

1. These are Oslo District Court, Bergen District Court, Sarpsborg District Court, Romerike District Court, Gjøvik District Court, Alstadhaug District Court, and Eiker, Modum and Sigdal District Court.
2. Only a few district court decisions are published in the Norwegian judicial database Lovdata.no. No cases concerning emergency orders from the Supreme Court or the Courts of Appeals were found in this database, making district court decisions a relevant source of law.
3. In Norwegian: *legalitetsprinsippet*. The principle has been developed by the Supreme Court, and has obtained constitutional status in national law.
4. See e.g. A. vs UK 1998, paras 20–24. See also Z. and Others vs UK 2001.

5. The term 'neglect' in CRC Article 19 includes physical neglect as well as psychological and emotional neglect.
6. The Norwegian child protection system consists of the municipal Child Protection Services (CPS), the County Board of Child Protection and Social Affairs (henceforth 'the County Board'), the Office for Children, Youth, and Family Affairs (Bufetat) with institution and foster home services. The CPS investigate referrals and decide and implement all voluntary preventive measures, as well as interim emergency care orders. The County Board is a regional, administrative court-like body with similar civil procedural regulations as a district court, and decides all coercive measures.
7. https://www.regjeringen.no/en/dokumenter/the-child-welfare-act/id448398/.
8. K. and T. vs Finland 1994, para. 166
9. K. and T. vs Finland 1994, para. 168.
10. Out of a total of 3492 claims in 2013, 902 of them concerned access rights for parents, 631 claims were concerned with care-order decisions, 491 with foster care placements, 483 with supervision and 317 with emergency placements by CWA section 4–6 (2).
11. I also did a search in the database for published emergency care order decisions and complaints from the County Boards. Out of 86 published emergency order decisions and complaints in 2008–2016, the summaries show that main reasons for emergency placement were: violence (21 cases), sexual abuse (4 cases), drug abuse (16 cases), psychological disorders/problems (7 cases), risk of abduction (2 cases), other forms of neglect (21 cases), not specified in the summary (15 cases).
12. See e.g. A. vs UK 1998, paras 20–24. See also Z. and Others vs UK 2001. The European Court has based its case law on these two cases in later decisions.
13. K. and T. vs Finland 1994, para. 168.
14. K. and T. vs Finland 1994, para. 168 i.f.

References

Baugerud, G. A., & Melinder, A. (2012). Maltreated children's memory of stressful removals from their biological parents. *Applied Cognitive Psychology, 26*(2), 261–270.

Detrick, S. (1999). *A commentary on the United Nations convention on the rights of the child*. Leiden: Martinus Nijhoff Publishers.

Gilbert, N., Parton, N., & Skivenes, M. (2011). *Child protection systems: International trends and orientations*. Oxford: Oxford University Press.

Stang, E. G. (2015). The child's right to protection of family life and private life. In S. Mahmoudi, P. Leviner, A. Kaldal, & K. Lainpelto (Eds.), *Child-friendly justice: A quarter of a century of the UN Convention on the Rights of the Child*. Leiden: Brill/Nijoff.

Melinder, A., Baugerud, G. A., Ovenstad, K. S., & Goodman, G. S. (2013). Children's memories of removal: A test of attachment theory. *Journal of Traumatic Stress, 26*(1), 125–133.

Sandberg, K. (2018). Children's right to protection under the CRC. In A. Falch-Eriksen & E. Backe-Hansen (Eds.), *Human rights in child protection. Implications for professional practice and policy*. London: Palgrave Macmillan.

Storhaug, A. S., & Kojan, B. H. (2017). Emergency out-of-home placements in Norway: Parents' experiences. *Child & Family Social Work, 22*(4), 1407–1414.

Viblemo, T., Gleinsvik, A., Meltevik, S., & Vestergaard, M. (2015). *Organisering, effektivitet og rettssikkerhet: Evaluering av Fylkesnemndene for barnevern og sosiale saker*. Stavanger: Oxford Research.

Open Access This chapter is licensed under the terms of the Creative Commons Attribution 4.0 International License (http://creativecommons.org/licenses/by/4.0/), which permits use, sharing, adaptation, distribution and reproduction in any medium or format, as long as you give appropriate credit to the original author(s) and the source, provide a link to the Creative Commons license and indicate if changes were made.

The images or other third party material in this chapter are included in the chapter's Creative Commons license, unless indicated otherwise in a credit line to the material. If material is not included in the chapter's Creative Commons license and your intended use is not permitted by statutory regulation or exceeds the permitted use, you will need to obtain permission directly from the copyright holder.

9

Rights-Based Practice and Marginalized Children in Child Protection Work

Bente Heggem Kojan and Graham Clifford

1 Marginalization: An Integral Part of the Picture in Child Protection

Marginalization is unavoidable in societies where exchange, distribution and accumulation of goods and services predominantly take place in the market. It follows from this that marginalization as such is not something that agencies and services can avoid, though they can seek to mitigate its negative effects in a variety of ways. When those outside the market are dependent on assistance of different kinds from several agencies, they will be especially vulnerable. The services will themselves, though not necessarily in any deliberate way, be agents of marginalization; they contribute to its often subtle and complex dynamics (Pusic 1972). Marginalization in the perspective Pusic provided is in part a product of services and provisions at the margins of the market that impose criteria and tests for providing help, or even penalties that may incur loss of status or integrity

B. H. Kojan (✉) • G. Clifford
NTNU, Trondheim, Norway
e-mail: bente.h.kojan@ntnu.no

© The Author(s) 2018
A. Falch-Eriksen, E. Backe-Hansen (eds.), *Human Rights in Child Protection*,
https://doi.org/10.1007/978-3-319-94800-3_9

for those who are helped. The economic costs involved are largely met by the state or its agents in an advanced welfare society such as those in Scandinavia. The moral costs fall upon the users of services.

Marginalization affects family life. Families in contact with child protection often have severely deficient social and helping networks and dysfunctional family relations. These tend to be associated with social isolation or poor social integration, not only for parents, but also for their children. To what extent might the implementation of CRC lead to better welfare for children and families who suffer most in terms of marginalization? This is an under-researched question, and important to investigate since it is a characteristic of child protection systems that social inequality as a marginalization generator and child protection intervention rates correlate significantly (Bywaters et al. 2015; Clifford et al. 2015; Kojan 2011). This does not necessarily mean that those with the greatest needs get most help. On the contrary, the least marginalized families seem to be the ones receiving most help (Clifford et al. 2015). Several findings from recent Norwegian research strongly suggest that reform and refocusing have not been sufficiently successful (Clifford et al. 2015; Hennum 2017). This can be naively interpreted as a 'failure' of the services. A more interesting approach is to examine how child protection and other services deal with the normative complexity and ambiguities that attend upon services for children. Welfare services do not operate only on the basis of legal rules and principles. They are embedded in the *mores* of a society that expects that families adopt child-rearing and socialization practices that meet the needs of the knowledge economy.

1.1 Marginalization in Egalitarian Societies

Norwegian Child Protection, as well as that in other Scandinavian countries, has been, at least partly, focused on equality as a goal in an egalitarian social system (Kojan 2011). In England and other Anglophone countries, equality is not really a goal of child protection and the social solidarity aspects of the broad spectrum of social provision have been greatly eroded during the past three decades (Featherstone et al. 2016).

At the same time, child protection systems across the world meet children and families that have much in common in terms of low education and low income, poor housing, and unemployment or at best insecure employment (Bywaters et al. 2015; Kojan and Fauske 2011). Health problems and especially mental health problems are widespread both for children and their parents. A lot of the children have difficulties at school, often from an early age. The families have restricted, attenuated networks and both children and adults are often poorly socially integrated. Family conflicts, often long-standing, affect relations both within and between generations. For instance, a recent Norwegian study showed that multi-challenged families still constitute the largest part of child protection's long-term clientele, comprising around 70 per cent of all families with contact lasting two years or more (Fauske et al. 2009; Clifford et al. 2015). In addition, this has changed very little over time. The socio-economic status and the difficulties children and parents face are the same; what has changed is that many more families are in contact with child protection. We see a greater gap between the favourable circumstances enjoyed by the majority of families and a minority who are marginalized. This has been a clearly apparent trend in Norway as well as in other countries in recent years.

The challenges child protection families and their children have to face do not seem to have changed much since 1990. Nor is there any evidence of a general improvement in the ways these families manage. The help that child protection provides to improve parental care for children living at home (assistance in the home, advice and guidance, and family preservation evidence-based interventions) is most often given to the least marginalized families. The multi-challenged families, in which the risks of poor care and breakdown of care are greater, seldom receive these forms of help. Children in these families often get help designed to provide better social integration (weekends spent in another family, support for leisure activities etc.) but help that might improve care in their own family is not provided (Clifford et al. 2015). Thus, the risks these children are exposed to will largely remain unmitigated as long as they continue to live at home. Such a state of affairs seems regrettable but in its very nature reflects the freedom to interpret children's and families' life circumstances, and decide how to intervene, which helping services at the margin of the market are allowed to do. Helping services within very broad limits are free to decide the terms of service: not even the most rigorous regulation can limit this power, and attempts to regulate it are often bitterly resented.

1.2   Individualization of Social Needs

Some researchers conclude that child protection has become rather one-sidedly preoccupied with parental competence and responsibility, without adequate attention paid to social and other factors that contribute to deprivation and deficient parental care (Christiansen and Hollekim 2018, Chap. 10 in this book; Featherstone et al. 2016; Lonne et al. 2009; Wastell and White 2017). The focus has shifted from family needs to a widespread tendency to expect that parents must themselves manage the risks for children that arise, however difficult the situation they face. Calder (2016) argues that this shift in focus is associated with a rights-based approach, reinforcing an already individualized practice and in effect not compensating for the role of the family in maintaining inequality and marginalization, for instance through not being able to offer their children sufficient help and support with their school work and social integration.

Assessing social needs as risk factors might result in a child protection system that operates in a socially discriminating way with too much attention focused upon marginalized families with serious shortfalls in economic and social capital. Consequently, we might see services and professionals operating at an even greater psychological distance from families and the realities of family life in deprived settings. Child protection is mostly concerned with the safety of children and imposes demands that parents must meet to guarantee their safety, and is not much concerned with help that might enable parents to provide better care (Clifford et al. 2015; Featherstone 2016). Social risk factors associated with marginalization become part of an objectifying calculation of risk. This has led, it is claimed, to a less holistic and contextually situated practice (see Christiansen and Hollekim 2018, Chap. 10 of this book).

2 The Implementation of CRC in Child Protection

For analytic purposes, we will draw a distinction between two kinds of rights in the CRC, applying the work of Onora O'Neill (2013, 2016). Protection rights can be viewed as freedom rights, as for example a right to personal security. It is often easy to see who offends against or restricts such freedoms for children. On the other hand, provision rights can be viewed as welfare rights. To understand who has the duty of securing another's rights to welfare, we have to understand the structure of obligations that underpins such rights. The question, as O'Neill puts it, is 'whose obligation?'

2.1 Freedom Rights and Welfare Rights: Two Sides of the Same Coin

As pointed out above, children and parents in child protection have to deal with the same challenges and difficulties as they have for decades. Further, we argued that CPS and a broader network of services have not succeeded in meeting the needs of those most marginalized. The question is in what ways implementation of CRC can change this situation.

Professional social work in child protection involves securing both children's freedom rights and (to an increasing extent) their welfare rights. Traditionally the question of whether child protection should intervene has been a matter of making children safe, ensuring that they are not exposed to grossly deficient care, neglect, violence or sexual abuse. Child welfare has had the task of preventing actions or gross omissions (usually by the child's parents) that may threaten his or her integrity or development, or represent an immediate threat or a potential for injury in the future. The current framing of child protection is still primarily concerned with protecting children, and lacks a clear focus on social suffering among the families (Featherstone et al. 2016).

However, dealing with welfare issues that affect children and their families should be a central concern for child protection and other helping services for children and families. Inequality strongly correlates with child protection interventions (Bywaters et al. 2015), and might be considered a risk factor for child abuse and neglect. In Norway, for example, protective actions due to deficient care, neglect, violence or sexual abuse have occurred in a stable proportion of child protection cases during the last three decades (Statistics Norway 2015). So these problems cannot account for the greatly increased numbers of children and families who receive assistance or intervention from CPS that we have seen since the mid-1990s.

In practice, it can be quite difficult always to draw robust distinctions between protection rights and welfare rights in child protection. At an empirical level we can see that child protection to an increasing extent intervenes in families, not because there is evidence that parents actively injure their children (Clifford et al. 2015) and by so doing deprive them of their freedom rights. Child welfare protection tends to be increasingly concerned that someone should actively work for and support a child's development. Nowadays, however, these trends are attended by a good deal of confusion. We can encounter statements that equate non-fulfilment of children's welfare rights with active deprivation of rights on the part of parents. There is a tendency to move from claims of preventability (that is the notion that children run developmental risks) to a preventive imperative (the notion that developmental risks warrant intervention if the family is unable to eliminate them).

2.2 Active Investment in Children

The striking growth in intervention rates in child protection might be seen as a consequence of social changes that affect families in a society promoting a public health approach in most welfare services, including child protection. Child protection has moved forward into a broader mandate and its development reflects social policies focusing on social investments in children. In this context child protection may have changed its reference from saving children from harm and serious abuse (protection) to concern about 'failing' lives and lifestyles (welfare).

Wyn and White (1997) described trends in western societies that have led to much greater attention being paid to children's functioning in school, their mental health, and problems that may indicate family difficulties or care deficits. The underlying trend is the emergence of the knowledge economy and the demands this makes with respect to child development, socialization and education. CPS are no longer only concerned with child abuse and neglect or children with serious behavioural problems. The services have been drawn into the orbit of the educational and health and welfare services where early intervention to secure optimal development and educational attainment for children with difficulties has become a major trend in policy (Stang 2007).

This turn toward active investment in children and a focus on welfare rights has profoundly affected child protection, not least seen in terms of expectations directed at the service, a multiplication of its tasks, and competing priorities within child protection's overall remit (Munro 2011). Scientific progress in the welfare disciplines (medicine, psychology, psychiatry, social work, education) nowadays pulls child protection in different directions, at the same time that we see that the service's horizon (in terms of research and practice developments) becomes ever broader.

3 Can the Implementation of CRC in Professional Child Protection Work Improve the Lives of the Most Marginalized Children and Families?

How might the CRC be applied to deal with the many deprivations and inequalities, spoiled life chances and disadvantages suffered by children in child protection? The answer is not too clear, and the question concerns what a broad range of services, and not only the CPS system, should offer to marginalized children and families. CRC contains various articles concerning children's welfare rights and the responsibility of the state in supporting parents' efforts to secure such rights: Articles 26 (social security), 27 (adequate standard of living), 28, 29 (right to education) and 31 (leisure, play and culture).

There is certainly no magic formula for how child protection can deal with the types of marginalization that children and parents struggle with.

A first step, however, is to realize that marginalization, leading to concrete obstacles when it comes to fulfilling all these rights properly, is a relevant issue for the challenges faced by parents and children in contact with child protection on an everyday basis. Social workers will have to understand this, and incorporate this understanding in their professional approach to children's situation and the quality of care they receive. Child protection is based both on the freedom rights and the welfare rights which are both embedded in the CRC, as mentioned above. Acknowledging this will provide a more holistic approach to children's and parents' situation. Featherstone (2016) argues that protecting children and promoting their welfare means that professionals need to reframe their approach. They must pay attention to the environments and contexts in which children live; families, school and leisure time.

4 School: One of the Most Important Generators of Marginalization

4.1 Education in the Knowledge Society

Poor educational attainment is often seen as a potential generator for marginalization, creating a foundation for exclusion from the labour market, and poor health and social problems in the knowledge economy (Frønes and Strømme 2010; Vinnerljung et al. 2010). It is important to examine how children in contact with child protection manage at school, the more so because they so often face serious challenges in other respects, such as family, health, social networks and integration. It is well documented that these children, whether living at home or after placement, have difficulties associated with completing schooling at all levels (Iversen et al. 2010; Forsman and Vinnerljung 2012; Skilbred and Iversen 2014; Dæhlen 2015; Valset 2014; Madsen and Backe-Hansen 2015). Official statistics also show that some children in contact with child protection need more time to complete their education (Backe-Hansen et al. 2014). Needless to say, this is a matter of considerable concern, since uncompleted education, and at whatever level, has a negative effect upon life chances. Young adults formerly in contact with child protection are over-represented among the unemployed, and receive social security and income support much more frequently than their peers (Clausen and Kristofersen 2008; Backe-Hansen et al. 2014).

Parents in contact with child protection have very often themselves had challenges at school, and many will not have completed secondary or even primary school (Clifford et al. 2015; Fauske et al. 2009). Their children often have a family background with poor network potential vis-à-vis employment and employers, or a lack of bridging social capital (Kojan and Fauske 2011). As well, they are much more likely than their peers to drop out of schooling or employment, and to a greater extent risk long-term dependence on social assistance. Research on non-completion of schooling at upper secondary level has shown that social factors, poor networks and mental health difficulties exert a clear negative effect, hindering completion of schooling and access to the labour market for many (Thrana et al. 2009). Of course, drop-out at upper secondary level is no absolute barrier to employment, but we have to recognize that many child protection children lack the network facilitation and support that could compensate for lack of formal qualifications. For instance, Collin-Hansen (2008) discussed how the development of CPS has led to changes in how responsibility for children's education is perceived. The school is expected to support upbringing and socialization on the part of the family. Parents are expected to support the aims and approaches of the educational system. If some parents are tacitly excluded from this community of interest, this will only serve to reproduce and reinforce marginalization.

4.2 How Can the CRC Guide Professional Practice in Meeting the Needs of Marginalized Children's' Situation in School?

Education is an example of how marginalization moves across sectors within state systems, and child protection must recognize these traits. However, child protection plays an ambiguous role in respect of children's education. This is especially evident in the case of the many children who receive various forms of help while living at home (Collin-Hansen

2008; Kojan and Thrana 2017). Marginalization affects family life at an everyday level and impacts upon children's daily lives. In practical terms (and in the theoretical terms provided by O'Neill) the first question is always that of who is obligated to secure welfare rights. The principle that parents are obligated to manage situations to secure welfare rights for their children is all well and good. But can marginalized parents reasonably be expected to provide adequate support and help for their children in school, particularly if the children have various learning problems? How can the CRC guide professional CPS practice in meeting the needs of marginalized children's situation in school? Article 28 of the CRC states that '*States Parties recognize the right of the child to education, and with a view to achieving this right progressively and on the basis of equal opportunity.*' This right concerns primary education, and also requires that different forms of secondary and higher education are available and accessible to every child according to their capacity.

Below we delineate four areas that are relevant in the sense that they can indicate what roles child protection might have in following children up at school, and in securing the rights of CPS children to access to education on a basis of equal opportunity. These recommendations are based on findings from an innovation study dealing with CPS children living at home (Kojan and Thrana 2017). Ten children in contact with CPS were followed for a school year.

4.3 Child Protection Workers Need Knowledge of Children's Situation at School

The study showed that CPS professionals had scant knowledge of children's situation in school. There was a one-sided approach focused on the home and family, and child protection's understanding of the children's lives was incomplete and, contextually speaking, quite deficient. Child protection risked putting too much emphasis on parents as the source of children's difficulties. To deal with the complexity of marginalizing factors affecting children, it seems important that child protection adopts a broad theoretical base in its inquiries about how children are cared for. Children's needs are to be understood as something broader than only being a matter of relationships within the family. That is after all the import of the shift toward an overlapping and sharing of responsibility for upbringing and socialization, as described by Collin-Hansen (2008). School seen as a social setting is important for children. They spend much of their time there, and an appreciation of their school situation ought to be part of any child protection investigation.

This does not (and this is an important point) mean that CPS should collect information directly from school in all investigations. CPS should set out to tell a different story (Featherstone et al. 2016). Implementing Article 28 requires an exploration of the school setting for the particular child. Child and parents should be asked about this. How does the child manage in particular subjects? Does she or he enjoy school, or not? What does he or she do in breaks between lessons? Who does he or she play with? Has he or she been excluded or bullied? How do parents see their contact with the school? Are they satisfied?

4.4 Child Protection Workers Can Take the Initiative in Defining Responsibilities

The boundaries between school and child protection are not clear in practice. The professionals involved can devote a lot of time to obtaining a shared understanding of how supports and intervention are to be framed and organized (Kojan and Thrana 2017). But we need an effective and operationally useful approach to sharing and assigning responsibility when children meet academic and social challenges at school. Children do not have the time to wait for the resolution of professional dilemmas, and they pay a price when things do not work properly and practical arrangements are not in place. CPS has of course an especially important responsibility in securing appropriate schooling for children in care. But the children living at home who are seen to be at risk need help too. Their parents often need support in their contact with school.

Parents with the most complex problems often wanted CPS to involve itself more (Clifford et al. 2015). One major consideration here is that most parents are very concerned and worried about their children, and they often feel unable to deal with the children's difficulties. They feel that child protection is actually committed to the child's best interests, even though they experience many setbacks and disappointments in their relations with the service. Parents in CPS are very often alarmed and anxious and feel unable to help their children. They trust child protection, if not to the bitter end, at least through long trials and tribulations. Some of them do not trust school and health services, these being seen as difficult to relate to, and likely to discriminate against their children. Parents see child protection as a partner in the sense that persuasion and negotiation are possible even if time-consuming and frustrating. They are acutely conscious of social difficulties and problems their children may encounter at school, and correspondingly preoccupied with the social advantages that can be gained by children through appropriate help. An expectation of fairness is the guiding principle for parents' efforts on behalf of their child, that she or he should have a chance, and not be excluded or discriminated, and as far as possible treated like other children. However, rights to help are not part of parents' perception of the service; as they see it everything has to be negotiated and struggled for (Clifford et al. 2015).

4.5 More Help Directed at the School Situation of CPS Children Living at Home

In Norway, CPS provide relatively few measures aimed at improving children's situation at school (Statistics Norway 2017). Out of 83,970 measures provided by CPS in 2016, only 536 were designed to enhance the child's development relating to education or employment. These numbers illustrate that measures in school are not the main domain of child protection. However, child protection does provide services for some children in cooperation with school, which are not shown in the child protection statistics.

Nevertheless, a review of the literature (Seeberg et al. 2013) shows that some academic approaches can help children in their social adjustment in school, and so enhance the likelihood of them completing their schooling. As we have shown above, children and families in CPS, especially the long-term clientele, have complex difficulties that reflect marginalization in a variety of arenas. On the one hand, this might imply a complexity of services, supports and interventions. On the other hand, this might lead to too elaborate and complex services, which could be avoided by using simpler devices, such as tutoring, mentoring, homework assistance and shared diary for school and home. Child protection does not need to be responsible for such forms of help, but should be more aware of children's situation at school and an initiator of practical and useful supports and interventions that can help children at school, whatever complex problems there may be that also involve the home. We need more knowledge about how CPS experience their own responsibilities to implement children's rights to education.

4.6 Recognize that Children in CPS Have Ability and Potential

A challenge associated with child protection's interest in the education of CPS children is that there have been persistently negative views about these children's capacities and abilities (Bufdir 2014). Article 28 in CRC uses the term *capacity*. An important aspect of professional work here is to acknowledge that CPS children have the same capacity to complete their education as other children, given real equality of opportunity. Vinnerljung and Hjern (2011) found that poor school performance among children placed outside the family was not due to weaker cognitive capacity than the child population as a whole, but rather school difficulties related to working memory. This can be related to burdens and anxieties that prevail when child-rearing is plagued by uncertainty and unpredictability.

5 Conclusion

A series of studies from many countries and over time has shown the extent of marginalization among child protection families. The question that has to be asked is, Who is responsible for this marginalization? Have parents denied children their rights because they have insecure employment, are without higher education and training, or as immigrants have not acquired cultural and linguistic competence? Or are there political constraints? Do we in effect deny children their rights because a reasonable distribution of goods and opportunities in society has not been arranged? O'Neill maintains that it is impossible to decide who has denied subjects their welfare rights unless there is a clearly established obligation for someone to see that the rights are observed. The question of rights is a matter of social order and duty, a social issue.

Our argument here has been that child protection services that examines the child's situation in school will have a better insight into what the child and its parents might need in the form of support and intervention. There will be a better grasp of the child's situation and a better chance of working with family and child. Of course, this will not always be easy. In such work, responsibilities have to be defined and assigned early on. Expectations relating to what other agencies might provide have to be adjusted to realities at the local level. If Article 28 in the CRC is to be taken seriously in child protection, the traditional boundaries whereby child protection is assigned what pertains to the home and family, while schooling remains 'the school's business', will have to be challenged to a much greater extent than we see today. At the same time we have pointed out that increased attention paid to children's situation in school will not in itself enable us to deal with complex problems related to marginalization. In some sense, the right to education is an approach that individualizes social problems, without enough attention paid to the societal causes of marginalization. In contemporary social policies there is a strong emphasis on education or work as a solution to socio-economic marginalization; everyone can have a share in society if their individual agency is improved (Davies 2015).

A stronger emphasis on rights will not necessarily lead to better child protection for children and families who suffer the most complex problems. The rights discourse can also reinforce and reproduce an already individualized, privatized responsibility for children's development, transferring obligations from the state to marginalized parents. This leads to a rights paradox: to secure welfare and development for children, marginalized parents are blamed. This can, or perhaps already does, create an ethos in which the importance of social conditions in shaping family problems and need for welfare is downplayed.

In a broader perspective, we have to ask whether a more trenchant rights-based approach would improve equality of opportunity for children in CPS. There is of course a danger that only rhetoric will change without any progress on the vital issue of who is obligated to help marginalized children and families. Nevertheless, CRC might help us to rethink the role of child protection in taking the welfare needs of children and families seriously, for example in relation to the situation of the child in school.

References

Backe-Hansen, E., Madsen, C., Kristoffersen, L. B. & Hvinden, B. (2014). *Barnevern i Norge 1990–2010. En longitudinell studie. NOVA Rapport 9/14.* Oslo: NOVA.
Bufdir. (2014). *Skolerapport. Hvordan bedre skoleresultatene og utdanningssituasjonen for barn og unge i barnevernet.* Oslo: Bufdir.
Bywaters, P., Brady, G., Sparks, T., Bos, E., Bunting, L., Daniel, B., Featherstone, B., Morris, K., & Scourfield, J. (2015). Exploring inequities in child welfare and child protection services: Explaining the inverse intervention law. *Children and Youth Services, 57*, 98–105.
Calder, G. (2016). *How inequality runs in families.* Bristol: Policy Press.
Clausen, S.-E., & Kristofersen, L. B. (2008). *Barnevernsklienter i Norge 1990–2005: en longitudinell studie.* Oslo: NOVA.
Clifford, G., Fauske, H., Lichtwarck, W., & Marthinsen, E. (2015). *Minst hjelp til de som trenger det mest? NF-rapport 6.* Bodø: Nordlandsforskning.
Collin-Hansen, R. (2008). *Barnets rett til opplæring og til vern mot marginalisering i skolen.* PhD dissertation. Bergen: University of Bergen.
Dæhlen, M. (2015). School performance and completion of upper secondary school in the child welfare population in Norway. *Nordic Social Work Research, 5*, 244–261. https://doi.org/10.1080/2156857X.2015.104201.
Davies, W. (2015). *The happiness industry: How the government and big business sold us well-being.* London: Verso.
Fauske, H., Clifford, G., Lichtwarck, W., Marthinsen, E., Kojan, B. H., & Willumsen, E. (2009). *Det Nye barnevernet: et forsknings- og utviklingsprosjekt i Barnevernet. Barnevernet på ny kurs? Sluttrapport fase 1.* Bodø: Nordlandsforskning.
Featherstone, B. (2016). Telling different stories about poverty, inequality, child abuse and neglect. *Families, Relationships and Societies, 5*, 147–153. https://doi.org/10.1332/204674316X14540714620085.

Featherstone, B., White, S., & Morris, K. (2016). *Re-imagining child protection: Towards humane social work with families.* Bristol: Policy Press.

Forsman, H., & Vinnerljung, B. (2012). Interventions aiming to improve school achievements of children in out-of-home care: A scoping review. *Children and Youth Services Review, 34,* 1084–1091.

Frønes, I., & Strömme, H. (2010). *Risiko og marginalisering.* Oslo: Gyldendal.

Hennum, N. (2017). The Norwegian child protection services in stormy weather. *Critical and radical social work. An international journal, 5*(3), 319–334. https://doi.org/10.1332/204986017X15029695863676.

Iversen, A. C., Hetland, H., Havik, T., & Stormark, K. M. (2010). Learning difficulties and academic competence among children in contact with the child welfare system. *Child & Family Social Work, 15*(3), 307–314. https://doi.org/10.1111/j.13652–206.2009.00672.x.

Kojan, B. H. (2011). *Klasseblikk på et barnevern i vekst.* PhD dissertation. Trondheim: NTNU.

Kojan, B. H., & Fauske, H. (2011). Et klasseperspektiv på barnevernets familier. *Tidsskrift for velferdsforskning, 14*(2), 95–109.

Kojan, B. H., & Thrana, H. M. (2017). *Aktiv støtte til hjemmeboende barnevernsbarn i skolen.* Trondheim: NTNU, Institutt for sosialt arbeid.

Lonne, B., Parton, N., Thompson, J., & Harries, M. (2009). *Reforming child protection.* Oxon.: Routledge.

Madsen, C., & Backe-Hansen, E. (2015). Barn og unge som mottok hjelpetiltak 1993–2010. In Ø. Christiansen et al. (Eds.), *Forskningskunnskap om barnevernets hjelpetiltak.* Bergen: Uni Research Helse, RKBU Vest.

Munroe, E. (2011). *Munro review of child protection: Final report.* London: DfE.

O'Neill, O. (2013). Session 4—Reason and evidence in ethics. Science, reasons and normativity. *European Review, 21,* 94–99.

O'Neill, O. (2016). *Justice across boundaries. Whose obligations?* Cambridge: Cambridge University Press.

Pusic, E. (1972). *Social welfare and social development.* Berlin: Walter de Gruyter & Co.

Seeberg, M. L., Winsvold, A., & Sverdrup, S. (2013). *Skoleresultater og utdanningssituasjon for barn i barnevernet. En kunnskapsoversikt.* Oslo: NOVA.

Skilbred, D., & Iversen, A. C. (2014). Unge voksne som har bodd i fosterhjem og tatt høyere utdanning: Suksessfaktorer? *Norges Barnevern, 4,* 161–176.

Stang, E. G. (2007). *Det er barnets sak. Barnets rettsstilling i sak om hjelpetiltak etter barnevernloven § 4–4.* Oslo: Universitetsforlaget.

Statistics Norway. (2015). *Tabell 1. Meldingar til barnevernet, etter konklusjon, innhald i meldinga, kven som melde saka og alder. Statistikkbanken.* Oslo: SSB.

Statistics Norway. (2017). *Measures from the child welfare services per 31 December, by measure.* Retrieved 21 February 2018 from http://www.ssb.no/en/sosiale-forhold-og-kriminalitet/statistikker/barneverng/aar

Thrana, H. M., Anvik, C., Bliksvær, T., & Handegård, T. L. (2009). *Hverdagsliv og drømmer: for unge som står utenfor arbeid og skole.* Bodø: Nordlandsforskning.

Valset, K. (2014). Ungdom utsatt for omsorgssvikt—hvordan presterer de på skolen? In E. Backe-Hansen, C. Madsen, L. B. Kristoffersen, & B. Hvinden (Eds.), *Barnevern i Norge 1990–2010. En longitudinell studie* (pp. 127–155). Oslo: NOVA.

Vinnerljung, B., Berlin, M., & Hjern, A. (2010). Skolbetyg, utbildning og risker for ogynnsam utveckling hos barn. In *Socialstyrelsen Social Rapport* (pp. 227–276). Stockholm: Socialstyrelsen.

Vinnerljung, B., & Hjern, A. (2011). Cognitive, educational and self-support outcomes of long-term foster care versus adoption. A Swedish national cohort study. *Children and Youth Services Review, 33*, 1902–1910.

Wastell, D., & White, S. (2017). *Blinded by science. The social implications of epigenetics and neuroscience.* Bristol: Policy Press.

Wyn, J., & White, R. (1997). *Rethinking youth.* London: SAGE Publications.

Open Access This chapter is licensed under the terms of the Creative Commons Attribution 4.0 International License (http://creativecommons.org/licenses/by/4.0/), which permits use, sharing, adaptation, distribution and reproduction in any medium or format, as long as you give appropriate credit to the original author(s) and the source, provide a link to the Creative Commons license and indicate if changes were made.

The images or other third party material in this chapter are included in the chapter's Creative Commons license, unless indicated otherwise in a credit line to the material. If material is not included in the chapter's Creative Commons license and your intended use is not permitted by statutory regulation or exceeds the permitted use, you will need to obtain permission directly from the copyright holder.

10

In-home Services: A Rights-Based Professional Practice Meets Children's and Families' Needs

Øivin Christiansen and Ragnhild Hollekim

1 Introduction

The Convention on the Rights of the Child (CRC) states that children are individual rights holders. Simultaneously, the Convention underlines that the family has the primary rights and duties to care for children and secure their well-being and positive development. According to the Convention, the role of state authorities is to protect children against maltreatment. Furthermore, state authorities have a preventive and supportive role, which is relevant at an early stage, before children experience maltreatment and severe risk within the confines of the family. When and under what kind of circumstances this supportive responsibility

---

Ø. Christiansen (✉)
Uni Research Health, Bergen, Norway
e-mail: oich@norceresearch.no

R. Hollekim
University of Bergen, Bergen, Norway
e-mail: ragnhild.hollekim@uib.no

materializes varies between nation states. Variations also exist concerning the mandate and role assigned to child welfare services (CWS) in this regard.

The overarching aim of this chapter is to discuss how relevant principles of the CRC inform and challenge the practice of professionals engaged in CWS preventive in-home measures. We explore the implications of several rights included in the CRC for child welfare professionals' work with children's needs within the family context. Further, we identify and discuss characteristics of current practice in relation to the CRC. The discussion centres on the threefold relationship between the child, the parents and the state and includes the following questions: Where to draw the line or place the threshold for public intervention in family life? How to realize children's rights to services when their parents do not give consent? What can explain and what are the consequences when support to children is primarily achieved through targeting parents?

In the CWS context, these questions concern the praxis with in-home measures aiming to provide necessary support for vulnerable children, prevent escalating problems in the family, and thereby prevent out-of-home placements. In-home services may entail a variety of measures, such as parent counselling, contact families and support persons for children, respite care, economical and practical support and leisure activities (Pösö et al. 2014; Christiansen et al. 2015). Norwegian policy and practice serve as examples to illuminate issues that are relevant in most jurisdictions.

1.1 The Relevance of the CRC to Professional Practice with In-home Services

The CRC clearly states the importance of (a) the family in children's lives and (b) the state's obligation to first and foremost provide support and assistance in the family context (e.g., Art. 18). According to Article 19, state parties shall take all appropriate actions to ensure that children receive necessary protection from abuse and neglect while in the care of parents/legal guardians. Only when children, in their best interests, cannot remain in their family environment shall out-of-home care be considered (CRC Art. 20). Article 3, where a superior value of the best interest of the child is incorporated, also underlines a need to take into account and respect parents' rights and duties when appropriate legislative and administrative measures are to be taken. Finally, CRC Article 16 ensures children's own right to protection from 'arbitrary or unlawful interference with his or her privacy'. This is a partner paragraph to the European Convention for the Protection of Human Rights and Fundamental Freedoms (ECHR) Article 8, which also underlines a superior value of respect for privacy and family life. Consequently, an overarching point of departure for rights-based professional work with children and families is assisting children and families. The importance of the family and biological bonds, a principle of legality and the least intrusive measure, as well as the value of voluntariness and participation, all underpin the predominant value of in-home measures or help within the family context.

Domestic law will in more detail guide how relevant rights for children can be implemented in professional social work with children and parents. Important services for children and families can be organized in different ways and by different institutions across countries. In Norway, in-home welfare and protective services for children are mainly regulated through the Child Welfare Act (CWA) § 4-4 'Assistance for children and families with children'. There has been an adjustment of various provisions in this law to coordinate it with main principles within the CRC. In-home measures shall be guided by the best interests of the child; services shall be provided in cooperation with the child's parents; children themselves shall be heard; and all services and interventions shall follow the principle of 'the least intrusive measure' (CWA §§ 4-1, 3-2, 4-3). Assistance and interventions offered shall be adjusted to individual needs and be adequate and of good quality.

Main challenges for professional rights-based in-home work concern how to, in context, navigate and negotiate sometimes disparate yet equally valued principles in the CRC. These same principles and built-in tensions are typically also part of domestic law. For example, while in-home measures are always to be guided by respect for the individual child's own rights and interests, measures shall at the same time help children in ways that also strengthen parents' rights, responsibilities and abilities to care for their children. The challenges for professionals are particularly related to situations where there is a conflict of interests or disagreement between service providers and parents concerning the best interests of the child.

2   When Does the State's Responsibility for Providing Services Occur?

Discussions of CWS in society—their role, mandate and areas of responsibility—concern how the relationship between the child, the family and the state is weighed and balanced. Numerous researchers have described different ways these relations have changed over time and differ between national and cultural contexts (e.g., Ericsson 1996; Falch-Eriksen 2012; Fernandez 2014; Parton and Reid 2017). As a starting point to explore the implications of the CRC for the intervention level and scope of child welfare engagement in children's and families' lives, we turn to Fox Harding (1997), who is often referred to in this respect. From a British context, she has outlined four perspectives that historically and in different ways have influenced child welfare policy and practice. The perspectives are, however, not only interesting as part of 'story telling'. They can even today be spotted as parallel undertones when CWS's decisions and professional practices are debated:

- laissez-faire and patriarchy;
- state paternalism and child protection;
- the modern defence of the birth family and parent's rights;
- children's rights and child liberation.

The four perspectives have in some respects emerged as reactions to one another. In this 'pattern of reactions', one can observe a pendulum, alternating between emphasizing the importance of a parent's perspective and a child's perspective in child welfare and protection work. *The laissez-faire and patriarchy* perspective implies that interventions in the family's private sphere from the side of public authorities should be limited to a minimum. This is the best way to show respect for parents' own particular responsibility, further underlining a notion that biological parents' care is superior for children. Only in extraordinarily serious cases shall child welfare authorities intervene.

State paternalism and child protection can be seen as the political and professional response to the (re)discovery of child abuse. Confidence in parents' ability to care well for their children has been replaced by 'a readiness to act', following notions that children are very much 'at risk' in the family sphere. For this reason, children need the vigilance and protection of relevant state authorities.

Fox Harding (1997) calls attention to the fact that this perspective may overlook the social situation such families often live in and the fact that child abuse and neglect must be understood as a consequence of various structural burdens and inequalities such as poverty and marginalization. This comprehension is therefore the point of departure for the third perspective listed here*: The modern defence of the birth family and parent's rights* (Lonne et al. 2016). Here, the value of relational ties between children and parents is underlined. Relevant state authorities shall neither choose a laissez-faire nor a paternalistic stand towards the family. However, they are expected to use an actively supporting manner in ways that increase the prospects of keeping the family intact in spite of various burdens. Families can be reunified even if at one point a temporary break-up was inevitable. In other words, there is a strong incentive in this perspective to establish large-scale in-home measures and services for vulnerable families.

As already suggested, the two perspectives that *state paternalism and child protection* and *children's rights and child liberation* have in common are that they both challenge a notion that children and parents always share common interests. However, there are clear divergences between the perspectives. State paternalism and child protection express a paternalistic view, emphasizing the child's need for protection. Children are perceived as objects and as victims of parental maltreatment. Children's rights and child liberation, on the other hand, highlight the value of children's dignity and children's position as individual subjects of rights. Further, in this perspective, protecting children's safety and development can only be realized when children are given a voice and an opportunity to express their own framing of their particular situations and needs.

2.1 The Threshold for CWS Involvement

The immediate assumption is that the children's rights and child liberation perspectives resonate with the United Nations CRC. However, how unambiguous is this parallel? Furthermore, does the CRC give any guidance for our considerations about when the responsibility of state authorities occurs with regard to securing children's well-being and engaging in the way parents care for their children?

When we address the specific role of child welfare authorities, our attention is directed to the CRC's declarations about the children's right to protection and especially how this is expressed in Article 19. The wording in Article 19 indicates that children's right to protection is at stake when their safety, well-being and development are seriously threatened due to violence or neglect. Article 19 para. 1 lists several forms of violence, both physical and mental, using concepts such as abuse, neglect and maltreatment. In their General Comment (GC) no. 13 from 2011, the Committee on the Rights of the Child has outlined a guide to all state parties on how to understand their obligations according to Article 19. The title is 'The right of the child to freedom from all forms of violence.' However, this text provides a broader and more comprehensive understanding of the concept 'violence'. This is especially the fact with regard to psychological and emotional neglect, which includes 'lack of any emotional support and love, chronic inattention to the child, caregivers being "psychologically unavailable" by overlooking young children's cues and signals, and exposure to intimate partner violence, drug or alcohol abuse' (GC no. 13, p. 9).

CRC promotes a holistic approach concerning state parties' responsibility for children (GC no. 13, p. 24). Further, it suggests that children's well-being is threatened not only by obvious and dramatic incidents of violence, abuse and maltreatment (children at risk) but also by deficiencies in the ongoing day-to-day interaction between the child and his or her carers, as well as between children's and parents' relationship to the wider society (children in need). This understanding represents an incentive to all public authorities to offer early help and a rather low threshold for supportive services and measures (see Chap. 9 for discussions on marginalization).

Norway may serve as an example of how the Nordic and other European welfare states have attempted to realize an early intervention and low threshold approach (Pösö et al. 2014). This concerns general services to all children and their families as well as the way CWS are designed and organized. Over the last decades, the number of children aged 0–17 receiving any kind of measures from CWS in Norway has increased gradually, from 20 per 1000 in 1996 to 30 per 1000 in 2016. According to national statistics, approximately one in ten children will receive at least one intervention from the CWS before they reach the age of 18, primarily in-home measures. This trend is definitely a result of political priorities 25 years ago, at the time when the current Child Welfare Act was implemented. Compared to the former act from the 1950s, the 1992 Act changed the concepts from Child Protection to Child Welfare Services, and lowered the eligibility threshold for assistance, all with the intention of strengthening the early intervention approach.

This policy and practice are recognized in a study where CWS workers reported the reasons why they provided in-home services to 245 children and their families (Christiansen et al. 2015). The findings demonstrated a large variety of problematic factors, and the majority of the children experienced a mix of such situations, as Table 10.1 illustrates.

Table 10.1 Reasons for providing in-home measures

Reasons related to parental care	%
Physical abuse	6
Sexual abuse	1
Psychological or emotional maltreatment	11
Neglect	8
Disciplinary problems	53
Mental health problems/substance abuse	43
Domestic conflicts/violence	38
Parent stress, exhausted, economic problems, lack of supporting network	53
Factors related to the child	%
Behavioural problems	21
Emotional problems	34
School-related problems: academic or social	32

$N = 245$

Supplemented with data on socio-demographic conditions, the reasons for offering services indicate that the recipients of in-home services are a heterogeneous but vulnerable group. Child neglect and abuse are recognized but constitute a minority of the causes for interventions. Instead, various combinations of parenting problems, mental health problems among parents and/or children, parental conflicts, challenges in school, a lack of supportive networks and financial difficulties, all trigger an intervention. These factors affect the children's daily care, well-being and development. Further, they entail deficient conditions and limited participative and coping possibilities for the children and may consequently lead to marginalization (Pelton 2015).

As indicated above, such a variety of factors may justify protection and support and resonate with the CRC. However, related to Fox Harding's perspectives, this (low threshold) approach corresponds as much to the modern defence of family perspective as to the children's rights perspective. Gilbert (1997) made comparative assessments of different national child protection systems and found that Norway and other Nordic countries operated according to a family service orientation. This description was applied in contrast to a child protection orientation represented by Anglo-American countries with parallels to Fox Harding's state paternalism perspective.

However, in their updated book, Gilbert et al. (2011) indicate that a much more complex landscape of perspectives has emerged recently both within and between different nations. This includes the addition of a 'child focused orientation' to the child protection and the family service perspectives (p. 252).

In Norway, we recognize a tendency towards greater complexity, as well. Several professionals, researchers and politicians have raised the question of whether the continually expanding family service approach has come at the expense of attention to and good quality follow-up of the most vulnerable children, especially children and young persons in public care (NOU 2016:16). Consequently, suggestions about the possibility of limiting the scope for CWS engagement has been raised.

In child protection-oriented countries, one can observe an opposite trend. There is a movement motivated from an increased acknowledgement of the fact that referrals to CWS concern children who more often suffer from diverse consequences of their families' living conditions than from incidents of actual abuse or maltreatment (Featherstone et al. 2016; Trocmé et al. 2014). The result is several initiatives to develop 'differential responses' in CWS making them capable to respond more adequately to the different kinds of problems, risks and needs children live with (Hughes et al. 2013). However, Featherstone and colleagues (2015) claim that the overriding ideology and practice still conform to risk investigation through 'child abuse lines'.

In a comparative study of child protection policy in five European countries, Spratt et al. (2015) found that despite differences in how the relationship between the state and the family is balanced, the countries shared a common ground of understanding concerning factors and conditions that are respectively harmful or supportive to children. Further, they shared a double mandate for the child protection system, including both support to families and intervention to protect children at risk. According to Spratt et al. (2015), this approach reflects values and rights enriched within the CRC (p. 1509).

3 Realizing Children's Rights to Services

For some decades, two distinct and parallel development trends have been present in the child welfare field. Both trends are of importance for realizing children's rights to adapted services. First, it has been continuously questioned whether children, in reality, do fully benefit from their status as individual subjects of rights. In a Norwegian context, this question has particularly been raised in relation to children's individual rights to services in the family context. Second, there has been a general development where child welfare in-home measures have become 'equal' to measures involving guiding and advising parents. In this chapter, we will discuss in more detail (a) children's individual right to services when parents do not give their consent and (b) targeting parents to secure children's individual right to adapted help and development. Illustrative examples of these development trends are derived from a Norwegian context.

3.1 Individual Rights to Services When Parents Do Not Give Their Consent

According to the current Norwegian CWA, while §4-4 in many ways satisfies demands put on a 'rights provision', one cannot speak of an unconditional right for children to in-home measures (Høstmælingen et al. 2016). At present, the state's duty to provide in-home measures (with a few exceptions rarely practised) is restricted by a need for consent from the parents, as well as from the children themselves if they have turned 15 years of age. This has led to at least three particular concerns of relevance for rights-based services for children. First, there is a concern that some children may not receive the help they need when they need it and that some groups of children do not enjoy the necessary help and protection (cf. CRC §§ 3 and 19). Second, lack of early and adapted intervention may ultimately result in more intrusive and radical measures, a consequence that conflicts with key guiding principles in the CRC. For instance, the Committee on the Rights of the Child has repeatedly commented on extensive use of out-of-home placements in their reports to Norway, urging more focus on children's rights to early help and intervention and efforts targeting children's needs within the family context. Third, there has been a concern that the voluntary aspect of in-home measures is being challenged or is in practice set aside. Parents may in some cases experience the use of 'concealed force', in the sense that they feel pressured to accept various in-home measures to avoid a situation where the child may otherwise be taken into care.

To address these concerns, we have in Norway seen a step-by-step move towards further acknowledgement of children as individual rights holders. In April 2016, new regulations were adopted that broaden the possibility to impose in-home measures against the will of the parents (BLD 2015). This regulation of the law strengthens children's individual right to services in the family context. It aims to secure early and adapted help and thereby also avoid more radical measures at a later stage. In March 2018 the National Parliament unanimously passed a bill declaring that children are granted 'legal claim' to necessary services. An important argument was that 'legal claim' on the part of the child means a harmonization with welfare rights in general. Welfare services have increasingly become rights-based and provided for by law. However, children have in general been left with a weaker position compared to adults. Subsequently, an Official Norwegian Report (NOU 2016, p. 16) proposed to strengthen children's participation rights by giving them the rights of a party to a case at the age of 12, as opposed to the age of 15 according to current law.

Granting children their own legal claims to necessary services may strengthen the contract between the state and the individual child. It increases the state's responsibility to secure that (a) children's rights are realized and (b) important rights are not challenged and breached, and consequently, it leads to a more active and engaged state in family matters. A legal claim to services has consequences for professional social work with vulnerable children and their families as well. First, legal claims on the part of the child make the image of an independent and participating child both more visible and more prominent (Hollekim et al. 2016, pp. 58, 59). This will further embrace an increased ability to pursue one's interests (Archard 2004). In many cases, legal claims for children will serve as a premise to secure important needs and interests in a more adapted and sustainable manner, as well as at an earlier stage. However, a development where individual rights for children too strictly guide services may also involve challenges for professional practice. In the worst case, interventions targeting the individual child against the parents' wishes may undermine the foundation of and context in which the child needs to develop well. As a narrowly guiding perspective, children may appear as 'an island in the family'. Professionals may more easily overlook 'the dependent, social and inter-acting child, who creates meaning and competence in context and in relation to close others' (Ulvik 2009, p. 1150).

Likewise, more rights on the part of the individual child will potentially imply a possibility for more conflict of interest across the three involved parties (the state, the parents and the child)—or even between siblings in a family who may have conflicting interests. Examples are situations where there is a disagreement between involved parties concerning how the problems are understood and whether or not there is a problem, when help and intervention are necessary, which measures need to be implemented, and how far-reaching they need to be. A development where various in-home services for children become more clearly rights-based will therefore inevitably mean increased demands for competence, professionalism and high ethical awareness on the part of the service providers. In-home measures when there is a conflict of interests will also increase demands for the quality of measures and good documentation that such measures are indeed in the best interest of the child. Compulsory in-home services make particularly current the need for a successful manoeuvre between securing individual children's needs and interest in a landscape that touches on ECHR § 8 and CRC § 16. These provisions aim to secure that measures are necessary and lawful and protect the child and the family from arbitrary or unwarranted intervention.

4 Targeting Parents to Secure Children's Right to Timely and Adapted Help

According to CRC Article 19, state parties shall provide *all the necessary support* to children and their caretakers (a) to protect children from all forms of maltreatment and (b) to secure children's health and development. Traditionally, child welfare preventive measures have had a clearly supportive character. In a Norwegian context, typical aims have been to secure for children contact with and developmental support from several adults and to facilitate children's taking part in positive leisure activities, thereby also building relationships with peers. Concerning the parents, measures have typically been various kinds of relief care and economic support. However, preventive in-home measures have also implied advice and guidance, as well as implicit and implicit measures of a more controlling character.

Following this situation, several related debates were raised. First, while preventive and supportive measures have been widely used and grown quickly in number, very limited research exists about the effect of such measures (NOU 2012, p. 5). Second, the measures chosen have typically had a *compensating* approach, without actually *improving* (in a sustainable manner) the situation for the child (BLD 2013). It has been questioned whether the most frequently used measures actually targeted a core problem, namely, parents' lack of proper (or at times even harmful) parenting skills. An understanding evolved that more systematic follow-up of parents through supervision and guidance would secure a better potential for positive change.

Raising these questions has led to a distinct shift in the kind of measurers CWS offer to children and their families. Different kinds of parent education, training and guidance have become the main in-home measure, according to national statistics. In the study previously referred to, the reasons for in-home measures varied broadly. Nevertheless, the selected measures were rather uniform. For more than 80 per cent of the 245 children, parent counselling was the chosen measure (Christiansen et al. 2015). Parent counselling was the most frequently used intervention independently of the reasons that triggered CWS engagement with the family. The main focus in this work was on the parent–child dyad and parent–child interaction.

4.1   Parents in Society

Assisting and supporting parents is a core value in the CRC. However, in a wider societal context, a situation where in-home measures in CWS have come to equal targeting the parents and the parent–child relationship must also be understood in relation to other interrelated societal development trends.

Parenting has during the last few decades acquired a certain connotation that has changed both the meaning and making of the concept. An understanding of parenting as a technical matter has developed, and related to this, parenting has become understood as something that can be generalized about. Parenting now implies a particular focus on how parents behave and perform (Furedi 2002). Implicit is also a view that the child–parent relationship in its nature is a problematic thing. Further, to parent is something that cannot be performed intuitively or naturally. Good parenting has become a form of learned interaction that requires particular knowledge and practice (Lee 2014).

Intertwined with this trend is a notion that children are more at risk than ever (e.g., James and James 2008; Featherstone et al. 2016). Faircloth (2014) claims that the status attachment theory has attained within developmental psychology and professional social work with children and families has driven such understandings. For example, there is the apprehension that much can go wrong, and that if it does, it is very hard to make it right. According to Gillies (2011), we also see a development where society continuously assigns more social responsibility to parents and a notion that parents are 'wholly deterministic in an individual child's development and future' (Faircloth 2014, p. 26).

More generally, these developmental trends have underlined a risk and deviation focus that increasingly makes parents and parenting a target for state interest, supervision and intervention (Gillies 2011). It has further paved the way for controlling and disciplining groups of parents through, for example, social work intervention in families (Hennum 2015; Ericsson 2000). Picot (2014) found a change from explicit state control of families to the presence of much more implicit and hidden control strategies embedded in state measures and interventions in vulnerable families, as present today. There are claims that the main aim for intervention is to normalize parenting and parenting practices and 'to confirm and reinforce existing social order' (Hennum 2011, p. 344). This makes measures and interventions particularly relevant for families that in some way diverge from the norm or are disadvantaged or marginalized (Gillies 2008; Hennum 2011; Juul 2011). Consequently, child welfare measures and interventions can be understood as tools, which are used by the authorities to ensure that families live up to contextually valid norms. 'The controlling power of child welfare is both exercised through interventions in families that are considered deviant, and through creating images of good and bad families' (Ericsson 2000, p. 17).

4.2 In-home Services and the Case of Immigrant Families

The question of homogenization and disciplining of parents in CWS has long been a discussion in relation to class (Vagli 2009; Egelund 2003; Kojan 2011; Gillies 2005). It has more recently also been made particularly current in relation to culture. The meeting between immigrant families and CWS in various countries is at present often problematized (Chand 2008; Johansson 2010; Kriz and Skivenes 2010). In an increasingly diverse and multicultural society, we see a situation in Norway where (a) children with an immigrant background are highly over-represented in child welfare in-home services and (b) there is a predomination of measures that target parenting practices and parent–child relations. This particular situation has brought to the public agenda heated discussions related to the concept of culture in child welfare work, what cultural rights mean for children in this area, and finally, consequences for professional approaches (Fylkesnes et al. 2017; cf. CRC Art. 30).

It is fair to say that in a historically equal society such as Norway, culture and cultural rights have not been a prominent focus within CWS, which is also reflected in the current CWA. References to children's rights concerning ethnicity, religion, culture and language are made once only and then related to the choice of placements when out-of-home care is decided (CWA § 4-15). However, during the last decade or two, a focus on culture has become increasingly prominent when understanding and assessing needs in immigrant families with children (Chand 2008; Johansson 2010; Kriz and Skivenes 2010; Rugkåsa et al. 2017). There has been an inflation in the use of concepts such as 'culture sensitivity' and 'culturally sensitive approaches' in child welfare and protective work. Rugkåsa et al. (2017), for example, claim that cultural explanations for immigrant families' challenges hold the field in Norwegian child welfare services. Typically, while what this comprehension means and implies has been unclear as well as contested, it has affected professional social work with immigrant families in important ways. According to Bredal (2009), on one hand, it has led to a certain constraint or aloofness on the side of professional workers and consequently a lack of timely and necessary measures and interventions. On the other hand, it has at times led to too intrusive and consequently less helpful and sustainable measures. Importantly, Rugkåsa et al. (2017) claims that it has narrowed an understanding of complexity when assessing immigrant families' challenges and needs.

5 Challenges to Rights-Based Practice

The case of immigrant families meeting CWS illustrates three important challenges for professional rights-based preventive services. These are, first, homogenization of parenthood; second, a reduction of complexity and a narrowing of understanding of CWS users' challenges and needs; and third, marginalization of children themselves. The challenges are relevant for CWS users in general. They also illustrate the relevance of Fox Harding's perspectives when trying to understand the way professional in-home services appear. In particular, *state paternalism and child protection, the modern defence of the birth family and parents' rights* and *children's rights and child liberation* are made current in the discussion below.

5.1 Homogenization of Parenthood

There is a frequently argued and seemingly generally adopted notion in Norway that immigrant parents need to be educated and trained to become proper parents. Further, good parenting in Norway is child-focused and circles around parent–child interaction and dialogue (Hollekim et al. 2016). Homogenization processes concerning acceptable parenting may mean less respect for parents' rights and responsibilities when bringing up children and a more general devaluation of diversity. For example, CRC Article 5 takes context into consideration when referring to the need to respect parents' own rights and responsibilities when bringing up children. It is, in the context of professional in-home services, important to reduce processes that may make parents feel disempowered, devalued and perhaps deficient (Hollekim et al. 2016). Such processes are counterproductive, as they will invariably trigger counter-reactions, such as withdrawal or open protest. This will further fuel marginalization processes for particular groups of children and parents.

5.2 Reduction of Complex Needs

In-home measures continue to target parenting practices (Christiansen et al. 2015). However, an increasing amount of research confirms that living conditions greatly affect children and families' well-being and possibilities. According to Staer and Bjørknes (2015), socio-economic factors more than cultural factors explain the challenges immigrant families face as they settle in a new country. Importantly, cultural explanations may remove the gaze from a variety of other societal injustices affecting many families, for example, low income, poor housing, inequality and discrimination. There is a need for a broader and more contextualized understanding of CWS users' needs to establish and offer more adapted and sustainable help (Andenæs 2004). If this understanding is absent, in-home measures and intervention offered may not be what the children and families need or ask for to better their life conditions (Rugkåsa et al. 2017; Fylkesnes et al. 2017).

5.3 Marginalization of the Child

In a situation where in-home measures are primarily focused on educating and guiding parents, there is a need to problematize how this may affect the position of the child and child participation, main concerns of the CRC. In spite of efforts securing children's voices in law and increased knowledge concerning the value of involving children in accordance with their age and maturity, children are not much involved and are even marginalized in situations of relevance to them. For example, in many structured and manualized programs such as Marte Meo, Circle of Security (COS) and Parent Management Training Oregon (PMTO), children are not even meant to be involved. It is only the adults' descriptions and understandings of problems and challenges in the parent–child dyad that define the needs for help and intervention. This is also most often the case when parent support and guidance do not follow structured programs (for example, are less specific in content, form, intensity and duration), as demonstrated in Norwegian research (Christiansen and Moldestad 2008; Christiansen et al. 2015).

To what extent children are involved in cases of relevance to them affects the way problems are described and explained as well as what kind of help CWS offer families. Heimer et al. (2017) found when interviewing family workers that without exception they based their work on the parents' way of describing the problems. Further, they found that a variety of problems and concerns were 'reframed' into problems with structure, routines and border setting, making them fit for parent counselling within a family treatment frame (Heimer et al. 2017). Likewise, Bakketeig (2015) found that while children were often heard at a very early stage, information sought was more about how they were doing in general and less about what kind of help they wanted. Follow-up talks with children concerning their experiences and wishes regarding in-home measures were exceptions. The value of guiding and educating parents is firmly embodied in the CRC. However, when deficient parenting is apprehended as the only 'answer' to perhaps very diverse family challenges, it will guide the kind of services offered, as well as who needs to be included in this work. Consequently, children's own views become less important, and children's own interests may remain under the radar, in glaring contrast to conditions in CRC Article 12, for example.

6 Conclusion

Working as a professional with preventive CWS in-home measures implies addressing challenges concerning the threefold relationship between the child, the parents and the state. Realizing a rights-based practice in this field is not a clear-cut path towards an unambiguous aim. Instead, it comprises a wide range of questions and implies balancing different interests and relating to several perspectives informing this threefold relationship. In fact, we can recognize input from all of the four perspectives introduced by Fox Harding (1997) when we look for implications of the CRC for CWS in-home measures. We may consider a proactive state performing early intervention to protect children versus a state taking a more withdrawn role in respect of parents' responsibilities, rights and duties to care for their children. In addition, we may consider a state offering support to and surveillance of parents with severe challenges versus a state obligated to give priority to the child's individual rights to protection and developmental support.

Regardless of the blurred character of this field, we will suggest some guiding principles for a rights-based professional practice with CWS preventive measures.

Primarily, there is a need for vigilance concerning children's position as subjects of their own individual rights through the entire process concerning in-home measures. To realize children's rights and for children to be able to pursue their own interests in a family context presupposes an active and responsible state, with institutions such as CWS that carry out this responsibility in a professional and child-focused manner.

Currently, the main approach to in-home services is targeting parents (and other carers) and parenting practices. While there is clear support in the CRC concerning supporting parents who struggle with their upbringing responsibilities, we will, following this particular development, point to three areas that deserve special attention.

First, it is necessary for relevant institutions mandated to help and intervene in a family context to *respect the parents' superior rights to organize family life in the way they see is in the best interests of their children*. In this way homogenization of parenthood, based on narrow contextual norms, can be avoided.

Second, *complying with children's needs for protection and developmental support requires a holistic understanding and service approach*. Even if the quality of the interaction between children and their parents is vital to children, a wider comprehension of the children's as well as the parents' needs is urgent. This includes considering the significance of social inequality and the family's living conditions, which in turn will lead to a broader array of measures than those limited to parent counselling.

Third, *even if the main target for intervention is parents and parenting practices, children should play an active role* in describing current problems and the kind of changes they want, in addition to communicating what they themselves consider helpful. This principle is vital to prevent marginalization of the child in her or his own case.

Finally, the overall challenge to professionals following the CRC is the day-to-day ethical awareness professionals should practice in their interaction with children and parents. High ethical awareness is important in order to acknowledge and address various parties' needs and interests when vulnerable families meet a responsible state actor. Ethically informed practice is necessary to secure the children's overall developmental needs in a short-term as well as a long-term perspective.

References

Andenæs, A. (2004). Hvorfor ser vi ikke fattigdommen? Fra en undersøkelse om barn som blir plassert utenfor hjemmet [Why do we not see the poverty? From a study about children who are taken into care]. *Nordisk Sosialt Arbeid, 1*, 20–34.

Archard, D. (2004). *Children: Rights and childhood.* London: Routledge.

Bakketeig, E. (2015). Ungdoms opplevelse av medvirkning. In Ø. Christiansen, E. Bakketeig, D. Skilbred, C. Madsen, K. Havnen, K. Aarland, & E. Backe-Hansen (Eds.), *Forskningskunnskap om barnevernets hjelpetiltak* (pp. 193–209). Bergen: RKBU Vest, Uni Research Helse.

Barne-, likestillings- og inkluderingsdepartementet. (2013). *Prop. 106L (2012–2013) Endringer i barnevernloven.* Oslo.

Barne-, likestillings- og inkluderingsdepartementet. (2015). *Prop. 72L. (2014–2015) Endringer i barnevernloven (utvidet adgang til å pålegge hjelpetiltak).* Retrieved from https://www.regjeringen.no/nb/aktuelt/ paleggehjelpetiltak/id2401784/

Bredal, A. (2009). Barnevernet og minoritetsjenters opprør. Mellom det generelle og det spesielle [Child welfare services and minority girls' rebellion. Between the general and the particular]. In K. Eide, N. A. Qureshi, M. Rugkåsa & H. Vike (Eds.), *Over profesjonelle barrierer. Et minoritetsperspektiv i psykososialt arbeid med barn og unge* [Across professional barriers. A minority perspective in psychosocial work with children and youth] (pp. 38–58). Oslo: Gyldendal Norsk forlag AS.

Chand, A. (2008). Every child matters? A critical review of child welfare reforms in the context of minority ethnic children and families. *Child Abuse Review, 17*, 6–22.

Christiansen, Ø., & Moldestad, B. (2008). *Evaluering av hjemmebaserte tiltak i barnevernet: med Årstad familiesenter som case.* Bergen: Barnevernets utviklingssenter på Vestlandet/UNIFOB Helse.

Christiansen, Ø., Bakketeig, E., Madsen, C., Havnen, K. J. S., Aarland, K., & Backe-Hansen, E. (2015). *Forskningskunnskap om barnevernets hjelpetiltak.* Bergen: Uni Research Helse.

Egelund, T. (2003). 'Farlige' forældre: den institutionelle konstruktion af dem, der afviger fra os. In M. Järvinen & N. Mick-Meyer (Eds.), *At skabe en klient: institutionelle identiteter i socialt arbejde* (pp. 59–81). København: Hans Reitzels Forlag.

Ericsson, K. (1996). *Barnevern som samfunnsspeil*. Oslo: Pax.

Ericsson, K. (2000). Social control and emancipation ambiguities in child welfare. *Journal of Scandinavian Studies in Criminology and Crime Prevention, 1*, 16–26.

Faircloth, C. (2014). Intensive parenting and the expansion of parenting. In E. Lee, J. Bristow, C. Faircloth, & J. Macvarish (Eds.), *Parenting culture studies* (pp. 25–50). Basingstoke, Hampshire: Palgrave Macmillan.

Falch-Eriksen, A. (2012). *The promise of trust: An inquiry into the legal design of coercive decision-making in Norway*. Oslo: Høgskolen i Oslo og Akershus, Senter for profesjonsstudier.

Featherstone, B., Gupta, A., Morris, K. M., & Warner, J. (2016). Let's stop feeding the risk monster: Towards a social model of 'child protection'. *Families, Relationships and Societies*, ISSN 2046-7443.

Fernandez, E. (2014). Child protection and vulnerable families: Trends and issues in the Australian context. *Social Sciences, 3*(4), 785.

Fox-Harding, L. (1997). *Perspectives in child care policy* (2nd ed.). New York: Longman.

Furedi, F. (2002). *Paranoid parenting: Why ignoring the experts may be best for your child*. Chicago: Chicago Review Press.

Fylkesnes, M. K., Iversen, A. C., & Nygren, L. (2017). Negotiating deficiency: Exploring ethnic minority parents' narratives about encountering child welfare services in Norway. *Child & Family Social Work*, 1–8.

Gilbert, N. (Ed.). (1997). *Combatting child abuse. International perspectives and trends*. New York: Oxford University Press.

Gilbert, N., Parton, N., & Skivenes, M. (2011). *Child protection systems: International trends and orientations*. New York: Oxford University Press.

Gillies, V. (2005). Raising the 'meritocracy': Parenting and the individualization of social class. *Sociology, 39*, 835–853.

Gillies, V. (2008). Perspective on parenting responsibility: Contextualizing values and practices. *Journal of Law and Society, 35*(1), 95–112.

Gillies, V. (2011). From function to competence: Engaging with the new politics of family. *Sociological Research Online, 14*(4), 1–11.

Heimer, M., Näsman, E., & Palme, J. (2017). Vulnerable children's rights to participation, protection, and provision: The process of defining the problem in Swedish child and family welfare. *Child & Family Social Work*, n/a–n/a. doi:https://doi.org/10.1111/cfs.12424.

Hennum, N. (2011). Controlling children's lives: Covert messages in child protection service reports. *Child & Family Social Work, 16*, 336–344.
Hennum, N. (2015). Makten i barnet [The power in the child]. *Norges Barnevern, 92*(2), 124–138.
Hollekim, R., Anderssen, N., & Daniel, M. (2016). Contemporary discourses on children and parenting in Norway. Norwegian child welfare services meets immigrant families. *Children and Youth Services Review, 60*, 52–60.
Høstmælingen, N., Kjørholt, E. S., & Sandberg, K. (eds). (2016). *Barnekonvensjonen. Barns rettigheter i Norge.* Oslo: Universitetsforlaget.
Hughes, R. C., Rycus, J. S., Saunders-Adams, S. M., Hughes, L. K., & Hughes, K. N. (2013). Issues in differential response. *Research on Social Work Practice, 23*(5), 493–520. https://doi.org/10.1177/1049731512466312.
James, A., & James, A. L. (2008). Changing childhood in the UK: Reconstructing discourses of 'Risk' and 'Protection'. In A. James & A. L. James (Eds.), *European childhoods. Cultures, politics and childhoods in Europe* (pp. 105–129). Hampshire/New York: Palgrave Macmillan.
Johansson, I. M. (2010). The multicultural paradox: The challenge of accommodating both power and trust in child protection. *International Social Work, 54*(4), 535–549.
Juul, R. (2011). Diskursive analyser som kritisk korrektiv av barnevernets praksis [Discursive analysis as critical corrective of child welfare practice]. *Barnläkaren, 2*, 83–102.
Kojan, B. H. (2011). *Klasseblikk på et barnevern i vekst.* Trondheim: NTNU.
Kriz, K., & Skivenes, M. (2010). 'Knowing our society' and 'fighting against prejudice'. How child welfare workers in Norway and England perceive the challenges of minority parents. *British Journal of Social Work, 40*, 2634–2651.
Lee, E. (2014). Introduction. In E. Lee, J. Bristow, C. Faircloth, & J. Macvarish (Eds.), *Parenting culture studies.* New York: Palgrave Macmillan.
Lonne, B., Harries, M., Featherstone, B., & Grey, M. (2016). *Working ethically in child protection.* London: Routledge.
NOU 2012:5. Bedre beskyttelse av barns utvikling. Ekspertuvalgets utredning om det biologiske prinsipp i barnevernet (Official expert committee report).
NOU 2016:16. Ny barnevernslov (Official expert committee report on new Children's Act).
Parton, N., & Reid, J. (2017). The recent history of central government guidance about child protection. In *Safeguarding and protecting children in the early years* (2nd ed., pp. 9–30). Abingdon: Routledge.

Pelton, L. H. (2015). The continuing role of material factors in child maltreatment and placement. *Child Abuse & Neglect, 41*, 30–39. https://doi.org/10.1016/j.chiabu.2014.08.001.

Picot, A. (2014). Transforming child welfare: From explicit to implicit control of families. *European Journal of Social Work, 17*(5), 689–701. https://doi.org/10.1080/13691457.2014.932273.

Pösö, T., Skivenes, M., & Hestbæk, A.-D. (2014). Child protection systems within the Danish, Finnish and Norwegian welfare states—Time for a child centric approach? *European Journal of Social Work, 17*(4), 475–490. https://doi.org/10.1080/13691457.2013.829802.

Rugkåsa, M., Ylvisaker, S., & og Eide, K. (2017). *Barnevern i et minoritetesperspektiv.* Gyldendal Akademisk.

Spratt, T., Nett, J., Bromfield, L., Hietamäki, J., Kindler, H., & Ponnert, L. (2015). Child protection in Europe: Development of an international cross-comparison model to inform national policies and practices. *The British Journal of Social Work, 45*(5), 1508–1525. https://doi.org/10.1093/bjsw/bcu109.

Staer, T., & Bjørknes, R. (2015). Etnic disproportionality in the child welfare system: A Norwegian national cohort study. *Children and Youth Services Review, 56*, 26–32.

The Committee on the Rights of the Child. *General comment No. 13* (2011). *The Right of the Child to freedom from all forms of violence* (CRC/C/GC/13).

The European Convention for the Protection of Human Rights and Fundamental Freedoms (ECHR). https://www.echr.coe.int/Pages/home.aspx?p=basictexts&c.

Trocmé, N., Kyte, A., Sinha, V., & Fallon, B. (2014). Urgent protection versus chronic need: Clarifying the dual mandate of child welfare services across Canada. *Social Sciences, 3*(3), 483.

Ulvik, O. S. (2009). Barns rett til deltakelse—teoretiske og praktiske utfordringer i profesjonelle hjelperes samarbeid med barn [Children's Right to participation—Theoretical and practical challenges in professional helpers' cooperation with children]. *Tidsskrift for Norsk Psykologforening, 46*, 1148–1154.

UNCRC. United Nations Convention on the Rights of the Child. https://www.unicef.org.uk/what-we-do/un-convention-child-rights/.

Vagli, Å. (2009). *Behind closed doors; exploring the institutional logic of doing child protection work* (PhD thesis). Bergen: Universitetet i Bergen.

Open Access This chapter is licensed under the terms of the Creative Commons Attribution 4.0 International License (http://creativecommons.org/licenses/by/4.0/), which permits use, sharing, adaptation, distribution and reproduction in any medium or format, as long as you give appropriate credit to the original author(s) and the source, provide a link to the Creative Commons license and indicate if changes were made.

The images or other third party material in this chapter are included in the chapter's Creative Commons license, unless indicated otherwise in a credit line to the material. If material is not included in the chapter's Creative Commons license and your intended use is not permitted by statutory regulation or exceeds the permitted use, you will need to obtain permission directly from the copyright holder.

11

Embodied Care Practices and the Realization of the Best Interests of the Child in Residential Institutions for Young Children

Cecilie Basberg Neumann

1 Introduction

In Norway, we have recently witnessed a shift in the public critique of the child protection services (CPS), from legal and economical shortcomings within the services, lack of professionalism, care ethics and knowledge in social work, towards an increased emphasis on the concept of love (Thrana 2016; Barnevernpanelets rapport (2011)). Here, love is used to denote what professional social work cannot promote unless the social workers invest themselves deeply in emotional involvement with the children. Although I acknowledge this shift as an attempt to meet children's need for love, and as embedded in a legitimate criticism based on client's experiences with CPS as cold and sometimes alienating bureaucracies, I worry that the privileging of deep emotions like love represents a setback for the continuous goal to professionalize social work. While the conduct of competent social work takes years to master, love invokes an image of

C. B. Neumann (✉)
Department of Social Work, Oslo Metropolitan University, Oslo, Norway
e-mail: nece@oslomet.no

'natural' and 'innate' abilities that all good persons potentially are in possession of, including social workers. Hence, the privileging of love may imply a de-professionalization of social work instead of furthering professional social work with a care ethics that departs from awareness of self and others, responsibility and sensitivity towards power that may be seen in connection with the securing of children's rights. In this chapter, I make the case for social workers in residential childcare institutions and ask, What is it that social workers do when they provide care to young children in residential childcare institutions? Moreover, what are the features or specific qualities of that care, which would justify the labelling of their caring activities as good care? Finally, what do these good care practices have to do with the realization of the best interests of the child and children's right to participate?

These questions depart from a larger research project on residential institutions for young children in Norway, where my part of the project was to explore social workers care practices through fieldwork and interviews. In addition, a particular focus was to investigate how the children's rights to participate, figuring most notably in the United Nations Convention on the Rights of the Child (CRC) Article 12, was handled by the social workers. However, as the study evolved, I found that in order to be able to understand the realization of the children's rights to participation, I first had to understand how the best interest of the child was secured (CRC Art. 3).

The ideal childhood proposed in the CRC's preamble states that all children should grow up with warmth, love and security, hence, the quality of care and the caring practices the child is a part of must be pivotal to the overall realization of the rights-principle referred to as the child's best interests (cf. CRC Art 3.1). In a residential context, one obvious approach to understanding the realization of the best interest of the child is to explore what kind of care the children receive.

Although I worry that the CRC's idealized view of childhood would be translated into an emotional requirement of love in professional social work settings (Neumann 2016), good care should, and does, serve as a guideline for professional social work practices in residential institutions, not in the sense that social workers should love the children they look after, but that they should engage professionally with the children in sensitive, responsible and respectful ways (see Kendrick 2013; Lorentzen 2015). This way of thinking is indebted to and departs from an ethics of proximity where the social worker is interpellated to act when he or she sees the pain in the Other's face (see Levinas 2006). As I hope to demonstrate in this chapter, this is also what good social workers in residential institutions do.

The background for the study, and for my part of the study in particular, is that there is a paucity of knowledge with regard to how (good) care is provided for young children in residential care (Backe-Hansen et al. 2017; Storø et al. 2017; Smith 2010). In addition, exploring good care practices in everyday residential contexts as realizations of children's rights is even rarer to come across, even if the law professor Kristen Sandberg has created opportunity for this connection on some occasions (see for example Sandberg 2016, p. 103).

In the following, I depart from the premise that social workers' accessibility and attentive presence towards the children is conducted within the framework of care and care practices. My aim is to specify that which may be characterized as the 'good' in the social workers' care practices with young children, seen in connection with, and as expressions of, the securing of the child's best interest in residential institutions. While the body is central to these articulations, I am not attempting to reduce good social work practices solely to a matter of the connectedness of embodied care practices and the child's best interest. Rather, I wish to investigate and articulate the meaning of the bodily aspects of the social workers' care work with young children in residential institutions, as these aspects intersect with an ethics of care that is already grounded in the social work ethos on sensitivity and responsibility towards the vulnerable Other (Lorentzen 2015).

2 Discovering the Body

Precisely because of the paucity of knowledge on how good care is practised in residential institutions for young children, the fieldwork took place in an institution that achieves good results and has a good reputation. This reputation was confirmed in my study, as the children

I followed over a period of almost one-and-a-half years appeared to heal, socially and physically.

An everyday interpretation of my observations of the children's improved social and physical health and skills, is that there was something going on in the institution that was good for the children that had to do with the particularities of the care they received and were a part of. What struck me as key to this care was how central the body was in the interactions between the children and the social workers.

Hence, my preliminary proposal for conceptualizing the relationship between good care practices and the securing of the best interests of the child is related to the social worker's bodily awareness and sensitive presence when interacting with and caring for children (see also Leseth and Engelsrud 2017, p. 2 on the relationship between teachers and pupils). Leseth and Engelsrud thus states:

> Thomas Fuchs, taking a phenomenological perspective, argues that human sociality does not originate in isolated individuals, but through intercorporeality and embodied affectivity (Fuchs 2016). Applying the concept of embodied inter-affectivity Fuchs (2016) asserts that in face-to-face encounters, intertwined subject-bodies resonate with each other; this inter-affectivity creates situations in which mutual empathy and understanding can develop. (Leseth and Engelsrud 2017, p. 3)

Following Leseth and Engelsrud, I see these embodied care practices as intertwined with an ethics of proximity, or ethics of care, that is intimately connected to and serves as a prerequisite for the realization of the best interests of the child. Moreover, I understand embodied care practices as a particular form of social work professionalism, namely, that it is intertwined with how practices are conducted and the rationale behind those practices (Freidson 2001, p. 35). Still, even if the interconnectedness of care ethics, the social worker's relational responsibilities, embodied care practices and the realization of the child's best interests are clearly present as theoretical and practice-based prerequisites and possibilities in social work, this cluster, that lies at the core of social work thinking and doing, is not often clearly articulated (see Pösö, Chap. 6 in this book, and Neumann 2016).

3 Good Practice, Knowing Bad Practices Occur

Before I continue, I should address a reservation. The Scottish researchers Joan Shaw and Andrew Kendrick (2016; see also Steckley and Kendrick 2008) have studied residential institutions for children in protective care and have interviewed former social workers with experience from residential institutions. They worry that Scottish and English care practices in residential child protection institutions have lost, or are in danger of losing, the bodily aspects of the social workers' care practices (p. 13) due to recent disclosures of violence and abuse in residential institutions. For the same reasons, social workers are prohibited to physically touch or be touched by the children in some residential institutions in Scotland (Smith 2010). As history and research on institutions in a variety of settings have taught us (Goffman 1961/1990), not all touch is good touch, and there is always a potential danger of the misuse of intimacy, power and authority in the child–social worker relationship (Ulset 2010; Munro 2008). While acknowledging both the possibilities for violence and abuse, my aim here is not to focus on bad social work practices, but on the unfolding of good care practices.

In the following, I will give a brief account of my methodological entry before I introduce some central phenomenological insights on embodiment, which provide a focused entry to understand the embodied conduct of care for young children in residential institutions.

4 A Methodological Consideration of Embodiment

The findings and discussions in the present chapter are based on ethnographic data from fieldwork and interviews with social workers in one residential institution for young children, and on interviews (but not fieldwork) with social workers in another residential institution for young children. Young children in this context are from the age of six to around twelve years.

The study consists of 20 field observations in a residential institution for young children that lasted 3–4 hours each time. I observed the interactions between social workers and the children. In addition to this, I conducted qualitative interviews with five social workers in this institution as well as with four social workers in an additional institution.

It was especially one incident with a child, in which I was directly involved, that made me acutely aware of the importance of the bodily aspects of the social worker's good care practices. One afternoon I sat at the dining table in the living room and followed the interaction between the children and the social workers. One of the children asked me if I wanted to throw a ball with him. I answered yes and left the chair in which I had been sitting. While I attempted to sit down at the floor beside him I lost my balance and came to touch his arm with my left hand. He pulled his arm quickly away and looked anxiously at me.

The incident made me feel shameful, and I feared that my touch could be harmful for the boy. Later, in one of the interviews, I asked the social worker who had been present in the situation what her opinion of the situation was. She told me not to worry and offered an alternative interpretation, namely that the boy had marked a clear bodily boundary for himself.

This incident changed my analytical focus; from a generalized focus on relational care work and participation, to a more specific focus on the meaning of the bodily aspects of the social workers' care work and thus the securing of the children's best interests (see Neumann and Neumann 2018 Chap. 2 on situatedness as an entry to specific analyses).

5 The Body in Care Practices, or the Embodiment of Care

That the body is involved in human practices—in our thinking, our actions and our ways of being in the world—has been highlighted and theorized in many different contexts. To Mauss (2004), the body was the site where the mental, social and biological system met. For Bourdieu, the body, captured in his conceptual concept habitus, was the point of departure in his analyses of our classed and gendered ways of being in the world

(Bourdieu 1999). Foucault (1997) articulated the body as the site for power, and feminists have focused on the body in their investigations of gender and gender relations in a number of different thematic contexts (for example Butler 1999; Sedgwick 2003; Mol and Law 2004).

In a passage on the body that is always with us, but at the edge of our consciousness, Merleau-Ponty wrote,

> Now the permanence of my own body is entirely of a different kind: it is not at the extremity of some indefinite exploration; it defies exploration and is always presented to me from the same angle. Its permanence is not a permanence in the world, but a permanence on my part. To say that it is always near me, that I cannot array it before my eyes, that it remains marginal to all my perceptions, that it is with me. (2002, pp. 103–104)

In other words, the body is the basis for our being in the world and for our communication with others (se also Lakoff and Johnson 1999; Leseth and Engelsrud 2017). It is precisely because of these and other phenomenological insights on our bodies and embodied being in the world that Twigg et al. (2011) calls for research that sees concrete bodies as important conditions and contexts for care work and the practising of care.

The question then is how the bodily aspects of care can be central to the conduct of good care practices, and if and in what ways these bodily aspects may be seen as normative prerequisites for good caring practices in social work with young children, as concrete realizations of the child's best interests.

6 Towards a Specific Understanding of Social Work Professionalism: Care Ethics, Good Care Practices and the Child's Best Interest

The starting point in research on the practice of care is that care means that one person cares for and looks after another person (Leira 1992; Ungerson 2005). For Levinas (2006) the essence of care was connected to the essence of being human. One becomes a moral person by recognizing the subjectivity of the other, and feeling responsible for acting when one sees the pain in the Other's face. This is a central premise in the ethics of care (Martinsen 1993; Held 2006; Lorentzen 2015), and can also be understood as the central feature in empathy (Lakoff and Johnson 1999). Thus, care is fundamentally relational, and the sociological point of departure for analyses of professional care work in institutions is that it is one person's task to look after and care for another person, who for different reason relies on this care (Wærness 1992; Kittay Feder 2011).

In theorizations of care, and what care practice is or could be, emphasis is placed on the ways this work is performed; for example with regard to 'warm' emotions (Wærness 1992), or with regard to collaboration around practicalities (Mol 2008). Emphasis is also placed on the professional practice of care relationships with the exercise of power and control (Ericsson 1996, 2009; Hennum 1997; Skau 2013) as well as with the conditions for the exercise of (good) discretion in the conduct of care work (Freidson 2001; Skau 2013; Skivenes and Sørsdal, Chap. 4 in this book).

It is especially in discussions of the *ways* care is given, as experienced by the recipients of care, that one talks about good care and bad care. Annemarie Mol's (2008) point of departure is to reserve the term care for the conduct of a specific set of concrete actions such as washing, feeding and attending to physical wounds. The body and embodied practices are central premises for Mol's exploration of care, and her project is to identify the logic of care and to show what good care is. She disconnects her analyses of care from more traditional understandings of good care practices as something that has to do with care conducted with the right feelings of compassion and love (Noddings 1984; Wærness 1992). Instead, she locates her understanding of good care as activities and practices that are carried out in specific, flexible and mutually respectful ways (Mol 2008, p. 2).

The conduct of good care is demanding and takes as its point of departure that the patient deserves support (Mol 2008, p. 37). This, Mol emphasizes, does not imply that health personnel should always do what the patient wants, nor is it an undermining of professional knowledge and responsibility. It rather means that health personnel recognize the patient's own knowledge, include the patient as a part of the care team and encourage the patient to take good care of herself. In good care, this is a collaborative endeavour (Mol 2008, p. 29).

Although Mol has explored good care as practices unfolding in collaboration between grown-ups with chronic diseases and health professionals, I believe she has identified some generic elements in good care that are valid when attempting to identify what good care may mean in residential child protection institutions for young children (see also Lakoff and Johnson 1999, Chap. 14).

Good care is something practical, involving collaborative actions and practices, and important values in this work are recognition, equality and sensitivity (see also Held 2006). This way of understanding good care resonates with the way Per Lorentzen (2015) views ethical action and responsibility in social work in residential institutions. Lorentzen, who grounds his thinking in the ethics of proximity, examines the ethical challenges and demands of social work, and, as for Levinas, it is a dialogical and relational approach that forms the basis of his thinking. What Lorentzen understands as ethical action in social work are actions based on a responsibility that is explicitly directed at and sensitive towards the Other. Like Martinsen (1993), Lorentzen emphasizes that it does not make sense to set out firm ethical principles in advance, but that they must be adjusted by the professional to particular, specific and flexible behaviour based on what a particular situation requires (see also Mol 2008).

The emphasis on the responsibility of the social worker means that the social worker acknowledges being part of the event (a meeting between two people) as she perceives it, and that she is doing her best with the resources, knowledge and skills at her disposal. It is the experience of responsibility, says Lorentzen, which is the reality of the social worker in her meeting with the child or client, and for this reason, professional approaches to children and clients should be based on such a condition (Lorentzen 2015, pp. 50–51).

By adding to this argument Virginia Held's emphasis that care as practice seeks good caring relations (Held 2006, p. 36; see also Mol 2008), we have a ground from where we can articulate the space where the children's best interests may be realized.

7 Connecting Embodied Care Practices with the Best Interests of the Child

During my fieldwork, I observed the social workers in the residential institution as they were acting with warmth, humour and flexibility, and at the same time, maintained routines such as serving regular meals, helping the children with their homework and following up the children's leisure activities. They also made sure that bedtime rituals were adapted to the needs and wishes of the individual child. It is here that I gradually came to understand this work as much more profound than merely securing the children's formal rights to participation, such as ensuring that house meetings are held regularly, that the child has good information about his case, receives regular health-care follow-ups and is allowed to decide what to eat for lunch. Although such activities are important elements of participation, and also in this institution's policy, it nevertheless constituted only a small part of what I eventually came to understand as the child's participation in practice; which was largely based on securing the child's best interests as integral to good embodied care practices. Here, the body itself is key to my understanding of good care, as connected to the realization of the child's rights to have her best interests tended to.

Liv Holmen (2009) has described how the body is a necessary prerequisite for pedagogical care with deafblind children:

> Kasper was so fond of rolling around on the floor; so we rolled around on the floor. We were constantly bumping into one another, and finally I was allowed to hold him in my arms while we rolled around, body to body. He was very excited; he hollered and shouted for joy, but because we were physically close to each other, it was possible for me to regulate his discomfort with my body movements. (2009, p. 47, my translation)

Holmen shows in an insightful manner what it could mean to work with and through the body. The disabled child who cannot see and cannot hear communicates directly through the body, and Holmen must follow her own and the child's body to be able to do a job, and to provide care for the child. The question is whether these are valid observations only for children with severe physical impairment. I will start my exploration of the bodily aspects of good caring practices by showing how the social workers caring practices unfolded in interaction with the children, and then go on to analyse some important reasons for their particular approaches to embodied care practices, that became evident in the interviews with the social workers.

Here is an extract from my field notes:

> I am sitting at the dining table in the living room outside the kitchen. Like all the other rooms in the institution, the living room is bright and cosy. Throughout the institution, the walls are painted in bright colours, white, light grey and light yellow, and the curtains and pillows match the colours of the walls in the different rooms. There is a cosy corner with a large couch at the far end of the living room. A few metres outside the corner with the couch is the dining table where I am sitting. From here I have an open view into the kitchen, as well as to the adjacent TV-room. Today, two regular social workers are present, in addition to a social worker trainee and a visiting social worker from another residential institution.
>
> The atmosphere among the adults is cheerful. They prepare dinner, talk, laugh and set the table. Two of the children come home from school and sit down in the adjacent living room to watch TV while waiting for dinner. The phone constantly rings, and the social workers plan the afternoon and evening for the three children living in the institution, apparently not distracted by the interruptions. They have a couple of options for each of the children and talk about what the children might want to do. The dinner is at four o'clock. Then the children have to do homework. They consult with each child, and together they decide that one child is going on a bike ride, while another child is going to the gym. The third wants to be at home.
>
> One of the children has received a new cover for his mobile phone. He comes out of the TV-room periodically, appears to be very happy, jumps around and says that this cover must surely be the coolest in the world. Then he sits down on one of the social worker's lap and gets a hug.
>
> When he leaves, the social workers talk about a new child that will come later that evening or the next morning. They discuss how they should arrange the day so that the child may feel welcome and secure. The social workers agree to let the child decide. They prepare for the possibility that the child might just want to greet the other children, and then go to her room and get to know the social worker who will have the main responsibility for her while she is in the institution.

It is when I am sitting at the large dining table watching the social workers and children's interaction on the couch in the corner that I can observe the bodily dimension of their caring interactions. This is one of many examples:

John has just returned from school. I hear him in the hallway. He takes off his shoes and outerwear in a hurry and comes storming into the room, crying 'Ellen!' to one of the social workers. He jumps onto her lap, and Ellen gives him a big hug, sniffs his hair and starts stroking his back. 'Well, have you had a nice day today?' she asks warmly. He looks up at her, smiles and says 'yes' while sitting on her lap. Another social worker, Karin, enters the room from her office and sits down at the edge of the big couch. John bounces out of Ellen's lap and says to Karin: 'Karin, can we play helicopter? Please, please!' Karin smiles and says 'yes, we can.' She then adds, addressed to the rest of us: 'It will be a good workout for my thighs this one.' She lays down on her back and lifts John into the air with her legs. He hangs with his belly over her feet and laughs. When she puts him down, he asks her to do it again, and they go on for a while until Karin says 'no, now I'll have to take a break.' 'Look here' she shows him her arm, 'I'm totally sweaty.' John touches her arm and goes back to sit on Ellen's lap, who resumes stroking his back. 'Ellen, can you read to me?' Ellen says yes and together they find the book he wants her to read for him.

What is so special about this example? First, it is the body's involvement in the social workers' care work that is striking. Second, it is the importance of touch, and third, it is the willingness of the social worker to enter into the bodily interaction that the child has invited to and asked for. This was what I observed, and that the social workers themselves did not articulate, until I began to ask them directly about the meaning of the body in their embodied care practices.

When I asked the social workers directly in the last four interviews about what the most important thing about the care they provide to the children was, everyone replied that it was about knowing and using their own bodies in their interactions in ways that gestalt therapists would call awareness (Neumann and Neumann 2018). They described their care practices as very physical, and gave many examples of how the job was largely about relating to and receiving the bodies of the children, with and through their own bodies and bodily consciousness and awareness (as in the example with John).

On my question about the importance of the body in their care practices with the children, a social worker responded this way:

> It really starts with the social workers own body … that we are conscious of how we appear towards the child. We need to be aware of things like: How do I move [when I'm stressed]? How do I keep my body when I talk to the child? Do I stand a bit like this [showing physically] backwards and with my arms crossed over my chest, or am I keeping my body in an open and relaxed position? You must also be aware not to use abrupt movements. There was a boy standing next to me while I was cleaning the dishwasher a few months ago. I turned a little abruptly while I held a lid in my hand and he threw himself at the floor. He waited for a blow … If the child is sitting on a couch and we want to talk to the child about something that might be uncomfortable for the child, we place ourselves on the couch beside the child, or kneel down beside him. They are so fragile. We try to keep this consciousness with us at all times.

Here, the social worker clearly expresses her reflections on her own bodily expressions as linked to her responsibility for the child in the situation (Lorentzen 2015). She connects her awareness and knowledge of her own bodily expressions directly to the care for the boy in the example above, with a further search for knowledge of the boy's situation. The bodily aspects of the good care practices are therefore not just about the child's body, but also about the social worker's own bodily involvement and understanding thereof.

Moreover, in order for the conscious and feeling body to be integrated into the social, there must be someone who responds to and accepts our bodily expressions. Central to Kari Martinsen's descriptions of the body in care and care work is touch, and the way this touch is performed (Martinsen 1993, p. 49). Translated to the understandings of the good care I have accounted for above, the touch must be perceived as something good by the recipient, in order for it to be claimed as good care (see also Mckinney and Kempson 2012). This resonates with Mol's (2008) emphasis of the collaborative, sensitive and respectful aspects of good care and the logic of care.

The social workers I encountered were willing to enter into interaction with the children that involved a high degree of bodily contact and touch.

John was hugged and lifted up in the air when he asked for it. The interaction between the social workers and John showed that they were focused and sensitive towards John's specific bodily expressions and needs.

However, embodied care practices and touching in child–social work relationships in residential child care institutions have also, as mentioned earlier, been problematized (Smith 2010) because touch is not always good touch, but may on the contrary be experienced as, or in connection with, abuse and coercion (Ulset and Tjelflaat 2012; Goffman 1990). Hence, the emphasis on the social workers' professional responsibility for the relationship with the child. Conversely, the good touch will have a lot to do with empathy and sensitivity. In a description of moral sympathy, Lakoff and Johnson say that sympathy can be understood as 'a feeling based on empathy that moves us to ensure that the other experiences well-being' (1999, p. 318). Thus, the warranting of a child's best interests while in residential care depends on the social workers' collaborative, responsible and sensitive efforts to respond to the child's presence in the world with and through their own bodies, in a fashion that responds to and respects the child's needs and boundaries. This, I think, is also the crux of social work professionalism in institutions, read through their actions as expressions of an ethics of care.

8 Conclusion

When social workers provide children with good care, I understand their care work as practices where they show the children that they see it as their responsibility to answer to the needs the children express. In doing this, they show empathy, and that they have the ability to take the child's perspective and to imagine the world as the child may see it, and to make an effort to feel what the child may feel (Lakoff and Johnson 1999, p. 309). Central to this care practice is the body; or embodied care practices. The young children invite the social workers in interactions that involves their bodies, and the social workers answer with their own bodies.

Precisely because of this, good care practices for young children depend on the social worker's own bodily awareness and knowledge, and her sensitivity towards the needs of the child at all times. When the child asks or invites the social worker to give him a hug, he will get a hug, even if the social worker is on the phone or is preparing dinner. Interpreted with Lorentzen, this corresponds to their 'sensitivity in the situation' (Lorentzen 2015, p. 64), which is also connected with their embodied presence, and awareness of self and others (Lorentzen 2015, p. 72). Seen in relation to the child's best interest and his rights to participate, this does not mean that the child should be allowed to decide whether or not to attend school or do his homework, or to decide that he will eat chocolate all day long. The situational sensitivity, and embodied care, is linked to the position of the social worker as the responsible party in the relationship, thus warranting a secure social space in which the child's best interest and right to participate are respected and welcomed. More than securing the children's rights to be protected and provided for, these care practices potentially allow the children to experience participation similar, but not equal, to the (ideal) care received by children in secure family settings. This implies an understanding of the securing of the child's best interest as something that is located in the continuous interactions between the children and the social workers, where the bodily aspects of the social workers' care practices play a central part, as they unfold in their day-to-day interactions with the children.

References

Backe-Hansen, E., Løvgren M., Neumann, C.B. & Storø, J. (2017). *God omsorg ibarnevernsinstitusjoner*. Oslo: Nova rapport nr. 12.
Barnevernpanelets rapport. (2011). Oslo: Barne-, likestillings og inkluderings departementet.
Bourdieu, P. (1999). *Meditasjoner*. Oslo: Pax.
Butler, J. (1999). *Gender trouble*. New York: Routledge.
Ericsson, K. (1996). *Barnevern som samfunnsspeil*. Oslo: Pax.
Ericsson, K. (2009). *Samfunnets stebarn*. Oslo: Universitetsforlaget.
Foucault, M. (1997). *Ethics*. London: The Penguin Press.
Freidson, E. (2001). *Professionalism, The third logic: On the practice of knowledge*. Chicago: Chicago University Press.
Goffman, E. (1990). *Asylums*. New York: Anchor Books.

Held, V. (2006). *The ethics of care. Personal, political, and global.* Oxford: Oxford University Press.
Hennum, N. (1997). *Den komplekse virkelighet.* Oslo: Nova Rapport nr. 11.
Holmen, L. (2009). *Pedagogikk og kjærlighet.* Oslo: Skådalen Publication Series No. 29.
Kendrick, A. (2013). Relations, relationships and relatedness: Residential child care and the family metaphor. *Child & Family Social Work, 18,* 77–86.
Kittay, E. F. (2011). The ethics of care, dependence and disability. *Ratio Juris, 24*(1), 49–58.
Lakoff, G., & Johnson, M. (1999). *Philosophy in the flesh. The embodied mind and its challenge to western thought.* New York: Basic Books.
Leira, A. (1992). *Welfare sates and working mothers.* Cambridge: Cambridge University Press.
Leseth, A., & Engelsrud, G. (2017). Situating cultural diversity in movement. A case study on physical education teacher education in Norway. *Sport, Education and Society,* 1–12. https://doi.org/10.1080/13573322.2017.1414694.
Levinas, E. (2006). *Humanism of the other.* Chicago: University of Illinois Press.
Lorentzen, P. (2015). *Ansvar og etikk i miljøarbeid.* Oslo: Universitetsforlaget.
Martinsen, K. (1993). *Fra Marx til Løgstrup. Om etikk og sanselighet i sykepleien.* Oslo: Tano.
Mauss, M. (2004). *Kropp og person. To essays.* Oslo: Cappelen Akademisk Forlag.
Mckinney, K. G., & Kempson, D. A. (2012). Losing touch in social work practice. *Social Work, 57*(2), 189–191.
Merleau-Ponty, M. (2002). *The phenomenology of perception.* London: Routledge.
Mol, A. (2008). *The logic of care.* London: Routledge.
Mol, A., & Law, J. (2004). Embodied action, enacted bodies. The example of Hypoglycaemia. *Body & Society, 10*(2–3), 43–62.
Munro, E. (2008). *Effective child protection.* London: SAGE.
Neumann, C. B., & Neumann, I. B. (2018). *Power, ethics and situated research methodology.* New York: Palgrave Pivot.
Neumann, C. B. (2016). Children quest for love and professional child protection work: The case of Norway. *Scottish Journal of Residential Child Care, 15*(3), 104–123.
Noddings, N. (1984). *Caring, a feminine approach to ethics & moral education.* Berkeley: University of California Press.
Sandberg, K. (2016). Barnets rett til å bli hørt. In N. Høstmælingen, E. S. Kjørholt, & K. Sandberg (Eds.), *Barnekonvensjonen. Barns rettigheter i Norge.* Oslo: Universitetsforlaget.
Sedgwick, E. K. (2003). *Touching, feeling.* Durham: Duke University Press.

Shaw, J., & Kendrick, A. (2016). Reflecting on the past: Children's service workers' experiences of residential care in Scotland from 1960 to 1975. *British Journal of Social Work, 47*, 1–17.
Skau, G. M. (2013). *Mellom makt og hjelp: om det flertydige forholdet mellom klient og hjelper.* Oslo: Universitetsforlaget.
Smith, M. (2010). Victim narratives of historical abuse in residential child care. *Qualitative Social Work, 9*(3), 303–320.
Steckley, L., & Kendrick, A. (2008). Hold on. Physical restraint in residential child care. In A. Kendrick (Ed.), *Residential child care. Prospects and challenges*. London: Jessica Kingsley Publishers.
Storø, J., Backe-Hansen, E., & Løvgren, E. (2017). Kunnskapsoversikt til prosjektet 'Barneverninstitusjoner som arena for omsorg'. *Tidsskriftet Norges Barnevern, 94*(3), 166–184.
Thrana, H. M. (2016). Kjærlighetens inntreden i barnevernet—en utfordring for den profesjonelle relasjon? *Tidsskriftet Norges barnevern, 93*(2), 96–109.
Twigg, J., Wolkowitz, C., Cohen, R. J., & Nettleton, S. (2011). Conceptualising body work in health and social care. *Sociology of Health, and Illness, 32*(2), 171–188.
Ulset, G. (2010). Tilværelse og oppvekst i ungdomsinstitusjon. *Tidsskrift for ungdomsforskning, 10*(1), 49–71.
Ulset, G. & Tjelflaat, T. (2012). *Tvang i barnevernsinstitusjoner.* Trondheim: NTNU Rapport20/2012 Skriftserien fra Barnevernets utviklingssenter i Midt-Norge.
Ungerson, C. (2005). Care, work and feeling. *The Sociological Review, 53*(2), 188–203.
Wærness, K. 1992 (1987). On the rationality of caring. In Showstack Sasson, A. (ed.), *Women and the state.* London: Routledge.

Open Access This chapter is licensed under the terms of the Creative Commons Attribution 4.0 International License (http://creativecommons.org/licenses/by/4.0/), which permits use, sharing, adaptation, distribution and reproduction in any medium or format, as long as you give appropriate credit to the original author(s) and the source, provide a link to the Creative Commons license and indicate if changes were made.

The images or other third party material in this chapter are included in the chapter's Creative Commons license, unless indicated otherwise in a credit line to the material. If material is not included in the chapter's Creative Commons license and your intended use is not permitted by statutory regulation or exceeds the permitted use, you will need to obtain permission directly from the copyright holder.

12

Formal and Everyday Participation in Foster Families: A Challenge?

Elisabeth Backe-Hansen

1 Children's Participatory Rights and Professional Work

Children's participatory rights are defined in the UN Convention on the Rights of the Child (CRC), particularly Articles 12 and 13. While Article 12.1 concerns all children, Article 12.2 assures extra rights to children who become affected by judicial and administrative proceedings, for instance children placed outside their homes by Child Protection Services (CPS). Article 13 assures the child freedom of expression. Norway serves as the example in the chapter, illustrating a point that is valid across different countries. Since the CRC was adopted in 1989, The Norwegian Parliament has amended Norwegian legislation, and incorporated the CRC in the Human Rights Act (2003), and *Grunnloven* (the Constitution) (2014), which has precedence over other national legislation. The *Grunnloven* states that

---

E. Backe-Hansen (✉)
Norwegian Social Research, Oslo Metropolitan University, Oslo, Norway
e-mail: ebha@oslomet.no

Children have the right to respect for their human dignity. They have the right to be heard in questions that concern them, and due weight shall be attached to their views in accordance with their age and development. (§ 104, para. 1)

In addition, legal requirements following from various other laws may be relevant, concretizing the rights defined by the CRC for more specific purposes. In Norway, for instance, there is the Kindergarten Act, the School Act, the Health Care Act and the Child Welfare Act. The last has been amended several times during later years, resulting in quite detailed regulations about children and young people's participation when they are in contact with CPS. I return to this Act below, since this chapter concerns foster families, but I will not discuss consequences of the other legal requirements here.

The overarching theme of this book is how the principles of the CRC can become an integral part of all professional child welfare and child protection work, in ways that ensure that these principles are implemented in practice. The CRC states that foster care is the preferred alternative when a child or a young person needs to be looked after by those other than their family of origin. This is the case in Norway and many other European countries. Most foster parents have children of their own, and these children as well as foster children have participatory and other rights accorded to them by the CRC, ensuing legislation and further regulations. Thus, one important question is what happens when the formal approach to participation, which follows from the regulations of the Child Welfare System, enters the private sphere where children's participation evolves as part of the process of growing up in a family, and as part of the relationship between parents and children. This issue has been only scantily addressed in the literature, where it is far more common to investigate to what extent foster children's formal participatory rights are assured before and during placement.

The chapter seeks to address this lack of knowledge through discussing the intersection between formal and everyday participation in foster families, and how the relationship between foster children, foster parents and other children in the foster home may be influenced by this. For the purposes of this chapter, a relational perspective on children's participation is useful because it serves to highlight both similarities and differences between foster children and children who already live in the foster family as both are children in relation to the same adults. This view has become more and more prominent during the last 10–15 years (Fitzgerald et al. 2010). After discussing this, I go on to describe foster children's participatory rights, and discuss how these may influence daily life in a foster family. Then I describe participation in decision-making as this is usually organized and negotiated, as a contrast to the formal and legalistic approach, before discussing possible consequences of the interaction between these two ways of implementing children's participation rights. Finally, I offer suggestions about how professional social work can address these issues. Although the Norwegian system is used as a case example, the issue of children's participatory rights in the intersection between being a public and private family should have wider relevance along with the importance ascribed to foster care as a care alternative.

2 Rights, Relationships and Generations

Many different rationales are offered about why children's participation and listening to children are appropriate and essential. In addition to the rights-based approach, which is the main focus of this book, better services, the promotion of citizenship and social inclusion, and personal and social education and development can be listed as worthwhile outcomes. Thus, a professional approach to children's participation may be inspired and justified by more than the CRC.

With reference to Warshak (2003), Mannion (2007) lists four different rationales, highlighting both advantages and disadvantages with regard to whether children actually participate. The first is dubbed *The enlightenment rationale*. Children have important information which may change decisions adults make on their behalf, again an important issue in relation to children as service users in the child welfare system. Such information provides important knowledge to adults about how they might better care for children's health, welfare and education, but at the same time what children say can easily be scripted by adults with their own agenda (Kjørholt 2002). She argues that discourses on 'children and participation' are deeply embedded in discursive fields other than children and their rights, as she found in her research about children's participation in local development in Norway. Here, an underlying agenda was how to maintain sustainable local communities in an era of centralization, rather than children's participation per se, making participation more tokenistic than real in Hart's (1997) terms.

The second rationale is political and is called *the empowerment agenda*, and is usually grounded in the CRC. In countering ideas about children as 'incompetent', this rationale positions children as complete individuals or citizens with adult-sized rights and responsibilities. If not seen in conjunction with children's needs, however, we risk an individualization of children's rights, which ignores children's all-important relationships with significant adults in their lives (Brannen and O'Brien 1995).

The third rationale is called *the ambiguity of the citizenship rationale*. This rationale argues that children's preparation for and participation in civic activities help them develop a sense of responsibility and obligation to society. Real citizenship may thus be seen as deferred while children prepare themselves through participation. But children may also be seen as citizens in the here and now, who as a minority group strive to be seen and heard while still children. School pupil councils may be seen as examples of practices where these competing views sit in tension—children can report that they participate in 'small' decisions, but not in really important ones, particularly not ones involving decisions about how to allocate the school budget (Holte 2009).

The three first rationales can all be understood as instances of an individualistic approach to children's participatory rights. On the other hand, criticism of these approaches, as exemplified by Kjørholt (2002) and Holte (2009), underlines how grown-ups play an important role in facilitating or limiting children's possibilities. Thus, it can be argued that it is not possible to leave the unequal power relationship between children and adults out of the equation (Punch 2005).

Warshak's (2003) fourth and final rationale is called *outcomes for children / outcomes for adults*, concretized as outcomes for adults and improved relationships between young people and adults. With regard to outcomes for children and young persons as a consequence of increased participation while growing up, not much research exists. In their research review, Vis et al. (2010) conclude that children's participation in planning and decision-making may have positive effects on their health, but the evidence is not very strong. However, research with children and young people, which focuses directly on their experiences with and views on participation, usually concludes that they want to participate, and want their voices to be heard, although they know that their wishes cannot always be granted. In their state-of-the-art review of children's and young people's participation within child welfare and CPS, van Bijleveld et al. (2015) sum up that the personal relationship between the child / young person and the social worker is mentioned as one of the most important facilitators for participation. Again, the relational perspective comes to the fore.

We know that relationships are fundamental in families, both for good and bad; between parents and children, between siblings, and between other members of the family network. Thus, it is easy to imagine that children will reflect on their participation within their families as part of the ongoing relationship with parents and siblings (Backe-Hansen 2009; Sagøe 2008). However, attempting to understand children's participation in a relational perspective has not been very prominent in the research literature until the last 15 years or so (Backe-Hansen 2011; Bell 2002; Élodie et al. 2017; Fitzgerald et al. 2010; Mannion 2007).

If we accept a relational perspective on children's participation, we also need to include context. This means reframing discourses about children's participation to include adults as important players, or so-called generationing practices that help us delineate between the generations, position us as adults and children, and demarcate how we relate to each other at different ages (Mannion 2007). Wyness (2012) advocates an interdependent and intergenerational approach to children's participation, recognizing the respective roles and positions of children and adults. Since foster children enter into relationships with both foster parents and foster siblings, this seems like a useful approach.

3 Formalized Participation for Children in Foster Care

3.1 Legislation and Regulations

Children in contact with Norwegian CPS have a series of participatory rights grounded in the CRC Article 12.1 and 12.2. A social worker is responsible for ensuring these rights in his or her work with a family, while judges are responsible for hearing the child or young person directly, or through appointed experts or a guardian *ad litem*, when a case is contested and brought into the legal system. Here, I will limit my discussion to instances of participation related to foster care placement and children's lives as foster children after a placement decision has been made, and a child or young person is to be part of a new family.

Besides the overarching laws mentioned in the introduction, the Child Welfare Act, together with regulations, accords several rights to children within the remit of CPS. The child has a right to participation, which means being given sufficient and adapted information, and the possibility to freely voice his or her point of view (cf. CRC Article 13). The child is to be listened to, and his or her point of view is to be taken into consideration in accordance with age and maturity. Further, CPS are obligated to inform the child, as early as advisable and in ways the child understands, about situations where he or she can participate, the case and his or her situation, possible services and rights, and finally the choices and decisions which have to be made, and the consequences of these.

In other words, existing regulations describe a rational decision-making process following steps of information and choice, based on knowledge about possible alternatives based on available information. As well, participation is to be seen as a process that goes on throughout the case. Although the regulation stresses the right to participation in the case as a whole, themes that are important from the point of view of CPS are underlined. The elements in the text are case-driven, not seen in relation to what may be important in children's daily lives. The decision context is fairly narrow, nor do the regulations problematize how children's relationships may influence their ability and desire to participate in these case-based processes.

The person who is responsible for hearing the child must talk to him or her, with special attention to children who may have difficulties in understanding the situation and voice their point of view. Further, the perspective and opinions of the child have to be included in the assessment of the child's best interests, and taken into account in accordance with age and maturity, and the child is to be informed about decisions that are made and why.

Children must not be pressurized to participate, although CPS must document the child's participation as part of the case notes, of which an important part is the obligation to speak with the child if he or she is to be consulted. Thus, the focus and drive is on ensuring the child's participation, and alternatives in case the child refuses to participate are not addressed. The question may as well be raised as to whether participation really is voluntary. Nor is there any discussion about possible situations when participation may even be contrary to a child's best interests.

3.2 Enforcing Foster Children's Participatory Rights

The Child Protection worker is responsible for ensuring foster children's participation rights. This entails giving a child or young person age-appropriate and understandable information about his or her situation as a whole, and what will probably happen over time. As well, it entails having contact with foster children to ascertain their views about their life and their situation—not only in a 'one-off' fashion, but again as a process over time.

Information from the child or young person has to be part of the ongoing casework, and will, thus, be available to parents and foster parents as well. Some themes are particularly salient, particularly if there are new decisions to be made about the case from time to time. Parents may ask to have their child return home, or there will be discussions about the best way of organizing contact with the family of origin or siblings living elsewhere. These are emotionally charged issues, where the outcome and the justification for decisions that are made will influence the well-being of both children and adults. This implies that children's participation can entail more than just talking to them, and raises the question of the kind of relationship that needs to be established between social worker and child in order to make participation a positive experience for the child as well as ensuring that the child feels able to talk openly (Bakketeig and Bergan 2013; Bergan 2017).

In addition, a foster child should be able to talk about how she or he likes the foster home, whether there are any problems at home, at school or with friends, leisure time activities, holidays or other ordinary matters. How social workers discuss such themes with foster children has not been much researched, perhaps because of the ongoing focus on more formal participatory rights.

In addition to the social worker, a foster child in Norway is entitled to have a personal contact which follows the child directly, and is supposed to be a person to talk to if things are difficult in the foster home. Neither needs to actually see the children more than a few times a year. Children in care may as well be allowed to choose their own so-called 'person of trust', who can, for instance, accompany them to meetings and be a spokesperson for them. This means that even when there are no conflicts involving the court system, both the caseworker, the contact person and perhaps a person of trust will be involved in the foster home to safeguard children's interests in general, not only their participatory rights.

To sum up, children move into foster care with a set of legal expectations connected with participation that are formal, accompanied by several adults who have the authority to enforce their fulfilment. These expectations concern the relationship between the child, his or her parents, the social worker and the legal and professional aspects of the case. At the same time, the implementation of participatory rights concerns the foster family's daily life in many ways, which I will elaborate in more detail below.

4 Participation as a Natural Part of Everyday Family Life

Family life exemplifies how provision, protection and participation are intertwined as children grow up, and how the relative balance between the three shifts over time until a young adult is expected to fend for herself or himself. Typically, children will be successively more involved in decisions that are made within the family as they grow older, and their influence on the outcome will increase, albeit in different ways, depending on the type of decision that is being made. Children may also achieve some age-specific legal rights before they attain their majority. For instance, in Norway young people can decide how to use money they have earned themselves from age 15, and the age of sexual consent is 16, which is also the age when one is allowed to start taking driving lessons with a grown-up.

4.1 Age and Type of Decision Matter

In Western countries a pre-school girl might well be allowed to decide whether she will wear trousers or a dress in kindergarten, but as long as the children are small, parents will usually decide unilaterally if they want to move the family somewhere else, for instance, or make other more life-changing decisions. This exemplifies how participation in decision-making within a family will vary according to the kind of decision that is being made, and the age of the children. In addition there will be an interplay between the parents' views on how and when their children should be involved, which will, of course, vary as well, as will children's agency in demanding to become involved. But within such variation, it is possible to find some research on how children and parents 'do' participation in their daily lives.

The relational and generational aspects of participation which were discussed above become obvious in research on how decisions are negotiated in families. In her Scottish study, Punch (2005) gives several examples of children who discuss parental authority and accepts that parents have authority over their children, much more so than for instance an elder sibling over a younger one. This might be understood within the context of protection, with children thinking that their parents are motivated by an earnest concern for their best interests, but also within the context of power relationships. Sagøe (2008) did a study of 52 Norwegian primary school children aged 7 to 12, and their participation in family decision-making. Her general findings were that the children felt they could ask and make suggestions, and discuss with their parents. Many situations were open for negotiation as well, and the children described instances when their parents listened to them if they found their arguments good. At the same time the parents had the deciding power. The children did not always feel that their parents justified their decisions properly, or they felt that parents might use vicarious arguments. At the same time the younger children preferred the situation as it was, while the older children would have liked more influence.

Sagøe (2008) found that children did participate in some everyday areas, for instance when it came to deciding what to have for dinner, or the kind of goodies to be bought on Saturdays. The children could state their preferences when it came to choosing what clothes to buy, while their parents had a say when it came to cost, quality and to a certain amount style. The children also participated in the choice of leisure-time activities they were to join. The older, but not the younger children were in addition involved in deciding what to do during weekends and holidays. All the children had rules concerning when they had to come home, most had to tell their parents where they were, and come home at the appointed time. Bedtime was usually *not* open for discussion, in the sense that the parents usually decided a time limit or a usual bedtime. Many parents wanted their children to join in at least one leisure-time activity, which in Norway will usually be some kind of sport, and some were not allowed to quit this even if they wanted to. In addition, some of the older children had duties at home, but were not allowed to decide which.

One will expect children's autonomy and influence to increase with age. There are limits to how long children can be forced to participate in activities they are not motivated for, and one expects children to become successively more competent as they grow up. Thus, negotiation and efforts to motivate will become much more important over time than just using parental authority.

At a more general level, Sagøe (2008) found that parents organized their children's lives based on time. They decided when the children had to get up in the morning, when they had to come home from school/after school activities, when they were to have dinner, come home in the evening and go to bed. As well, many parents set limits to how much time the children could spend watching TV, use a PC or play data games. The oldest of her participants were 12–13 years old, however, so one would expect the parents' monitoring of their children's time use to become less intense with age although parents of teenagers still want to know the whereabouts of their children.

4.2 Participation Is Relational and Entails Compromise

When children are asked directly about what participation means to them, the relational dimension becomes evident. Backe-Hansen (2009) asked 44 10- and 13 year olds to write short essays about how they would define 'participation'. Although particularly the oldest girls wrote more in detail, there were not fundamental differences between the responses.

First, it was obvious that the children themselves understood participation as a relational phenomenon. They gave many examples that underlined the importance of achieving agreement, that nobody has to give in. They could motivate others to join them, or they could be happy to have a say. Examples were given in relation to parents, siblings or friends. They gave examples from their daily lives, like where to go on holiday, what to eat for dinner or what to do after school. The examples underlined the importance of making decisions in collaboration with others.

As well, the examples underlined that participation is a process that takes time, and does not necessarily end well. The children described how they could discuss with their friends over time, and how agreements could be reached and undone, and how they sometimes had to talk for a long time before reaching an agreement. Sometimes they did not manage to agree, and had to find a workable compromise—or leave.

The participants in this study were specifically asked about participation, and were not asked to describe limits to participation or situations where they were not invited to participate. Still their examples correspond well with the findings from Sagøe's (2008) study, which was based on interviews. The focus on relational aspects of participation also resonates well with more recent theorizing about children's participation (Fitzgerald et al. 2010).

Seeing decision-making in the daily lives of families in relation to Warshak's (2003) four categories, the final one, outcomes for children / outcomes for adults, seems most appropriate since it concerns improved relationships between adults and children through the involvement of children. The research literature does not necessarily discuss this in a children's rights context, but rather as a question of roles and expectations of adults and children, negotiations and processes within an ongoing and changing, close relationship.

Parents will also see participatory rights in relation to responsibilities, thus a give-and-take relationship with parameters that may be defined by both grown-ups and children. Part of raising children is to teach them that you have to contribute with something to earn the right to increased privileges, and you may have to accept the withdrawal of privileges if you do not contribute. This does not pertain to all rights, as children have a series of rights that do not presuppose this kind of exchange. But the issue of fair distribution of responsibilities as well as rights, preferably in agreement between all family members, will be important within a family setting.

4.3 The Decision to Become a Foster Family

The decision to become a foster family can involve many persons—the foster parents themselves, their children, other family members and members of their social network. The processes prospective foster parents have to go through in particular before a child or young person actually moves in entail a transition from being a family with the right to define their own family life with large degrees of freedom, to being a 'public' family. As such, the foster family has to submit to assessment and control by CPS through formal assessments, contracts and counselling and supervision.

One question is to what extent the foster family's own children are involved as actors in this process, or to what extent the decision to foster is seen as primarily a grown-up concern, which will be presented to the children as more or less a fait accompli. In their literature review about the impact of fostering on foster carers' children, Höjer et al. (2013) point out, first, that being involved in the decision to foster enhances subsequent adaptation. This was a key finding in the 17 studies that were included in the review. Children and young people need to be involved in family discussions concerning the decision to foster, and should not be seen as less significant or passive members of the family. Second, the review shows that being informed about fostering and about each particular child beforehand reduces conflicts. These findings underline the need for collaboration between prospective foster parents and social workers about how foster parents' own children can be involved in the process leading to a placement. Consequently, the second question is to what extent social workers see prospective foster parents' own children as important participants in the placement process, and to what extent only older children are involved.

Nordenfors (2016) combined qualitative and quantitative methods and investigated the experiences of foster parents' own children of growing up with foster siblings. Two-thirds of the 684 children who answered a questionnaire reported being asked their opinion by their parents before the decision to start fostering was made. Some explained that they were too young, however, although how young they actually were, varied. The article does not describe these processes in detail. On the other hand, the foster parents' own children could be described as non-participants in the official part of the process. As many as 44 per cent of the children had not been asked by the social worker what their thoughts were, while 29 per cent had been asked and 27 per cent did not know. As might be expected, the oldest children were most frequently consulted by the social workers. This meant that many of the children were deprived of the possibility of information from professionals about what it means to be a foster child, as well as what it means to get a foster sibling—information which might be crucial to later adaptation, particularly if the gap between expectations and reality becomes too large (Höjer et al. 2013).

5   Interactions in Everyday Life

What, then, are the most important differences between being a foster family and a family without foster children, and how do they affect interactions in everyday life? First, being a public family with a renegotiable contract, subject to being overseen by CPS, takes authority away from the parents in relation to the foster child. Although foster parents are supposed to make everyday decisions concerning a foster child, they still have to relate to social workers and to parents when these have retained parental rights. If, for instance, a child asks where he or she is going to spend the next summer holidays, or whether it is OK to start playing football, the foster parents cannot answer directly, but must check with the social worker.

This loss of authority on the part of the foster parents illustrates that foster parents do not have the same authority over foster children as they have over their own. For instance, being oppositional and wanting to move somewhere else is not uncommon amongst teenagers living with their parents. In these situations, parents might well want to exert their authority and refuse this as an alternative until a child gets older. This is not possible with a foster child, who will, in addition, have the possibility to engage the social worker or the person of trust because of the way participatory rights are defined—and might end up moving somewhere else. Sometimes this is the right decision, but in many other situations, the young person might be significantly worse off losing what has been a stable home over time. Some young adults can also look back and think that a precipitate move was a bad decision, since she or he could not envisage all the consequences at the time.

The existence of public persons who have the right to visit the family and have opinions about their life will as well influence the relationship between foster children and the other children. Not much is known about how these influences unfold in practice, but a couple of reflections may be useful. One important question concerns imbalance—that a foster child and another child in the family have different status. While the former partly lives this 'public childhood' as it were, the other children in the foster family must relate to the parents as they always have done, with the parents having authority that can be questioned by the children, but which does not depend on acquiescence from outside of the family. Consequently, foster children and the other children will have different ways of negotiating issues that may arise, and both may feel that they are unfairly treated compared to the other.

6 Professional Practice with All Children in a Foster Home

When a foster home is approved, CPS presuppose that children will be provided for and suitably protected. Ensuring this is part of the run-of-the-mill system of following up foster children. However, ensuring participatory rights is something over and above this. Thus, I suggest three guiding principles for a rights-based, professional practice in foster care with regard to participatory rights.

The first is *to see all children in a foster home on an equal footing as bearers of participatory rights*, even though social workers do not have any responsibility for the children already there, and even though foster children are assured extra rights according to Article 12.2. Although there will be case-relevant matters that are just as relevant for the foster child, life in the foster family will entail questions where it may be important for all the children in the family to be able to talk with the social worker, as equal members of the child generation. In addition comes the findings from research (Höjer et al. 2013; Nordenfors 2016) showing that informing children already in the home and including them as actors improves the probability of adaptation on their part. Although there will always be room for conflict, as in any family, it can help the children to feel that they are heard and seen by someone who actually has some authority. As well, this might help them accept that foster children may need extra attention and work, which gives their parents less time for them.

The second principle concerns parental authority on the part of the foster parents. Balancing parental authority between CPS, the parents and the foster parents can be tricky, but if a child is to have a stable foster home, *the carers need to be able to exert sufficient authority as responsible parents*, even or perhaps particularly when there are conflicts. In Norway, foster parents do not have this authority, since any conflict may end up as a question of what jurisdiction foster parents have, whether the contract should be cancelled and so on.

The third and overarching principle needs to be *participation as relational and contextual*, as discussed earlier in this chapter. Foster children need to be incorporated into the foster family. This is done through engaging with the daily life there, including taking part in decisions that are made, and not remaining aloof. For the foster parents to engage with their new family member, they need to feel that he or she belongs, which means fully incorporating them in their daily life with all the usual ups and downs. This underlines the need for foster parents to be allowed to involve foster children in these processes, as well as being allowed to act as parents.

To sum up, these three principles entail changing the balance between social worker, foster parents and all children in the foster home in order to ensure professional work with children's participatory rights. All children need to be treated equally, foster parents need more authority and social workers need to involve the family as a whole, not just the foster child.

References

Backe-Hansen, E. (2009). Barns medbestemmelse sett med barns øyne [Children's participation seen through the eyes of the children]. In R. Hjermann & K. Haanes (eds), *BARN* (pp. 52–61). Oslo: Universitetsforlaget.

Backe-Hansen, E. (2011). *Teoretiske perspektiver i synet på ungdoms medvirkning— en litteraturgjennomgang* [Theoretical perspectives on young people's pariticipation—A literature review]. Vedlegg til NOU 2011:20—Ungdom, makt og medvirkning.

Bakketeig, E., & Bergan, L. T. (2013). Om ungdoms medvirkning ved plassering i fosterhjem [Young people's participation when placed in foster care]. In E. Backe-Hansen, T. Havik & A. B. Grønningsæter (eds), *Fosterhjem for barns behov. Rapport fra et fireårig forskningsprogram* (pp. 85–101). Oslo: NOVA, rappot 16/2013.

Bell, M. (2002). Promoting children's rights through the use of relationship. *Child & Family Social Work, 7*, 1–11.

Bergan, L. T. (2017). *Barns medvirkning under barnevernets omsorg. En kvalitativ intervjuundersøkelse av hvordan barn i fosterhjem opplever å medvirke* [Children's participation in care. A qualitative study]. Oslo: VID vitenskapelige høgskole, Master's thesis.

Van Bijleveld, G. G., Dedding, C. W. M., & Bunders Aelen, J. F. G. (2015). Children's and young people's participation within child welfare and child protection services: A state-of-the-art review. *Child & Family Social Work, 20*, 129–138.
BLD. (2014). FOR-2014-06-01-697. *Forskrift om medvirkning og tillitsperson* [Regulation about participation and a person of confidence]. Oslo: Ministry of Children and Equality.
Brannen, J., & O'Brien, M. (1995). Childhood and the sociological gaze: Paradigms and paradoxes. *Sociology, 29*, 729–737.
Élodie, M., Paulsen, V., & Goyette, M. (2017). Relationships matter: Understanding the role and impact of social networkds at the edge of transition to adulthood from care. *Child and Adolescent Social Work Journal, 54*, 573–582.
Fitzgerald, R., Graham, A., & Taylor, N. (2010). Children's participation as a struggle over recognition: Exploring the promise of dialogue. In B. Percy-Smith & N. Thomas (Eds.), *A handbook of children's participation* (pp. 295–305). London: Routledge.
Hart, R. (1997). *Children's participation: The theory and practice of involving young citizens in community development and environmental care.* Firenze: Innocenti Research Institute.
Höjer, I., Sebba, J. & Luke, N. (2013). *The impact of fostering on foster carers' children. An international literature review.* Oxford: University of Oxford, Rees Centre for Research in Fostering and Education. Downloaded November, 2017.
Holte, J. (2009). *Barns deltakelse i skolen—slik det fortoner seg fra barns synsvinkel* [Children's participation in school—As the children see it]. Bergen: Universitetet i Bergen, Senter for barnevernsstudier. Masteroppgave.
Kjørholt, A.-T. (2002). Small is powerful. Discourses on 'children and participation' in Norway. *Childhood, 9*, 63–82.
Mannion, G. (2007). Going spatial, going relational: Why 'listening to children' and children's participation need reframing. *Discourse: Studies in the cultural politics of education, 28*, 405–420.
Nordenfors, M. (2016). Children's participation in foster care placements. *European Journal of Social Work, 19*, 856–870.
Punch, S. (2005). The generationing of power: A comparison of child–parent and sibling relations in Scotland. *Sociological Studies of Children and Youth, 10*, 169–188.
Sagøe, U. (2008). *Barnets stemme hjemme. Om barneskolebarns stemme hjemme sett fra barns synsvinkel* [Children's participation at home—As the children see it]. Bergen: Universitetet i Bergen, Senter for barnevernsstudier. Masteroppgave.

Vis, S.-A., Strandbu, A., Holtan, A., & Thomas, N. (2010). Participation and health—A research review of child participation in planning and decision-making. *Child & Family Social Work, 16*, 325–335.

Warshak, R. (2003). Payoffs and pitfalls of listening to children. *Family Relations, 52*, 373–384.

Wyness, M. (2012). Children's participation and intergenerational dialogue: Bringing adults back into the analysis. *Childhood, 20*, 429–442.

Open Access This chapter is licensed under the terms of the Creative Commons Attribution 4.0 International License (http://creativecommons.org/licenses/by/4.0/), which permits use, sharing, adaptation, distribution and reproduction in any medium or format, as long as you give appropriate credit to the original author(s) and the source, provide a link to the Creative Commons license and indicate if changes were made.

The images or other third party material in this chapter are included in the chapter's Creative Commons license, unless indicated otherwise in a credit line to the material. If material is not included in the chapter's Creative Commons license and your intended use is not permitted by statutory regulation or exceeds the permitted use, you will need to obtain permission directly from the copyright holder.

13

Conclusion: Towards Rights-Based Child Protection Work

Elisabeth Backe-Hansen and Asgeir Falch-Eriksen

1 Introduction

The purpose of this book has been to critically explore what child protection policy and professional practice entail if they claim to abide by a human rights standard in order to be justified. To achieve this aim, contributions were commissioned that addressed the question of rights-based, professional child protection work at three levels: the systems level, the policy level and through examples from child protection practices.

In various ways, the authors have responded to the call for critical exploration, which altogether paints a picture of possibilities as well as challenges if rights-based child protection work is to be implemented successfully. One of the strengths of the book is the varied professional backgrounds of the contributors, which have enabled pertinent issues to be addressed from the point of view of the law, political science,

E. Backe-Hansen (✉) • A. Falch-Eriksen
Norwegian Social Research, Oslo Metropolitan University, Oslo, Norway
e-mail: ebha@oslomet.no; asgeirer@oslomet.no; asgeir.falch-eriksen@nova.hioa.no

psychology, social work and sociology. This has both added important richness to the arguments presented throughout, but also insights into the importance of building bridges between academic fields of interest in order to give birth to more accurate and needed research for professional practice and policy development.

Another strength of the book is the choice of empirical examples from a series of countries. One chapter draws on data from 14 countries, while the other chapters utilize examples from Denmark, England, Finland and Norway. All examples were selected analytically because we think readers from any country claiming to enforce the Convention on the Rights of the Child (CRC) will find them both relevant and useful. Each chapter thereby seeks to be relevant to Child Protection Services (CPS) across borders.

In the rest of the chapter, we sum up the most important conclusions and draw out implications for practical child protection work.

2 The Systems Level

Chapters 2, 3, 4 and 5 addressed several overarching themes and principles. To be able to explore and critically discuss rights-based professional work within child protection, we need to immerse ourselves in children's rights, and how these rights ought to be understood as human rights. Since the book concerns child protection, Article 19 in the CRC, that is the right to protection, was a logical point of departure (Sandberg, Chap. 2). In addition comes theorizing about rights-based child protection work (Falch-Eriksen, Chap. 3), comparative analyses of legislation concerning the principle of the best interests of the child (Skivenes and Sørsdal, Chap. 4), and how to achieve rights-based child protection work through reorganizing the system (Munro and Turnell, Chap. 5).

In some settings it is pedagogical to divide children's rights into categories, like participation rights (Article 12), protection rights (Article 19) and provision rights (Article 27). One essential reminder form Sandberg's discussion of Article 19 is that children's rights are indivisible. One cannot pick and choose rights, but must see all rights under the umbrella of a human rights standard, as a perspective and in relation to each other.

Thus, child protection workers need to know not only the CRC from a formal and semantic point of view, but also what the CRC implies as a human rights standard set to govern 'all actions concerning children' (cf. CRC Art. 3). Hence, rights are not only viewed in relation to formal decisions regarding a child and his or her parents, but must also become an integral part of the investigation and assessment process.

Article 19 states that children have the right to be protected from all kinds of maltreatment, which can also justify out-of-home placement if absolutely necessary. A challenge resulting from the formulation in Article 19 and the specifications in General Comment (GC) No. 13 is that the definition of maltreatment is extremely wide. In a sense, anything a child is exposed to has the potential to be classified as maltreatment. Thus, practitioners must depend on national legislation for definitions of maltreatment that justify intervention from CPS. As Skivenes and Sørsdal (Chap. 4) point out, however, national legislation varies considerably when it comes to describing relevant situations and the scope of discretion delegated to professionals. Thus, practitioners need to be familiar with national legislation and regulations and the position of professional discretion in decision-making, and use this knowledge as an important basis for their decision-making.

Both Falch-Eriksen (Chap. 3) and Skivenes and Sørsdal (Chap. 4) remind us that the principle of the best interests of the child is indeterminate. Making a decision which is really and truly in a child's best interest thus necessitates taking into account the individual child's situation, wishes and prospects. But this does not necessarily mean that these are the only considerations. As Skivenes and Sørsdal argue, sufficient general knowledge about what children need exists for us to use this as a factual basis for decisions as well. However, as Falch-Eriksen underlines, if a decision does not approximate the principle of the child's best interests in decision-making, but relies too heavily on general knowledge, the practice departs from the human rights ethos of the CRC. Furthermore, as Christiansen and Hollekim argue (Chap. 10), general views about children's needs become problematic if they become too ideological and lose sight of the large variation that exists in conjunction with the commonalities. Not in the least, class, culture and gender influence our general views of children's needs. Thus, child protection workers need to address indeterminacy in an adequate manner, through combining individualized assessments with factual knowledge, while at the same time taking into account that generalized knowledge might be flawed or unfit for a child.

This conclusion resonates with Munro and Turnell (Chap. 5), who argue that a truly rights-based approach presupposes decision-making designs and systems that open up in the direction of a critical, reflective and collaborative practice at the street level. This shift has to be endorsed by the administrative level if it is to succeed, which is a well-known result from other research on the implementation of systems changes. Munro and Turnell also give an example of an approach that can accommodate a human rights-standard in decision-making (Signs of Safety). Signs of Safety is designed to ensure children's participation throughout a child protection case process, involving the parents as well. Implementing this method depends on the kind of practice they endorse. Thus, the child protection system needs to endorse critical and reflective practices if a rights-based professional practice is to have any chance of success.

3 The Policy Level

Chapters 6, 7, 8 and 9 concern rights-based child protection work at the policy level or what professional child protection practice can learn through researching various policies. First, in Chap. 6, Pösö addresses collective participation by groups of child welfare youth. Hestbæk shows how there is a need for improvement in rights-based work in CPS, particularly in residential care (Chap. 7), while Gording-Stang (Chap. 8) discusses how protection rights can be enforced in emergency placements. Finally, we are reminded about the need to also keep provision rights at the forefront when aiming to protect children from maltreatment as well as realizing other rights (Heggem Kojan and Clifford, Chap. 9).

Experts by experience as a form of collective participation have gained a large impact during the last decade or so. As Pösö (Chap. 6) argues, the impact is perhaps greater on policymakers than on street-level workers. Experts by experience share their biographies in ways that resonate with today's individualized society, and with our wish to make a difference for a group of children and young people who have had a bad deal by society and their parents. One reason why street-level workers may be less influenced is that experts by experience do not address systems and structures (nor can they be expected to do so). Thus, child protection workers need to listen carefully to what experts by experience can tell them, but at the same time they need to relate this knowledge to the system of which they are a part in order to be able to use the knowledge professionally.

While Pösö discusses collective participation as a matter of right, Anne-Dorthe Hestbæk (Chap. 7) uses information collected from individuals through a survey study among children and young people in foster and residential care. This creates different but no less important knowledge. It rather illustrates the variety of areas where rights-based practice needs to be developed. Hestbæk found significant differences between the well-being of those in foster care and those in residential care, with far greater challenges associated with the latter. What she shows as well is that it is fairly easy to 'translate' often-used questions about safety and well-being to children's rights terms. This gives new insights about possibilities and challenges when it comes to developing rights-based professional practices in out-of-home care, particularly residential care. Thus, child protection workers need to use knowledge about children's rights and national legislation and regulations as a basis for framing residential care in ways that promote rights-based practices.

The use of emergency out-of-home placements challenges decision-makers both in CPS and the courts, as Elisabeth Gording-Stang (Chap. 8) shows in her analysis of decisions that were made in ten court cases from Norway. Provisions for such placements exist across jurisdictions, but they are often contested, and sometimes accepted for assessment by the European Court of Human Rights. There is a need for provisions enabling CPS to overrule other considerations when a child's need for protection through out-of-home placement is sufficiently paramount. However, the threshold is high, maybe too high, and it is important for CPS to assess carefully whether a case should rather be accorded full judicial treatment. Thus, child protection workers again need to know both the CRC and national legislation and regulations, besides comparable decisions already made, as a decision aid in concrete cases.

Bente Heggem Kojan and Graham Clifford (Chap. 9) use as their point of departure the fact that social and economic marginalization is widespread among families in contact with CPS. As well, there is across countries a well-known correlation between being marginalized and coming into contact with CPS. This makes it important to ensure that children's provisions rights, or welfare rights, are enforced by CPS or adjacent social or welfare services targeting children and families. The authors point out that protecting children and promoting their welfare mean that professionals need to reframe their approach. Child protection workers need to pay attention to the environments and contexts in which children live; like families, school and leisure time.

Kojan and Clifford use children's right to education (CRC Article 28) as a practical example, since poor educational attainment is a risk factor for later marginalization in today's knowledge-based societies. As they point out, we cannot expect all parents in contact with CPS to be able to help their children sufficiently by themselves. Parents often lack resources to do so, have often themselves had trouble at school and ended up with poor educational attainment, besides having trouble coping with their daily lives. Thus, child protection workers need to engage themselves in children and young people's schooling, and the authors suggest four areas. *First*, child protection workers need knowledge about the school situation of all children they are responsible for. *Second*, they need to be proactive in their contact with the children's school, ensuring ongoing and updated knowledge. *Third*, helping children living at home with their school work and situation needs to be part of what CPS prioritizes for children receiving in-home preventive services. *Finally*, but not least importantly, child protection workers need to know the children they meet, what abilities and cognitive potential they have, something which is too often undervalued by social workers and others alike.

4 Three Examples from Child Protection Practice

The final three chapters in the book delved into important areas of child protection practice in greater detail. In accordance with CRC Article 19, in-house preventive work is prioritized whereas out-of-home placements are to be avoided if possible. Øivin Christiansen and Ragnhild Hollekim

(Chap. 10) discuss some challenges that may arise if this kind of practice, which presupposes collaboration with both parents and children, at the same time can succeed in being rights-based on the part of the children. In her chapter, Cecilie Basberg Neumann (Chap. 11) analyses the provision of care in a residential unit for severely troubled children, and how it is possible to ensure that children's protection and participation rights are met through the use of bodily contact. Finally, Elisabeth Backe-Hansen (Chap. 12) addresses participation rights for children in foster families when foster children and children already in the foster home do not have the same standing.

As Christiansen and Hollekim show, there will often be many reasons why in-home preventive services are initiated. Child maltreatment need not play a very prominent part, as parents' mental health issues, drug abuse or more general family problems often dominate. And in many cases, there are multiple problems to be addressed, including poor educational attainment on the part of the child, or even serious behavioural problems. However, whatever the reason for initiating services, they are supposed to realize children's rights, that is help improve the child's situation at home.

Christiansen and Hollekim discuss two important challenges in this respect. The *first* is how to realize children's rights when the parents do not consent. This may lead to children not getting sufficient help, which may again necessitate more intrusive interventions at a later stage, or to parents consenting anyway because they feel coerced to do so for fear of the consequences if they refuse. The *second* challenge is related to today's trend to target parents with guidance and advice, and whether this is actually sufficient in the way stated in CRC Article 19. Kojan and Clifford (Chap. 9) pointed out that it might seem as if today's choice of interventions do not help those with the most serious problems.

Finally, Christiansen and Hollekim warn against current trends to homogenization of parenthood, a narrowed understanding of the complexity of children and parents' needs, and a marginalization of the child following from the present trend to educate and supervise parents. Thus, child protection workers need to be aware of the delicate balance between motivating parents and children and recognizing their right not to consent. It is also necessary to keep in mind the complexity of the lives children and parents in contact with CPS lead, and remember the indivisibility and indeterminacy following from rights-based work.

Cecilie Neumann (Chap. 11) asked what care workers do when they provide care to young children in residential settings, and what good care has to do with realization of the principle of the child's best interests and children's right to participation. Through fieldwork in one such setting, she came to the conclusion that good care of children was related to care worker's bodily awareness, and a sensitive presence when interacting with and caring for the children. It is important to focus on positive practices involving bodily contact in today's climate of scepticism and fear of abuse in institutions.

Working with children in residential units, child protection workers thus need to pay attention to how the children's need for physical contact or regulation of physical contact is met by the care workers, and how positive interactions also increase the children's ability to participate and be part of life on the unit. The ways this happen will vary with the children's age and what their problems are, but the principles remain the same.

Backe-Hansen (Chap. 12) chose as her point of departure what may happen when a child is placed in a foster home with participatory rights that follow from CRC Article 12.1 and 12.2, in a formal way, in contrast to how participation is an integrated part of daily life in the family. CPS also tend not to involve children already in the foster family when a child is to be placed within that family, but concentrate on the latter. In contrast, foster families are 'public' families, and foster parents have to accept that they have less authority as foster parents than they have as parents, and have to accept more intrusion and control from outside.

Backe-Hansen argues that these factors create imbalances in foster families, which may lead to less stable placements. Thus, three things are important for child protection workers. *First*, they need to reduce the imbalance between children in the foster family by involving those already there in the placement process—through informing them, and asking about their views. *Second*, workers need to accede foster parents sufficient authority to enable the parents to actually act as parents in the daily lives of the family, thus being able to protect them sufficiently as well. *Third*, it must be remembered that children's participation is relational in nature—children always participate in relation to someone, be that parents, foster parents, siblings, friends, other grown-ups and so on.

5 Conclusion

The book contains far more discussion, suggestions and insights than it has been possible to sum up in this concluding chapter. It also contributes theoretical insights and developments that need to be studied in depth in the chapters. For this concluding chapter, we aimed to draw out the most important lessons for child protection work at the street level. In other words, what can and should child protection workers do in order to develop rights-based, professional practice? Many answers have been given here.

Open Access This chapter is licensed under the terms of the Creative Commons Attribution 4.0 International License (http://creativecommons.org/licenses/by/4.0/), which permits use, sharing, adaptation, distribution and reproduction in any medium or format, as long as you give appropriate credit to the original author(s) and the source, provide a link to the Creative Commons license and indicate if changes were made.

The images or other third party material in this chapter are included in the chapter's Creative Commons license, unless indicated otherwise in a credit line to the material. If material is not included in the chapter's Creative Commons license and your intended use is not permitted by statutory regulation or exceeds the permitted use, you will need to obtain permission directly from the copyright holder.

Index[1]

A

Abduction-risk, 157–158
Approximation rule, 51–53
Australia, 61, 65–67, 71–77, 82, 83, 84n6
Austria, 61, 65–67, 69, 71–75, 82, 84n6
Awareness campaigns, 23

B

Bad practice, 213
Balanced assessment, 91, 92
Basic negative right, 44, 46, 47, 50
Berlin, Isaiah, 43
Best interests of the child, 154
Body, the, 214–215

C

Canada, 61, 65–67, 72–74, 76, 77, 84n6
Care order, 63, 66, 78, 150
Care practices, 209–223
Child centric, 79, 83
Childhood, 53–54
Children's views, 27–29, 32, 34, 116–117
Child rights approach, the, 34
Child's best interests, 31–33, 45, 211
  basic negative right to liberty, 45
  rational self interest, 45
Child's integrity, 46
Committee on the Rights of the Child, 17, 31
Comparative research, 64–65
Compliance culture, 90, 94, 98

---

[1] Note: Page numbers followed by 'n' refer to notes.

Continuity, 131, 132
Convention on the Rights of the
    Child (CRC)
  Article 3, 9, 31, 33, 210,
    218–222
  Article 9, 139
  Article 12, 112, 118, 132, 227
  Article 19, 3, 16, 17, 19–21, 23,
    24, 26, 28, 33, 132, 148, 190
  Article 20, 132, 140
  Article 25, 132
  Article 26, 173
  Article 27, 173
  Article 28, 173, 177, 180
  Article 29, 173
  Article 37, 16
  Article 39, 18
  Article 43, 17
  Article 44, 17

D
Decision-making, 75–76
Defensive culture, 93
Defensive practice, 93
Denmark, 61, 66, 67, 71–73, 75,
    76, 84n6
Discourse principle, 52
Discretion, 5–6, 49–51, 64
  best interests, 61–64
  formal restriction, 50
  strong and weak, 78–82
Drug abuse, 155–156
Dworkin, Robert, 59, 61, 62, 83

E
Educational measures, 23–24
Education in the knowledge society,
    174–175

Embodiment-method, 213–214
Emergency placement, 150
England, 61, 66, 67, 69, 72–75, 77,
    83, 84n6
Estonia, 61, 66, 67, 71, 73–75, 78,
    79, 84n6, 85n9
European Court, 149, 151, 162,
    164n12
Experiential knowledge, 113–115,
    119–121, 123
Experts by experience, focus on
    expert and experiential
    knowledge, 113–115

F
Family life, 74, 149
Family service-oriented systems, 64, 65
Finland, 61, 66, 67, 69, 71, 72, 74,
    75, 84n6
Follow-up, 28–30
Foster care, 131, 228
  age, 235–237
  decision-making, 235–237
  interaction, 239–240
Freedom rights, 171
Front-line practice, 121–123
Future of the child, 75

G
General Comment (GC), 16–33
Germany, 61, 66, 67, 71, 72, 76, 77,
    82, 84n6
Grunnloven, 227

H
Habermas, Jürgen, 52
Harding, Fox, 188–189